SAMUEL L. JACKSON

The Unauthorised Biography

Jeff Hudson

For Angela

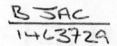

First published in Great Britain in 2004 by
Virgin Books Ltd
Thames Wharf Studios
Rainville Road
London
W6 9HA

A catalogue record for this book is available from the
British Library.

ISBN 1 85227 024 1

Typeset by TW Typesetting, Plymouth, Devon
Printed and bound in Great Britain by
Creative Print and Design (Wales), Ebbw Vale

CONTENTS

PART THREE: THE 'L' STANDS FOR LUCKY

ACKNOWLEDGEMENTS

First and foremost to the king of cool himself, Mr Jackson. Unfortunately, I was not able to interview him for this book, but never has there been a better excuse to watch nigh on seventy films. Also to my editors at Virgin – Mark Wallace, for once again suggesting a subject of no little importance and even greater merit, and Kirstie Addis for running with the ball.

On the writing front, I will be forever indebted to those who gave their time so graciously to the preparation and completion of this book. They know who they are (send SAE for full list). To the British Film Library and its Institute for providing the leading movie resource in the world; and to Helena, for her unbeatable and ever-changing writing environment.

To fellow captains of the low seas, Mr and Mrs H for continued support in the face of many incomprehensible decisions; to the Marshall gals Dredd, Abigayle and Harriet; Nan and Frank; Dave and Caroline; Martin; Neville; the chaps at Infinity and beyond; The Good Fairy and The Bad Fairy; Dr Smirnoff and Mr Jack; and that other Jackson clan: Roo, Miguel, G.J. and Debs.

A pleasure doing business with you.

Finally, to Pangelina, for whom a dedication is not enough. In the words of the man himself, it's my duty to please the booty . . .

Part 1
I AM SAM

INTRODUCTION: I'VE SEEN *ED WOOD*

'Shit.'

It is March 1995, Oscar night at Los Angeles' prestigious Shrine Auditorium. The great and the good rub shoulder pads with the shining lights and Beautiful People of Tinseltown. A global audience of 2 billion is watching the live television broadcast. Anna Paquin has just announced the latest winner. And Samuel L. Jackson has just sworn. On stage, the heavily jowled Martin Landau begins his acceptance speech. Watching the live feed relayed outside, a phalanx of the world's press starts to write. They've just been given their story.

When the nominations for the 67th Academy Awards had been announced at the start of the year, a lot of industry eyebrows were raised for a couple of reasons. For a start, did *Pulp Fiction*, a relatively small-budget movie from Harvey Weinstein's Miramax and Danny DeVito's Jersey Films really deserve to appear in the Best Picture, Best Director, Best Screenplay, Best Actor and Best Supporting Actor/Actress categories? Whatever the public's opinion of new *enfant terrible* on the block, Quentin Tarantino, there was a sizeable school of thought in Hollywood that questioned whether the Mekon-headed one should be so lauded for only his second film. It said more for the quality of Miramax's shameless pamphleteering than the actual film, went the rumour.

In the Jackson household, however, questions were being asked for another reason. Of *Pulp Fiction*'s two lead actors, was it not odd that comeback kid, John Travolta, had been nominated for Best Actor while the film's unquestionable star turn, Samuel L. Jackson, had to settle for Best Support? Travolta may have been in one extra scene (making cat eyes with Uma Thurman at Jack Rabbit Slim's), but didn't Jackson's Jules Winnfield have more lines? What's more, weren't they the best ones? Who could have failed to leave a screening of *Pulp Fiction* without the nostril-flaring threat of Jules's 'great vengeance and furious anger' resonating around their heads?

Responsibility for this decision to put Travolta ahead of Jackson goes, ironically, less to the Academy members themselves than to the film's biggest – literally – backer: Miramax. Before you can be a winner, you have to be a nominee and, regardless of public acclaim and box-office performance, no movie is guaranteed a nomination from the Oscar voters. But there are ways of improving a film's chances, and Harvey Weinstein was one of the first studio bosses to recognise this. His plan is simple: minimise the tiresome business of 'thinking' for the Academy members and make sure they not only know who you are but convey the feeling that they'd be fools to miss out on the opportunity to vote for you. In the months leading up to the nominations' announcement, well-placed interviews, adverts and promotions in the 'right' magazines and newspapers offering various films and actors 'for your consideration' have now become standard practice in Hollywood thanks to Weinstein's lead. His policy of aggressive ingratiation seems to work. In 2003, four of the five Best Picture nominees, including the winning *Chicago*, were his. (As a consequence, in May 2003, the Academy announced that it would be clamping down on such bullish canvassing.)

Keeping it simple for the Academy of Motion Picture Arts and Sciences' voters manifests itself in various ways. An obvious ruse is to present a united front for each film, campaigning for one person in each category only. In 2003, voters were encouraged to consider Nicole Kidman ahead of Julianne Moore for Best Actress in *The Hours*, despite Moore having more screen time. Moore made do with a campaign for Best Supporting Actress for that film, together with her own stab at the main honour for her leading role in *Far From Heaven*. (In the event, while the nominations went to plan, Moore lost out in both categories – to Catherine Zeta Jones and Kidman.) In 1993, given the Academy's track record, Denzel Washington was asked by Weinstein to campaign for the secondary award to give co-star Tom Hanks a clear shot at Best Actor for *Philadelphia*. He refused, insisting on going for the big one or not at all (he already had a Supporting Oscar for *Glory*). In the event, only Hanks was nominated. (He won. In tears.)

Learning from his friend Washington's precedent, relative newcomer to the big occasion, Samuel L. Jackson, was not going to take such risks back in 1995. According to the Miramax logic, if campaigns were run to promote each actor for different categories, the chances for both would be increased – which would have to be good for everyone. But that logic only goes so far. It does not answer the question about why Travolta got the preferential nod over his co-star.

The answer to this is likely to lie with Oscar history. By the time of the 67th Academy Awards in 1995, how many winners of the main acting categories had been black? Answer: one – Sydney Poitier for 1963's *Lilies of the Field*. It does the Academy of Motion Picture Arts and Sciences no credit at all. As 2002 nominee Will Smith says, 'The Academy is made up mostly of white Americans, so for the most part white American films are going to be nominated and white American actors are going to win.' While demographic statistics are closely guarded, it is no secret that the percentage of minorities represented among the 5,700 voting members is far lower than in the general population of the USA.

In 2002, a watershed situation appeared to be reached when Denzel Washington and Halle Berry walked off with Best Actor and Actress awards for *Training Day* and *Monster's Ball* respectively. Will Smith's nomination for *Ali* meant the ceremony also marked the first time since 1972 that three black actors had been in contention for the main acting awards. In addition, with Poitier receiving a lifetime achievement award, there was a real feeling of black talent finally getting not only its just rewards but also long-overdue recognition. Back in 1995, however, there had been no such landmark precedent and Samuel L. Jackson was compelled, many felt, to campaign for a nomination for Best Actor in a Supporting Role.

'Everybody called and wanted me to accept the fact that I should be in the supporting actor category,' he recalled in *Premiere*. 'It was presented to me as, "If you allow us to push you for Best Supporting Actor, it's pretty much guaranteed you'll get a nomination. But if we put you in the Best Actor category, then we can't say that it's a lock." '

That both he and Travolta duly won nominations in their respective categories was perceived in most circles as vindication for Miramax's rigorous divide-and-rule campaigning. No doubt Travolta was very happy with his nomination, the very public welcome back into the acting fold after a decade in the wilderness. By the same token, Jackson couldn't, as a relative newcomer, be too disappointed with a nomination for Best Supporting Actor. Could he?

Anyone who knows Samuel L. Jackson does not need to be told the answer to that question. In 1995, he was 46 (Travolta was 41) and *Pulp Fiction* was his thirtieth film. Regardless of what the Academy or even the media thought, he did not class himself as a newcomer. He certainly did not consider himself an inferior actor to John *Look Who's Talking* Travolta. And he was not afraid to say it. Despite already picking up Best Actor trophies from the Texas Film Critics among other bodies, he decided that letting his name go forward for the secondary category was the phlegmatic thing to do. 'I could have made a stink, but what good would it have done?' he continued. 'I know that people are going to see this film, and they're going to see this film for ever. People can judge for themselves the work that I did.'

He had a similar attitude of laissez-faire when it came to the actual ceremony. Looking around the auditorium on 27 March, Jackson felt quietly confident that he'd turned in the best performance of the year, whatever the result that night. But the omens were not good. Martin Landau had previously scooped the Golden Globe and the Screen Actors Guild awards for his role in *Ed Wood*. Despite the odds stacked against him, Jackson felt a glimmer of hope for one brief moment as the nominations were read out at the actual ceremony. 'I thought, "OK, Martin's won every award up till now, maybe the law of averages is about to catch up with him, and I'm going to win the big one," ' he told *Empire* in 1995. He didn't. 'I sat there and they said, "The winner is . . . Martin Landau," and I went, "Oh, shit." '

That, as anyone who has ever sat through an awards ceremony will know, is not the way it's done. Some might even call it bad form. The unveiling of the Best Actor name in 2003 was a case in point. Former winners Jack Nicholson, Daniel Day-Lewis, Michael Caine and Nicolas Cage sat transfixed for a second as the name 'Adrien Brody' sank in, then they were all smiles, quick to be seen to congratulate the star of *The Pianist*. Nicholson grabbed Cage to share a laugh; Caine was seen exclaiming 'Wonderful!' into the watching camera.

Now, that's how it should be done. When the screen split in time-honoured tradition in 1995 to reveal all five nominees' faces at once, no one expected Samuel L. Jackson's response. It certainly wasn't 'wonderful'.

'I made this bet with a friend that I would not be sitting there applauding and smiling like most losers,' said in *Premiere*. 'So when I didn't get it, yeah, I thought, "Shit." ' Platitudes like 'You'll be nominated a lot more, you're a fabulous actor, Martin Landau's old, he's been nominated a few times' counted for little as Jackson went home empty-handed. 'You know, Morgan Freeman's old, he's been nominated more times than Martin Landau,' he told the *Guardian*. 'And he's a better actor. I've seen *Ed Wood*. Give me a break!

'It was a sentimental vote.'

It was also a political vote. As Jackson points out, Morgan Freeman has been passed over more times than most, certainly more than Landau. Nominations received: four. Nominations converted: zero. Freeman, for those who don't know this great actor's work, is black. Statistically, his chances, like Jackson's, of taking home a gold statuette have never been good. Ignoring Poitier, Washington and Berry as the token winners in the Best Actor stakes, only five black actors have won Best Support awards since the Oscars' inception in 1929. That's around 2 per cent of all winners. Compared to the proportion of non-whites in the United States, this figure is little more than disgusting.

Samuel L. Jackson isn't afraid to say so. To the *Evening Standard* he admitted, 'I have very low expectations of the Academy and the whole Oscars process. I've reached a point where I don't believe having an Oscar is going to validate my career.'

Which is just as well. If talent were the barometer he believes he'd have a Kangol hatful: 'I guess in a fair world I would have had maybe four,' he said in *The Times* magazine. 'One for *Jungle Fever*, maybe *Pulp Fiction*, *A Time to Kill* and *Jackie Brown*.' But talent, it seems, is just one factor that goes through voters' minds when totting up Oscar worthiness. And, quite patently, it is not even the deciding one, not when skin colour appears to be in the mix.

Despite the statistics and despite the obvious, repugnant conclusions, it is still anathema in the current PC climate to suggest that racism plays any part in any group or individual's decision-making. It's just not the done thing. So to say that you have not won an Oscar because you are black immediately sends out signals of sour grapes. For fear of retribution, most people, even if they thought it, would not say such things to their friends let alone the international press. But Samuel L. Jackson did, and does regularly. And do you know what? He doesn't care what you or I or they think about that. He is what he is. Opinionated and self-confident; talented, charismatic and imposing. And, yes, cool. Very cool. Welcome to his world. Strap yourselves in. It's not a comfortable ride.

1. TALKING RUBBISH

'My name is Sam and I am an addict.'

Of all the lines Samuel L. Jackson has ever had to read, memorise and recite, one short sentence stands in his mind as the hardest of all. Obviously for a man earning his living on the New York stage, rattling off pages of complex dialogue night after night, the nine words he was asked to say by Narcotics Anonymous in 1990 were not taxing in their number. But as a personal statement, as an admission to others – strangers – that he was not in control of his own life at that time, they constituted a sobering moment. Literally.

Samuel L. Jackson is a fighter. He is determined, unrelenting and unflinching in his pursuit of a goal. 'I can't do anything on a small scale,' he said in the Guardian. 'I have a personality that is compulsive and obsessive.' It is these qualities that have seen his acting career eclipse those of most of his contemporaries. It is these qualities that have transformed his golf swing into that of a lower-ranking pro. And it is these qualities which meant that for 23 years he was in the grip of drug and alcohol dependency.

Fortunately, the same qualities, the same presence of mind and strength of will, meant that Jackson was not as disabled or disorientated as some when he arrived at his own personal crossroads. The same forceful stubbornness that had got him into the mess in which he found himself in 1990 would extricate him. He knew it. And, if you knew Sam, you knew it too. More than a decade later he stands vindicated. And, above all, dry and clean. 'I met people in rehab who had been in eight times,' he said, pity and disdain mixed in his voice. 'I only needed to do it once.'

For Jackson, control is all. As a black man in what is still perceived as a white man's world, there are enough things outside his sphere of influence already. As a consequence, he takes his personal dominion very seriously. He neither does nor says things by accident or because someone has told him to. For an actor, whose very existence depends on the patronage of others, that is rare. But although dedicated beyond average standards, Jackson is an actor second. He is his own man first. And a man not in control of his own actions is, in Jackson's view, not much of a man at all.

That explains the relative ease with which he kicked his various habits more than a decade ago and the fact that he has never looked back. 'I know I could never have just one drink and I still can't,' he admitted. But that is the pay off for the drug-fuelled years, and it is a debt he always knew he would have to settle. The chemical dependency thing was just something he did. It was a social thing, a private thing, a hobby. Most people did it to some extent, on their own or with friends. But not all of them were 'compulsive and obsessive'.

You don't have to read between the lines, then, to learn that unlike Ol' Blue Eyes, regrets do not rank too highly in Samuel Jackson's memory. 'Unhappy?' He bristled at the Guardian's suggestion. To be unhappy during that period would be an admission of weakness. 'No, I wasn't unhappy. I was happy. Hell, I was very happy. For a long time, heh-heh-heh.' He laughs incredulously at the notion and it is hard not to believe him.

An important stage of the twelve-point recovery programme for recovering alcoholics and drug addicts is talking to others, preaching the errors of your ways, using your mistakes as an inverse template for new sufferers' success. That is one step that Jackson will not take. 'I'd be a hypocrite if I did,' he explained in the weekend section of the Guardian. *Mistakes? 'For 23 years, I was having a good time. There's no way I can tell kids, "It's awful, don't do it." ' There is, after all, little worse than a pious reformed smoker.*

In his own opinion, after all, he had used drugs successfully for years. 'Life was good! I was going to work every day, money in the bank, making movies and playing on Broadway. I did things on stage that were phenomenal. And I was bombed every night.'

Bombed every night, drunk every day. But they were good times. For a while, the best times. And they had been raging for as long as Jackson could remember. And not just for him. His 'problems' were a result of his environment. And his environment, like that of so many young black men, had been built on shifting sand.

To a Caucasian European thirty-something writing in the 21st century, it is difficult, almost impossible, to imagine what life was like just a few decades earlier in the United States – the United States, the most advanced country in the first world. But the documentary evidence exists for anyone who has the stomach for it. America was a country of segregation even in our parents' lifetimes. Slavery was commonplace and economically essential in large parts of the country until Lincoln's dissolution of it as recently as 1865; even then, as a devout believer that 'the negro is not equal to the white man', he only acted in order to destroy the lifeblood of the South's slave-dependent plantation system after their opposition to him in the Civil War. One hundred years later, black citizens were still treated as second class; afforded the same 'rights' as cattle. And not just by the populace: laws had been passed by government to articulate and assert white superiority over blacks. It was federal policy, from the president down. For such a new country, and one which owed its very existence to a legacy of immigrants overpowering a territory's indigenous inhabitants, it was historically appalling behaviour. Words in a book such as this, in the space available, cannot truly do 'justice' to the scale of such evil.

In 1954, however, the Supreme Court finally outlawed segregation of public facilities following the landmark case of Brown vs Topeka Board of Education. Passing the law and enforcing it were two different things, however, especially given the micro-sovereignty of each individual state. The militant presence of the Ku Klux Klan in the South, along with the white population's staunch refusal to give up what it believed were its 'rights' meant that only force would win the day. For a black people who, despite being given the vote in 1870, had become disenfranchised through a generation of segregation and their inability to purchase land, it did not seem a fight they could win.

In Montgomery, Alabama, however, there was a mood for change. On 1 December 1955, black woman Rosa Parks was arrested for refusing to give up her bus seat – in contravention of state law – to a white man. In her support, black workers were encouraged to boycott the town's mass transit systems, either walking to work or being driven by black cabbies charging the same prices as the bus companies. In the face of arrests, bomb attacks and intimidation, the boycott dragged on for eleven months, resulting in the redundancy of many white drivers. Co-ordinating the movement was local pastor, Dr Martin Luther King Jr. In November 1956 the Supreme Court acted: segregation on public transport was declared illegal. From Rosa Parks's spark to Dr King's eloquent pacifism, life for millions of Americans would never be the same. Slowly but surely a revolution had begun. The Black Revolution.

The following year, 1957, national and international attention was drawn to the Arkansas town of Little Rock when its politicians voted, in the face of federal law, to repeal the anti-segregation policy of 1954. Nine black pupils due to join its Central High School that September were informed the day before term began of the state's decision to ban them. Overruled by the federal court, the Governor, Orval Faubus, simply ordered his state troopers to seize the school. Armed with bayonet-capped rifles, the guards were instructed not to let the black students onto the premises. For a period, the town descended into anarchy with each night bringing new attacks on black families. The pupils themselves faced incredible intimidation and interest from both sides as they became national figures thanks to news reports and the burgeoning TV network. Amazingly, only President Eisenhower's late decision to bring in the 101st Airborne Division ended the stand-off. Federal law had overruled state law but only because it had greater firepower. The symbolism was clear.

For those able to avert their eyes from the country's inherent divide, it was rammed home via other outlets. For years, audiences at Las Vegas's biggest hotel theatres had paid good money to be entertained by the likes of Nat 'King' Cole, Jackie Wilson and Sammy Davis Jr. But while they were considered good enough to be put on stage, cheered and applauded, it didn't stop the singers being banned from actually staying in the hotels they'd sold out; they were not even allowed to enter through the main entrances. (Ironically, the Mafia came to such stars' rescue: Nat 'King' Cole's personal entreaties to the local 'family' later meant he no longer had to use the tradesmen's entrance; Sammy Davis Jr was fine as soon as he stepped into Frank Sinatra's 'connected' Rat Pack.)

In 1954 a young singer called Elvis Presley scored his first hit single with 'That's Alright Mama'. A good old-fashioned southern white boy to look at, Presley shocked record companies, radio and TV bosses as soon as he started performing. Not only was his amazing voice the product of listening to dozens of black singers, but his movements below the waist – the reason he was nicknamed The Pelvis – had never been seen on a white performer. Parents were shocked, kids were enrapt, colour was irrelevant. The youth had spoken.

In the world of sport, Cassius Clay had exploited the rampant racist attitudes for his own benefit. In his famous title bout against Sonny Liston, he stoked a dangerous fire as he painted a clear divide between the 'evil, animalistic black man' and the 'conquering white saviour'. The damage done to Liston was untold. But Clay – another black man – achieved his purpose. By playing to his country's innate racism he had sidelined his opponent; at the same time he had subliminally won over many supporters who were as oblivious to his colour now as they had originally been anti it.

Lest he be taken for a white man's pup, Clay struck a crucial blow for equal rights in 1968. As Muhammad Ali he refused to take up arms and fight for America against Vietnam. Widely dismissed as a coward, his response was clinically precise: 'No Viet-cong ever called me nigger.' The implication, that fourteen years after segregation ended and with an Olympic medal under his heavyweight belt, he was still subjected to racial abuse in his own country, still resonates today.

Muhammad Ali may have been a focal point, but all around him thousands of individuals were mounting their own black revolutions. As a movement, it was gaining momentum. The twin strands of pacifist Dr King and the more controversial Malcolm X, who espoused the black man's right to take up arms to claim and defend his rights, were finding a worldwide audience. (Both men were eventually assassinated for their efforts. Which way was right?) Riots in Los Angeles and Detroit were the direct result of Malcolm X's call to arms. The sinister emergence of black 'freedom fighter' group, the Black Panthers, became his legacy.

While Malcolm X's tactics were certainly the more attention-grabbing, King's guiding message that black emancipation could not be achieved without economic equality had more far-reaching impact among the lawmakers. Modern European inner cities highlight the same problem: where there is a localised lack of employment, race-based or not, social groups drift as a whole towards lawlessness. In the late 1960s, as with today, a non-aggressive statement of lawlessness was drug-taking.

In 1967, revolution was the last thing on the mind of nineteen-year-old Sam Jackson. In fact, he was just starting out on his road to addiction. He had tried marijuana a year or two earlier and liked it, nothing more. Now he was lighting up regularly. For him, it was not a choice between a hash pipe and a gun; more a toss-up between fitting in and not. 'I'm a child of the 60s and when I started doing [drugs] there was something wrong with people who didn't,' Jackson told the *NME*. 'It was part of social development. Getting high, hanging out, talking rubbish.'

In his final years at high school, and with just part-time jobs for income, young Sam was certainly no square. A good student in every other way, marijuana was less a symbol of rebellion than acceptance. His peers smoked, so he did. If it didn't make him feel better, it certainly made his friends more interesting. It helped the days pass and it made a series of low-paid jobs bearable. Never, though, did it impinge on his life in a negative way; not to his mind, anyway. He was in control. Always. Even when he strayed from the weed.

'Angel dust,' Jackson said wistfully to the *Guardian* in 1998. 'I loved that stuff. See, I always knew it was a drug. I liked to sit in a room and watch people's eyes roll off their face, or just melt out of the chair.'

Proof that Jackson was in control came with his acceptance in 1969 into Atlanta's prestigious Morehouse College, America's number one academic institution for male black students. Morehouse is not the kind of place you fall into by accident. It is the apogee of hard work and dedication. Sam Jackson has never been afraid of either. Whatever his social habits, whatever cliques he was trying to be a part of, the work was getting done. His grades were good. Very good.

Morehouse College began life as the Augusta Institute in the basement of Springfield Baptist Church, Georgia, the oldest African-American church in the US. Currently sited on 61 acres of land among Atlanta's West End community, Morehouse can boast of such alumni as Dr Martin Luther King, Spike Lee and US Surgeon General David Satcher. In 1969, the college did not know it would one day be adding 'Samuel L. Jackson' to its headed paper.

The college introduced freshman Jackson to many things that would change his life for ever. It was at Morehouse that he envisaged a career in acting – it was not what he'd had in mind when he signed up for an oceanography degree course. It was through Morehouse that he met his wife

LaTanya Richardson. And it was at Morehouse that he fully engaged with the bewitching powers of drugs. Two out of three ain't bad.

Ironically, the US Government has to carry some of the blame. Even more ironically, the action they adopted was in accordance with the logic of Dr King. In the late 1960s, with Black Power dominating column inches the world over, radical measures joined the agenda to sort out the 'racial problem' in light of the sporadic social disturbances. King had argued that economic equality was the litmus test for unifying emancipation; the government of the late 1960s agreed. As a means of quelling the annoying black uprisings, they targeted a possible source of the discord: narcotics. Take away the black man's drugs, they reasoned, and you take away his power. (They did not ignore the fact that white kids were junkies too; but they could blame this fact on their being led astray by the African-Americans.) In the largest anti-drugs police clampdown ever seen, drug barons were arrested and their supply networks capped. Marijuana and the other drugs of the underground culture became temporarily unavailable. It was ironic that it had an anti-black policy at its core, but the result would benefit America as a whole for years to come. Or would it?

It didn't work with Prohibition. It was never going to work with drugs. How sad that, given the country's rife drug problem, it was civil unrest of such insidious origin which drove the whole clean-up campaign. Of course, there was a loophole and of course it was exploited. While it was true that marijuana was the drug of choice of a large proportion of blacks and other disenfranchised groups, it was also the number one narcotic among the beat anti-culture, which was picking up media interest. But federal overlords mistook each group's dependency on the drug. The truth was, it was the easiest and cheapest drug to find, use and enjoy; take it away and it would be replaced by another potentially more harmful alternative. It might be a subculture, but market principles still apply. In the event, this is exactly what happened. The late Richard Nixon is discredited enough in history thanks to Watergate but he could well have been remembered as the president who inspired a nationwide, potentially fatal heroin epidemic.

As one of the target audience, Sam Jackson was susceptible to the deadly charms of the drug. Fortunately, he remained unenchanted in the long term. 'When marijuana and the other stuff was taken off the streets to defuse the Black Revolution, heroin was all that was left,' he recalled in *Guardian* Weekend. 'It never became a problem for me because I used to OD a lot! Plus, I didn't like being depressed! I like being awake. And having fun.' Heroin, of course, can leave users destroyed and distraught. Jackson agrees, but insists his personal make-up was his defence. 'It all depends on your state of mind and your attitude when you do it,' he says. And his attitude was this: he was in control. And while he was in control, he would take what he needed. He would try what was available. He could handle it. He could handle anything. He was The Man.

2. SAM THE DORK

'Wake up. Get up. Sam! Sam!'

The panic in LaTanya Richardson's voice as she entered the family kitchen can only be imagined. Certainly, as she has revealed in several interviews, it is not something she ever wants to experience again. Returning home to find her husband of ten years slumped over the breakfast table, she experienced a flash flood of emotions: fear, guilt, panic and rage. Yes, rage. At herself for letting it get to this stage, for letting this happen where her daughter, Zoe, could see it. But mainly at the man in front of her. He was one of the greatest potential talents she had ever seen, he could have anything if he put his mind to it. He was a father, a husband and, she now realised, an addict and a drunk. Why hadn't she seen it happen? Why hadn't she helped him? Why somehow hadn't she prevented this?

However close a relationship is, you cannot help anyone – partner, friend, child – if they do not want to be helped. All the kind words, all the bullying in the world will not effect any change unless they want to listen, unless they want to help themselves. To get better, they have to do it themselves. For themselves.

Fortunately for LaTanya, for her husband, his family and for a generation of future movie fans, Jackson had spent a young lifetime doing things for himself. If anyone had the inner wherewithal to sort himself out, it was him. His inner resolve was impressive. It had had to be from an early age.

When your father elects to quit his job rather than earn a salary large enough to pay for your upbringing, you know you're in for a tricky start in life. That was indeed the fate that befell Samuel Leroy Jackson when he was born on 21 December 1948 in Washington DC. Rows between his mother Elizabeth and her lazy, selfish husband were constant and terrifying for the young boy. No kid wants to think ill of his father, but watching his mother work every hour she could to provide the things that her husband was too idle to broke young Sam's heart. When his dad finally left to start a new life in Kansas City, Missouri, it hurt but not as much as it should have done. The paternal bond had been irreparably broken and father and son would rarely meet again.

As a remote parent, Jackson Sr proved as ineffectual as when he had been at home. He rarely kept in touch and, when Elizabeth could find him, refused to pay maintenance for his family. 'His story was that he'd been in the army and my mom tried to get money from him for me so he got out of the army rather than pay it,' his son told *Premiere*. Without money and with sole responsibility now for two mouths to feed, life in Washington was hard. There was only one option open to Elizabeth and she took it. Packing their bags, she moved herself and Sam to Chattanooga, Tennessee, home of the fabled 'choo-choo' but, more importantly, home to her parents. They would help.

It was the best move she could have made. Her father had a steady job as a janitor, so there would always be food on the table, and her mother didn't work so she could look after the baby while Elizabeth held down a job in a factory. This set-up was so successful, in fact, that it would last until Sam reached the fourth grade, by which time Elizabeth's higher powered job as a buyer for a state mental institution and Sam's age meant that they could live together again as a unit. But back in the early 1950s, it worked just fine. Who needs fathers anyway?

Actually, the answer to that question is everyone, and it is to the credit of those involved that Sam emerged such a well-balanced child, considering his odd upbringing. It wasn't just a father his life lacked, it was a father figure – in fact, a male of any sort. With grandpa out at work all day and a succession of aunts and friends of his grandmother constantly visiting, young Sam's earliest environment was one of female company and attention. Surprisingly, considering the type of image he would acquire and the type of roles he would make his own, there was no macho influence around the house.

'I was a bit of a mommy's boy,' Jackson admitted to the London *Evening Standard*. 'My dad wasn't there. He didn't even teach me how to be a man. I had my grandfather and his brothers for my strong male role models.'

One of the upsides to his female-focused household was the lack of competition which tends to dominate some households. 'It saved me from having constantly to prove myself,' he admits. It also helped denude him of some stigmas, which could only be helpful in either his relationships or an acting career – not being afraid to show his emotions, for example.

'I guess you become a bit more sensitive to the way women look at things, because you've seen it and you understand it,' he has suggested. 'In my house it was OK to cry. So my world-view was different from an early age.'

Not only did Sam lack a father, of course, but neither were there any siblings to rub up against. Again, this was something he managed to turn to his long-term advantage as he perfected a nice line in using humour to defuse a number of situations, but at the time it often meant only one thing: trouble. 'Because I had no brothers or sisters there was no one else to blame,' he said in the *Guardian*. 'No dog, no cat. Anything got broken? It was me.'

While he obviously missed out on a level of companionship, on the plus side Sam learned to be comfortable in his own company, to make his own entertainment and, most importantly for his later career, to enjoy being centre of attention. At school he threw himself into learning the French horn and trumpet so he could perform in front of audiences with the school orchestra, staying from the third grade to the twelfth. He also showed an early aptitude for languages.

'Well, you know, I was always kind of memorable,' he admitted. That said, he used either to lock himself away with a novel or in front of a television show or film, although never at the expense of his school work. 'I lived in a sort of fantasy world, inside books and TV.'

Part of the TV ritual included *The Ed Sullivan Show*. One act in particular caught Sam's eye. 'I remember when Elvis showed up,' he recalls. 'That show was pretty much a tradition in my house on Sunday.' Everyone would assemble round the set to watch the latest stars. Like everyone else, Sam was puzzled by the treatment of the King. 'I remember them shooting him from the waist up and wondering, "Well, why are they doing that?"'

As a result of his TV watching, Sam liked nothing more than playing Cowboys and Indians with his friends. Being Sam, he went that extra mile. 'One time I took ketchup and bloodied up some Kotex pads and wrapped them around my head, and all the old ladies in the neighbourhood were chasing me around yelling, "Get that off!"'

Unfortunately, even for a young boy still in shorts, that fantasy world was not powerful enough to mask some of the unpleasant realities of the world in which he was growing up. The truth was brought home to Sam at an early age when, aged four or five, he whistled at a white girl from his porch. 'My grandmother, my mom, my aunt, everybody was out of the house, snatching me up, hitting me,' he told *Premiere*. 'Because I could have been killed for that.'

Regardless of what good legislative work was going on elsewhere in the early 1950s, southern states like Tennessee had yet to fall in line. Not only was integration a long way off, but actual hostility from the white community towards blacks was still commonplace. Signs on public buildings saying NO NIGGERS AND DOGS rammed the message home in the most degrading manner possible.

On the positive side, young Sam's first all-black Chattanooga school provided a welcoming haven from the divided world outside the play-ground gates. 'All my teachers were black, all the pupils were black,' he says. What's more, a lot of the teachers had taught Sam's mother and her brothers and sisters, so they knew what the expectations were for him. 'They set goals for me and helped me reach those goals.'

There was also the welcoming arms of the local church. Elizabeth and her family were very religious and Sam was inducted in the power of prayer at an early age. Every day, before bed and as soon as he woke up, Sam would pray, on his own in his room. Sundays, though, provided him with a more public way to show his faith as the entire household joined their black-only congregation. Even on days when he did not feel like attending, ten minutes in the company of his grandfather's friends and neighbours never failed to lift Sam's spirits and church became something he would look forward to as much for the social side as for the spiritual.

That cushioned environment, where everyone was like him, was in stark contrast to the rest of the town. More shocking for the young TV addict was the realisation that it was different to the fake world he loved watching on screen. No matter how long he sat in front of the small box in the corner of his grandmother's room, no matter how much he lost himself in the various programmes, one question was never far from Sam's mind: 'Where were all the brothers?'

'I accepted it,' he reflects. 'I grew up in a segregated society. I had a different outlook on the world and what was going on in it.' Even at such an early age, he was taught not to have any fantasies about the world being any place he could be a part of.

It would be this fact that caused Elizabeth, his mother, to be so against her son becoming a performer years later. 'When I told my mom I wanted to be an actor, it wasn't a viable career choice,' he says. How could he be an actor, she reasoned, when all the actors on TV were white? 'It was hard to convince anybody until they actually saw something up on screen.'

It was not just television that remained the domain of whites. 'I had the same heroes as everybody else,' Jackson says. That is, the same as 'white people'. 'Until *Shaft* came along I hadn't seen a hero who was like me on screen.' Just like his white neighbours, when Sam and his pals played, they too pretended to be Roy Rogers, Gene Autry or Errol Flynn – whoever was the matinee idol at the time. There were no black heroes, just Sidney Poitier. 'When we saw Sidney he was either a sidekick or a sacrificial lamb of some sort. You didn't want to pretend to be that.'

Sam spent a lot of time watching movies because his mother was a big film fan, but even those moments of escapism were tarnished by the racism of the day. 'We watched the same films as you guys,' he told the *Evening Standard*. 'You just had to watch them with your own people. That was how it was, that was how we lived.'

The physical apartheid of the South did not stop once you got inside the black-only theatres. Even the content of the films themselves was toned down for its audience, just like Elvis's appearance on *The Ed Sullivan Show*. If the abridged versions of movies we see broadcast on aeroplane flights are annoying enough, at least we know they have been watered down for a reason, usually because there could be minors watching who would not be allowed to see the film normally at a cinema. Imagine how galling, then, it must have been to be shown only diluted versions of pictures you have paid good money to see, all the while knowing that the crowd in the whites-only cinema across the road was seeing the unexpurgated reel.

Sidney Poitier's *Band of Angels* contains a scene where Poitier, as a Union soldier, is angered on returning from battle to find Yvonne De Carlo pretending to be the white mistress of the house. The fact that he slaps the white actress caused a stir throughout the industry. In fact, throughout the country. This was the film where Poitier, the black man's put-upon spokesman, got to stand up to the white oppressors. It was landmark film-making. In Chattanooga, *Band of Angels* could not arrive quick enough.

The cut that did arrive, however, did not live up to billing. 'That slap was a big thing in the South,' Jackson recalls. 'But when it got to my movie theatre, you never saw him hit her.' In Jackson's version, the argument started then cut to De Carlo sitting in a chair. Crucially, you never saw Poitier hit her – not if you were black. Of course, it was a different case in Chattanooga's segregated Grand or Liberty to just over the road. 'We'd see the same films shown to whites, but they'd be edited,' Jackson told *Premiere*.

The ignominy of having such offensive psychological abuse thrust at you on a daily basis gave young Sam a focus to his life, even at such a tender age. Elizabeth made sure of that. 'Brought up in that kind of environment, it was instilled in me from an early age that I had to be ten times smarter than everyone else in order to survive.'

Phase one of that policy of survival meant knuckling down at school. As he admits, the endless hours of TV watching did not seem to harm his grades. Nor did the play acting out in the streets with his friends. But then, Sam felt comfortable at school, among people like him.

For all his natural exhibitionism, however, there was an aspect of the young kid's life that caused him as much stigma as his skin colour. At least being black meant he was only picked upon by ignorant white people. But his stutter – and by the time he started school it had grown quite pronounced – meant that even friends, his own people, would sometimes snigger. Life was not fair. As a consequence, he threw himself into his text books, reputedly going a whole school year without talking to anyone. 'During that year I made the best grades in the class so everybody would leave me alone,' he reveals. 'I set the curve.'

The stutter is still there today, he says, on and off, but barely discernible. The first serious step towards combating it would be taken at Morehouse later, and that in turn would set him on the road to movie stardom. But a decade and a half earlier, it was smaller artistic fry which was concerning young Sam. And, to be honest, he did not like it one bit. His aunt Edna was a drama teacher who lived on the same block as her nephew. Every time she was short of boys for her productions, she came calling – whether the crying Sam wanted to take part or not.

'All the guys were out playing ball and she had me doing tap dancing and being the Sugarplum Fairy in *The Nutcracker Suite*,' he recalls. A Cowboy and Indian pageant was even worse. 'I was in a loincloth with bells on my ankles and some big headdress on.'

Crucially, however, there was one aspect the young performer liked. 'I enjoyed the attention. And that's what this is all about, at least at the start.'

Being known as a 'mommy's boy' was one thing, but playing dressing up games with girls was something else. Improbable though it now seems, the lad who would grow into 'Sam the Man' or 'The King of Cool' was not known as anything like that then. 'More likely, Sam the Dork,' he admits. And it wasn't just the acting that won him the accolade: 'I dressed pretty much the way my mom wanted me to dress.'

Elizabeth's devout preaching of the rewards of the work ethic was not just for her son's benefit. The factory work that had sustained them when she first moved her son to Chattanooga was soon replaced by more demanding employment. Eventually she won a lucrative post with the Tennessee health department buying equipment for one of the state's mental institutions. Finally, when Sam reached the fourth grade at school, she was able to move them out of her parents' home to a place of their own nearby. Her parents would still be around Sam, but at last he would have some freedom, and as a mother and son they would have time to themselves.

That time soon passed. Although still a dedicated student, Sam the teenager developed other interests that were not on the school curriculum. For a start, soft drugs were providing a one-way ticket into the fantasy worlds of his youth quicker than any TV show. Then there was the fact that he and his friends were becoming increasingly fired up by the racial situation around them. The news was carrying reports every day of new rights for minority groups, of new legislation meant to help his kind, but they were yet to see the results on the streets. Bigotry may have been outlawed by law, but on a day-to-day basis, it was as plain as the nose on his face. What became the issue now, however, was dealing with it.

'There was a survival mechanism,' Jackson says now. 'There were times when things happened and I would have loved to leap across and wrap my hands around somebody's throat. But you just stood there and showed nothing.'

When opportunities arose to demonstrate his feelings, though, Sam grasped them. The bigger the outlet the better. The day after Martin Luther

King was killed, he flew to Memphis to take part in the march. 'It was a great time to be young and to be part of that,' he admitted to *The Times*. 'A time of celebration and outrage and transition, which made wonderful changes to our society.'

Those times for Sam Jackson, by 1969, were black and white – literally. There were problems with his life and with the world, but he could identify the source. He was oppressed and he knew who the oppressors were. They would pay. But first he would finish his education.

Despite the loosening of the restrictions on segregated schooling, Morehouse College, America's number-one institution for black males, provided everything Sam was looking for in a higher learning establishment. For a start it had history – recent black rights pioneer Martin Luther King was an alumnus – but it also had promise of a future for him. There he could mingle with like-minded Americans, ones who were at the upper end of the learning scale but who shared his suffering, who understood what it was to be treated as a second-class citizen in their own country. And also by people whose grades were nowhere near as good.

When he arrived in Atlanta for his first days as a Morehouse boy, Sam Jackson was intent on a career in oceanography. Indeed, he had signed up for three years of marine biology study. For a guy raised as far from any ocean as possible, this was an intriguing choice. But by the age of nineteen, Sam had been consistently intriguing for some time. The fantasy worlds of his childhood had not left him, and the romantic lure of things he could not have – in this case the great seas – was an enticement to him, just like playing Cowboys and Indians on the streets had been years earlier. Years of hogging the TV set when *Sea Hunt* came on had left him with a taste for the aquatic that just would not go away. If he could channel this passion, he thought, higher education would be a breeze.

Standing proudly in its austere grounds in the Atlanta suburbs like some gothic Wayne Mansion from Tim Burton's moody *Batman* films, Morehouse College was almost a finishing school for the finest African-American minds around. A downside of assembling the greatest cerebral talents is that they often show a tendency to think 'off message'. Morehouse might have been a renowned seat of learning, but more than one of its student body thought he knew better. It was just a question of how they demonstrated it that mattered.

With black power raging on the streets of the United States, and the antics – indeed, the very existence – of the beret-wearing Black Panthers scaring the life out of a section of the white community, life in Morehouse seemed tame to its students. So what if the college was the leading one of its kind? What was it doing for black rights? Where was its syllabus purely on black history?

Fired up freshman Sam Jackson was a key figure in the movement to shake Morehouse out of its complacency. As America's leading African-American college it should stand for something, it needed to lead the debate on behalf of black Americans, not exist neatly and quietly on the white man's terms.

If the thinking was radical, the action of the student groups behind it was more so. When the Morehouse board of governors convened in the school for one of its regular meetings, a team of militant students entered the meeting room and declared the governors to be political hostages. The students' demands? A bespoke black history syllabus and more black members on the education board.

As part of the group, it never occurred to Sam Jackson that this was not the right thing to do. A lifetime of being taught by Elizabeth that things worth fighting for were the things most worth having had led him to the ineluctable conclusion that this was a Just Cause. He had read enough stories of people like King, like Rosa Parks, like Malcolm X fighting this war. He needed to feel part of it, part of the movement. And in confronting the board of governors of Morehouse College, he finally achieved that.

Looking back, the actions of Jackson and his fellow students do not seem to cover the perpetrators in glory. One of the governors affected by their actions was Martin Luther King Sr. If any man understood the need for sacrifice on behalf of his people, it was him. Locally, the action gained maximum news coverage. In the wider (white) press, there was unanimous condemnation. Rightly or wrongly, given the sentiment behind the action, the Morehouse authorities had no option but to expel the wrongdoers, Jackson among them. It was a tragic waste of excellent young minds. He, for one, was not impressed. 'As soon as I found something I liked about college, they kicked me out,' he moans. 'But that was the 60s rebellion – everybody was up in arms about something.' In their own way, Sam and friends had found something they wanted to change and created an avenue for them to have a voice.

Fortunately, after rigorous campaigning in the local press, Morehouse soon agreed with 'the voice'. High jinks, they said, rather than seriously vindictive intent, was at the root of the action. The sinners were welcomed back into the college. Other retribution would be required, but at least their learning would not suffer. Oh, and we've decided to start a specialist course in black history. Fair?

Samuel L. Jackson smiles at the memory. 'I've mellowed quite a bit since then,' he says, before adding, 'then again, maybe I haven't.'

While his desire for a black history syllabus may have seen him nearly evicted from the college, it was a different course that won him back.

Oceanography was going well enough, but more important to him at the time was a speech class that was finally having some healing effects on his stutter. When his teacher said that extra marks would be given to students who joined the local acting group, Sam decided to sign up. Since speaking unprepared in public was the main cause of the impediment, the logic went that speaking in public – but with previously rehearsed lines – would go a long way to improving the problem. For the extra credits it would win him, Sam was willing to try. It might even improve his stutter.

Although theoretically present on medical grounds, when it came to his first audition, he was won over. 'They were having "photo night",' he told the *Voice*, 'and all these girls were laying around in corsets and garter belts and I thought, "Hey, this might not be so bad . . ."'

That first Morehouse production was *The Threepenny Opera* and, thanks to the hours he had put in as a kid in his aunt's productions, Sam won a part. Immediately he was bitten. Not only did his stammer virtually disappear overnight, but he felt as if he had found his calling. A few meetings with his tutors later and oceanography was but a distant memory. There was a new major in town and its name was drama.

Switching courses was a no-brainer, Jackson admits. 'All of a sudden I found a place where I felt safe. I was eager to go to class. I was eager to perform. There was no fear about having this assignment or that deadline to meet. I wanted to do it.' The rewards made it worthwhile – he soon acquired a taste for the applause – but Sam was equally happy to be involved behind the scenes. 'I spent all day in the theatre building sets, hanging lights, and doing whatever we had to do. Then we rehearsed at night.'

His dedication and performances attracted another bonus, he admits: the attention of girls. 'Let's put it this way, there was nobody hanging around the biology department going, "Hey, you were really great in that test . . ."'

One girl in particular caught stuttering Sam's eye. And she his. LaTanya Richardson was a student at another Atlanta black institution – the girls' college, Spelman – when she came across town for the *Threepenny Opera* auditions and, later, rehearsals. One guy grabbed her attention: 'He was tall and lean and reminded me of my grand-daddy,' she told *Essence*. For his part, Sam was struck by her beautiful rich skin tone. 'I always wanted to be really dark,' he says. 'The first thing I noticed about LaTanya was that she was black. When I saw her backstage she looked even darker.' Then came the smile and the 'energy' she projected and he was hooked.

Before the production was over, the couple were an item. Their mutual love of acting had brought them together but their mutual love for each other would keep them that way for the rest of their lives. And all because a speech coach suggested taking up a little drama. With the all-or-nothing approach he would later show towards all aspects of his life, Sam was bitten by the acting bug. 'It felt so good I just kept doing it,' he says.

Famous last words . . .

3. DIE, WHITEY, DIE

The truth is, of course, that when you have a self-confessed 'compulsive–obsessive personality', the words 'it felt so good I just kept doing it' could refer to anything. And everything. That, after all, is the way Samuel L. Jackson lives his life; that's just the way he is. Today those obsessions include an encyclopaedic knowledge of martial arts films and, top of the list, his beloved golf. But thirty years ago? Well, where do you want to start . . .

Unfortunately, while theatre and acting and his new-found vocation for the stage began to consume Sam's study time at Morehouse, his extra-curricular hours were just as obsessively filled by partying, alcohol and drugs. At least when he enrolled at Morehouse there was some air between them – just. By the time he had graduated three years later, however, the boundaries were blurred beyond distinction.

Atlanta in 1972 offered the perfect place for Sam Jackson to begin his life as a man. He was 23, he had an excellent drama qualification behind him and the knowledge of having studied at one of the great institutions in America. Now, though, at the time he needed to find a career, he wanted to take the next step and that, quite naturally, was to become a full-time actor. A professional. Stage, TV, the movies – whatever came along he would take. Whatever the personal cost, whatever the effort required. Hard work? That didn't scare him. He was Elizabeth Jackson's boy. Hard work was his middle name.

Actually his middle name was Leroy, but not that you'd know it. In more than one interview during the last ten years, Jackson has replied to the question of the mysterious 'L' with the same answer: 'The L stands for lucky.' And for many observers he would be right.

Luck though, if you explore the Jackson definition, is not something totally beyond your control, like winning numbers on the Lotto. 'Somebody once told me that luck is the perfect meeting of preparation and opportunity,' he explains. And if Sam was serious about a subject, whatever that subject was, he would put in the preparation. No mistake.

Although an admirer of his endeavour and his enthusiasm, his mother was not impressed by Sam's career choice. 'Now it's become a viable choice,' he recalls, 'but back at the time when I chose to be an actor, my mom wanted to know what I was going to do for a living.' In other words, how would he support himself while failing to earn money on stage?

To Elizabeth fretting away in Tennessee, her boy's prospects would not have looked too encouraging. While she supported his right to follow his heart, she could not have helped worrying that he was taking a dangerous path. Again. Although proud of his integrity in doing what he thought was right (not that Elizabeth told him that), she had been furious three years earlier when Sam was temporarily expelled from Morehouse for following his heart rather than his head. How was he ever going to make something of his life if he didn't get an education? she had thought back then. And who was going to give him an education if he had a reputation as a troublemaker? And who would ever give him a job with no education?

Raised in an environment where keeping your head down and your nose clean was the only way to combat racism – the consequences of any alternative action were too frightening to contemplate – Elizabeth could not understand where Sam's new-found rage had come from. Of course she supported efforts to change racist attitudes and repeal segregation laws, but as she had seen on occasion with her own eyes, nothing good ever came of confrontation, not for the person in the front line, anyway. Why couldn't Sam keep himself to himself before he got into serious problems?

It was not just his outspoken views on racism and black advancement that worried Elizabeth, though. There were other changes, too, during his college years. The Black Revolution was more than just a political movement. For those of Sam's age in the late 1960s it heralded a new way of thinking, of behaving, even of dressing. Things that had previously been considered 'underground' were now more prominent for no other reason than the oppressive lid of fear had been lifted. Greater freedom of expression was sweeping across all strata of every society, and for the first time personal style – what you wore and how you wore it – said more about you than how rich you were. Your clothes became a statement of membership, affiliating you to one group or another. *Shaft*, released in 1971, must take a lot of the blame or credit, depending on your generation. Sidney Poitier may have gone to dinner with white folk, but Richard Roundtree's character was fucking them and spitting them out afterwards.

'It was different, exciting, powerful, inspiring,' Jackson says. 'I couldn't afford the leather coat but I developed that walk and grew my hair and some sideburns; tried to grow a moustache. All the girls wanted somebody who looked like Shaft.' Or if they didn't look quite like him, acted like him. The bolder you were, the closer you were linked to the cause. And Sam was bold. Gone was the boy that Mrs Jackson used to dress; in his place was smooth Sam, a sharp dresser with an eye for 'don't fuck with me' threads and an attitude to match. If Morehouse had opened his eyes to nothing else, the school had given him the confidence to evolve into this, once *Shaft* had shown the way.

With the clothes and the movement went the lifestyle, of course. The

1960s were a time of huge experimentation with narcotics, both legally and behind closed doors. No better example of the confusion surrounding them, particularly in America, is that of Jack Nicholson. When he and his wife Sandra Knight were going through difficulties they tried marriage guidance counselling. Considering that part of the couple's problems at the time stemmed from Nicholson's drug use, it seems bizarre today to learn that an analyst prescribed a course of LSD for each to take. It might not have saved the marriage – they soon after broke up – but it made trying all the more interesting.

So by the time Sam Jackson left Morehouse, drug-taking was an established part of his life. Like the clothes, the developing language and the political movement, it was another part of the statement of black identity. By dint of its being frowned upon by the white federal lawmakers, marijuana seemed an almost compulsory pastime. By smoking it, and by taking heroin or cocaine or whatever else was available at the time, he and his friends were in daily defiance of those power brokers running the country. It just so happened that it was extremely pleasurable too. Marijuana in particular, in the 1960s, gave Sam a confidence that he had rarely felt before. Alcohol, too, had the same effect. There was nothing he could not achieve under the influence of either.

The proof of this had come at his first drama audition at Morehouse. After a few beers first and a sly toke he took to the stage in front of his first audience as an adult performer. 'I had never been on stage without a substance in my body,' Jackson confirms of his pre-90s days. 'Never in my life had I gone onto a stage without alcohol, reefer, acid, something.' If he had struggled to get through the role, or if he had been told that his performance was ever let down by that spaced-out look he sometimes had, then maybe he would have curtailed the drinking and smoking. But nobody ever said anything. And why would they? He achieved great things on stage while high, and that couldn't have been a coincidence. The alcohol, the drugs – they were his chemical muse. Like Coleridge. Like Byron. Maybe he couldn't actually do it without something like this inside him?

'I thought that was how it was done,' Jackson admitted to *Movie Maker*. Theatre tradition is filled with great partyers and great drinkers like Peter O'Toole or Richard Burton. Why not him? 'The great ones could do it so you did it too, hoping it would give you some insight into greatness.' It was the same in movies. 'Listen, Oliver Reed wouldn't have been Oliver Reed unless he had twenty beers inside him. So why not me?'

Whether or not Sam ever found greatness is debatable, but he never once considered the alternative of looking for it while clean. The 'muse' element aside, there was more than a hint of Dutch courage to his actions as well.

'I wasn't confident I could still act because I'd never acted without a substance in my body,' he says. 'People used to ask if I ever got stage fright. I wasn't cognisant. I was fucked up.'

Like several accepted sayings, the phrase 'what doesn't kill you can only make you stronger' should perhaps come with a government warning. But in 1972 it did seem to be the motto Sam lived by. And you could see his point. As he emerged blinking into the sunlight of the rest of his life after three great years of college, he was convinced the only way was up. Whatever doubts his mother may have had about his aspirations, he was convinced that he could make it in the entertainment industry. And it wasn't just the drugs talking. Not only had he won great notices during his Morehouse years for the roles he had played, but he had even picked up some professional – that is, paid – work on the side.

Directed by Michael Schultz from a story by Lindsay Smith, *Together for Days* was an independent production produced on a budget of $600,000. As a first-time actor, and a student at that, Sam pocketed very little of that amount. But he got to travel and to see a proper production on location and he began to get a glimpse of the subtleties required for acting for cameras rather than the Upper Circle.

At the time, given his militant interests and the fact that his initial attraction to LaTanya was based on the darkness of her skin compared to his, the subject matter of the proposed film prompted mixed thoughts. On the one hand it featured black activism to the fore. On the other hand, the central premise of the film was that the lead activist would fall in love with a white girl. In a daring move for the time – on top of the bold step of featuring interracial sex on a general release picture in the US – the racism that occurred as a result of the liaison was viewed from the black perspective. Clifton Davis's character is subjected to massive guilt from the rest of his group and pressurised to step down as a spokesman; how can he fight for the cause if he is sleeping with the white man's daughter (Bond star Lois Chiles)?

Fortunately for Sam's entrenched student beliefs, the part offered to him was as Stan, one of the mouthy detractors. Regardless of the movie's overriding message – that love is colour-blind – he could get to appear on screen in a motion picture and be true to his personal beliefs. What's more, he got to spend a few days in LA for the first time in his life. Returning to Atlanta after that trip was something else and for a few days – probably longer if he's honest – there was an extra swagger in the Jackson stride.

The summer after Sam's graduation, *Together for Days* was released in cinemas. It didn't break box-office records and certainly didn't fire up critical interest, but sitting in the best row of the Atlanta movie theatre in December 1972, LaTanya Richardson was the proudest girl in the world. Next to her, Sam Jackson just smiled and nodded. He'd done good work and there it was, twice as large as life and booming out around him.

Variety, in its 6 December issue, led the way in the faint-praise stakes, describing *Together for Days* as 'hardly the worst of the indie species'. It also criticised the film's failure to predetermine its audience. 'While lacking the energy that is demanded of black audiences, it inadvertently insults whites who might have been attracted to the liberal underpinnings of this romantic tract.'

Nevertheless, if Sam had had his doubts about this career choice, they were shot down in flames now. He had appeared in a movie and picked up a character name in the rolling credit list. You could see his work in selected movie theatres all over the country. Although his performance was a case of blink and you'll miss him, it was still something for his résumé. And, if he had anything to do with it, it wouldn't be the last.

Movies, though, would take a back seat during those early 70s years as Sam diligently learned his trade. The hours that he put into his recreational drug use were nothing compared to the effort expended on his art. Anything to do with the theatre he pounced upon. If a job needed doing, and a play needed it to happen before it could go on, then Sam was there. Carpentry, lighting, general dogsbodying. Whatever the demands, whatever the hours, he was available. Inebriated maybe, but available all the same because this is how he wanted to spend the rest of his life, regardless of the sacrifices.

'I wasn't worried about making a living at it, but my mom did,' he recalls. 'She was like, "You won't be able to pay the rent." It wasn't a viable career choice as far as she was concerned.' But the professors at Morehouse encouraged students to go out and get agents and seek employment. As a result, Sam found work in underground and children's theatre, adding new techniques to his repertoire. At the same time he kept his hand in with the off-stage environment, building sets and learning other theatre-related skills.

It was during his Morehouse time that Sam and LaTanya hooked up with one of these 'underground' outfits, Atlanta's Black Image Theatre Company. The demands of college life, for all their impact on his grades, were not enough to entertain the prolific and oh-so-keen Mr Jackson. What's more, he was consciously looking for an outlet for his inherent political views. With the Black Image troupe he found it. Where Morehouse, as a public body, was bound to be more conservative in its approach to all things, private groups could be more controversial. They had no history to concern them, just a future. And that future was bright. That future was black.

'The Black Image Theatre Company was a kind of revolutionary street theatre at the time,' Jackson told Nasser Metcalfe in 1999. 'My wife hates for me to refer to it as the "Hate Whitey" theatre but essentially that's what it was.' Once they made the decision to take part, the couple spent all their time there, arriving at the theatre at 7 a.m. and staying sometimes until three in the morning. Clearly Sam's tendency to obsess was contagious.

There speaks a man dedicated to his art. There also speaks a man dedicated to his cause. White-hating or black-supporting – the result was the same. Intense dramas based on centuries of oppression for African-Americans everywhere. No production went without the white man being denigrated almost for existing. This was payback theatre with score-settling for an encore. And Sam Jackson was at its heart, lending a hand to every production in some capacity, starring when chosen. The fact that this was also the time of the Blaxploitation period on the silver screen, the fact that films like *Shaft* were just becoming accepted as mainstream, meant that more than ever there was a commercial audience for his work as well. What had started as underground was becoming more loud and proud by the week. And the audiences were beginning to match.

Of course, not even working twenty-hour days can be enough to sate the appetites of a true compulsive obsessive and it was not long before Sam and LaTanya left the company to set up their own: Just Us. The message was the same – black theatre for black people by black people – but if anything it was even more hardcore. ('Die, whitey, die – so black folk can take over,' is one of his recent interpretations, much to LaTanya's embarrassment.) And, if possible, it was more hard work. But that, Sam had decided, was the only way to achieve anything.

Just Us and the Black Image Theatre Company still formed only part of Sam's plan to crack the entertainment business. When he wasn't acting, auditioning, selling tickets or running cables, he was catching trains across the country trying to find more lucrative work in TV and film. In 1975 he got his first break.

Success is a relative concept – literally. A person can achieve great things in a career but for it to register back home with his relatives and family, it needs to enter their sphere of reference. When it comes to most arts professions, that sphere can be frustratingly narrow. For a writer, no number of years of consistently profitable magazine work or paperback releases can match a family's pride at seeing their darling's first hardback publication, often regardless of content. A photographer's work for the world's leading design magazines might pass quite unnoticed in his own family until he supplies a shot for his aunt's local rag. Equally for actors, all the good stage work in the world pales into insignificance against what most 'normal' people would consider the holy grail of the profession: a one-second spot on a TV commercial.

For all her many good attributes, Sam's mother was guilty of this. Even though oceanography offered barely more worldly application than fluency in Flemish, Elizabeth was still more comfortable with it as a 'serious' subject for Sam to study. Acting was a hobby, not a profession. Clowning around on stage was fun stuff, not hard work. And hard work is what got you places. At least if you were from Tennessee and you were black.

But all that changed one day when Elizabeth was watching TV with her folks. She knew it was coming but that did not diminish the proud anticipation in any way. For ages she sat there, only leaving the room during the shows themselves, but always back for the commercials. And then she saw it. For thirty whole seconds, there was her boy, Sam Jackson, on her TV screen. He was talking and everybody in town could see it. Make no mistake, her boy was an actor and she was going to let the whole world know.

'Once I did my first commercial and her friends called her and said, "Hey, I saw Sam on TV," she was like, "Oh yes, he's an actor now," ' Jackson laughs.

Not only did it not matter that it was a commercial, it did not even matter what that commercial was for. In fact, it was a fast food ad, for Krystal hamburgers, and Sam got to say one line, 'It's probably the little flame-grilled onions', in response to the question 'What makes Krystal hamburgers so good?' But it didn't matter. It was a start. And it was on TV. And it made his mother proud.

'That really proved to my mom that I was an actor,' he smiles. Before that, she never really believed that stage work qualified as acting, saying, 'Why don't you get a job in one of those soap things, one of those things on TV?'

As far as Sam was concerned, however, it was just a job. It was his first job, but it was not how he wanted to spend his life. He had to use it as a stepping stone to reach his real ambitions. And they, he admits, did not stop at sell-out TV spots – not at first, anyway. 'Being a movie star was one of those things that I thought about,' he says. 'So whenever the Academy Awards came on I sat at home practising my acceptance speech.' Over the years, aspirations were tempered by realism. From movie dreams to maybe hopes of a regular TV slot on a soap. When that didn't transpire, sights were lowered even further. 'Then it's like, "Damn, I wish I had a really good beer commercial lined up." '

Fortunately, although LA was not exactly begging him to elope, Sam was still getting the odd job from his Atlanta base that justified his and

LaTanya's stay there. The year before the Krystal commercial, on 8 May 1974, he could be seen in *In Tandem*, a TV film about two independent truckers who team up to help an orange grower get his fruit to market, despite his neighbours' best attempts to drive him out of business and buy his land on the cheap. Directed by Bernard L. Kowalski for D'Antoni-Weitz Productions, the film gave Sam another glimpse of life on a large set with retakes and a workable budget. It also opened his eyes to the impact special effects and stunts could have. Coming from the team that brought us *Bullitt* and *The French Connection*, it was no wonder that the trucking chase sequences were memorable. As the second offering in NBC's *Double Feature Night at the Movies*, *In Tandem* was well received by, among others, the *Hollywood Reporter*, who cited 'first rate direction' and 'a good deal of raw and raunchy humour' among the plaudits. That, today, no one remembers it – or Sam's very small role – is irrelevant to the part it played in his learning curve.

Similarly, *The Displaced Person*. As part of The American Short Story season which featured dramatised versions of works by Hemingway, Henry James and F. Scott Fitzgerald, this TV film of Flannery O'Connor's harrowing tale relayed how Father Flynn brings a Polish refugee family to work on a small southern farm in the 1940s. As a boy from this area, Sam could immediately identify with the story. The fact that the film centred on racial hostility in the South also rang true to his experiences. However, as one of the black hired hands cast to terrorise the newcomers – with tragic consequences – that is where Sam's identification with the piece ended. For the founder of a 'hate whiteys' group, it was hardly the ideal material.

For all its ideological faults, as far as he was concerned *The Displaced Person* proved another landmark for Sam. It was his third large-crew vehicle, another glimpse at the efficient production line of TV production, and another in which he had been awarded a character name in the credits – he played farmhand Sulk in the film alongside Irene Worth, John Houseman, Robert Earl Jones and Shirley Stoler. More than anything, though, *The Displaced Person*, shortly followed by a minor part in short-lived TV show *Movin' On*, fired up both Sam and LaTanya to take the next step in their careers. LA was still the last port of call on their acting journey; but for theatre, real theatre of the type the couple specialised in, there was only one place in the country.

In 1976 Sam and LaTanya packed their cases and caught the train to New York for the next stage in their destiny. Together.

4. WHERE ARE THE ETHNIC PEOPLE?

New York in the mid 1970s offered a wonderful chance for black actors. Gone were the days when you might turn on the TV and not see a non-white face for nights on end. The media was full of multi-cultural events and broadcasts. Blaxploitation was gaining momentum as an artistic movement, with the films of Pam Grier and *Shaft* star Richard Roundtree playing all over the country, and New York, like London, offered a welcoming base for talent of all denominations. Sam Jackson, for one, appreciated the timing.

'By the time I started acting it was the Blaxploitation period,' he says. 'Black actors were working and you could see them working – you knew there was a chance to get a break.'

In other words, black actors were trendy. For all its faults, Hollywood is at least transparent in its mercenary approach. When you're out you're out; when you're in you're in. It has little to do with you or your creed or your race, and more to do with whether you fit the demographics that are popular with majority audiences at the time. It's a kind of prejudice but only in as much as 'are you the next Brad Pitt?' would alienate women from casting sessions.

Jackson is at least alive to this distinction. He knows that Hollywood never set out to make him welcome because of his skin colour. He knows that Broadway never cut him any slack because of his history. But he also knows that when audiences want to pay to see black faces, then that's what they shall see. It really is as simple as that.

'Prejudice is part and parcel of the job,' he admitted to the *Independent*. 'Other actors go through the same thing, whether it's because they're young or blond.' The decision-makers, he realises, are 'business people rather than creative people' and it doesn't pay to take their decisions personally. 'Understanding who these people are prevents me from being frustrated by it.'

That is not strictly true. Even putting his Oscar gripes aside, twenty years later Samuel L. Jackson is convinced that the game is weighted in the white man's favour and it does bother him. Led by his hero Morgan Freeman, there is a sizeable number of very good black actors, but there could be more. Unfortunately, Hollywood, as an industry, doesn't seem too intent on unearthing them. 'Producers are out there every day trying to find the next Tom Cruise and Brad Pitt, when they should be trying to find the next us.'

The move to Harlem, though, was a major step in Sam and LaTanya's lives. Renting part of a brownstone house, they plotted their onslaught on the local theatres. It helped that they both came packing extra skills. 'By the time I moved to New York, if I wasn't acting, I was building sets,' Jackson says. He was doing anything, in fact, as long as it was in the industry. Unlike just about every other actor you care to mention, Sam had no intention of diluting his talent, or his passion, by taking up another job to pay the way. No Burger King for him. He would do things his way, not the LA way.

'You know, I never waited tables,' he says, proud at always finding a way to work where he was supported, rather than resented, by the people who were around him. 'If I said to somebody that I had an audition to go to, they said, "Good luck," not "Well, who the hell is going to wait on my tables?" '

That sense of camaraderie, of good wishes and brotherhood was also something he knew he wouldn't find in Hollywood. New York, at the time Sam and LaTanya decided to head there, was alive with openings for black talent and, more importantly, home to a real sense of community among its performers and artists, all of them just happy to have the opportunity to follow their dreams among like-minded people. 'We'd walk together from audition to audition,' Jackson says. 'We went to see each other's shows. We socialised together. It wasn't the kind of competition that I see going on in LA.' Part of New York's advantage over LA is its transport system. Most American cities outside of New York are very much car societies. There are no pavements or sidewalks; if you don't have a car, you don't have a life. On the east coast, however, there is a mass transit system at the core of New York's vibrant atmosphere. When everyone is travelling together to the same auditions on the same subway, it makes it easier to get to know your rivals. When you're all having to leap the barriers because you're too poor to pay the fare, you at least have a starting point. Friendships form and a sense of community is established. In LA, you never really get to know your rivals. Everyone turns up in their own personal vehicle and the first you see of them is in the audition hall.

'LA is very adversarial,' Jackson summarises. In New York, if he knew he wasn't going to get a part, he'd tell four other people about the audition and hope they were luckier. Not in LA. 'There you get to the audition and you look at the person across from you who is auditioning for the same role and you don't talk to each other.'

Harlem, Manhattan, Queens – New York City had everything that Sam could want at that stage in his life. Some things were more obvious to a man with his habits, but there were other distractions too. Movies were still a great passion and he would set aside a lot of his days to catch the latest releases. Audition at nine, drugs at eleven, movie at twelve; that sort of thing. In fact, the dark rooms of the cinemas often provided the perfect chill-out zone. His great love, at the time, was the sensationalist kung fu films coming out of Hong Kong.

His love affair with martial arts movies began as soon as he and LaTanya arrived in New York, when he could visit the movie theatres on Manhattan's famed 42nd Street. At the time, the strip's decaying theatres played either pornography (think *Midnight Cowboy*) or Hong Kong 'chopsocky' films. On stage only at night, Jackson and his young actor friends became regulars at martial arts matinees. 'There were at least four places that would show triple features of Hong Kong films,' he says. 'We would go all day, and watch three features a day.'

He barely remembers the first Hong Kong film he saw, a Shaw Brothers production. 'There were Bruce Lee films that happened, but most of them were kind of anonymous films like *The Seven Deadly Venoms*,' he says. His appetite was well and truly whetted. 'That was where I got my whole love for them.' He is now the proud owner of most of the films he saw back then, plus hundreds of new ones, and remembers *Master of the Flying Guillotine* as a particularly fine example. 'Back when David Chang was actually the One-Armed Boxer, that was totally cool. David was the man!'

Despite his love for martial arts flicks, Jackson was not so discerning to ignore other genres. This was partly to do with his love of film; equally to do with his being smacked out of his head. In 1977, quite the worse for wear, he caught a low budget sci-fi flick that would have an amazing impact on his life.

'I went to the very first showing of *Star Wars* at this movie house on 44th Street,' he says. The fact that he was far from sober, as usual, only added to the experience. 'I was sitting there zoomed out of my mind and this spaceship passes overhead. I was hooked immediately.' And when Samuel L. Jackson says hooked, you know he means it.

His former love, *Star Trek*, was instantly forgotten for this new, darker view of galaxies far, far away. 'I was like, "OK, that's hi-tech, but if I'm going to go into space these are the people I'm gonna be hanging out with and these are the places I'm going to go." '

Even though this was sci-fi, even though there were men with three eyes wandering around, the activist part of Sam still found fault. For a moment, anyway. 'I did wonder where the brothers were,' he admitted to *Empire*. 'But then I figured, "Well, these people are blue, green, orange and everything else, so I guess you don't have to have black people." ' Or perhaps you do. By the time the film's third sequel came to be filmed in 1997, that imbalance would be addressed. And how. (Whether he realised it or not, the most distinctive voice in the whole film was a 'brother'. James Earl Jones contributed the voice of the Empire's Darth Vader; former Green Cross Code Man Dave Prowse provided the physique.)

Being overwhelmed by the 'brothers' issue when watching a new film was understandable for Sam back in 1977. The Black Revolution may have lost some of its national appeal, and certainly the media was less intrigued by it by then, but for those like Sam, whose very living depended on playing a white man's game to white men's rules, the grassroots divisions were still very much in place. For all its cosmopolitan overtures, New York, like most major cities, still had its pockets of racial tension; Harlem was pretty much given over to its black population, and there were still problems between the NYPD and all non-whites. As a consequence, regardless of how high he was in the movie theatre, the question of equal representation would always float across Sam's mind. Almost thirty years later, he is appalled to admit it still does.

'Sometimes you look at a movie and say, "Where are the ethnic people?" ' he exclaims. He notes that he can watch films supposedly set in a city as large and diverse as New York and still leave asking, 'Where are we?' 'The world does have people like us in it,' he justifies. 'We do almost every job that's out there.'

Still burning today, this despair was at the front of Sam's mind when he arrived in NYC fresh from the race cauldron of Atlanta. The Black Image Theatre Company and Just Us had served his political ends well, but neither really helped his acting. In New York he would have the opportunity to develop both sides of his personality.

New York has had its share of bespoke black theatre companies over the years. The National Black Theatre, New Federal Theatre, Inc, Opera Ebony, Ujamaa Black Theatre, Urban Bush Women and New Ensemble Actors Theatre have all operated at various times. Arguably the most respected – and controversial – of them all, however, was the Negro Ensemble Company, formed in 1967 as part of the Black Revolutionary Arts Movement of the era.

The company was formed after director and playwright Douglas Turner Ward wrote an open letter in the *New York Times* in 1966 challenging American theatre to produce work relevant to black society. American community theatre was outdated and out of its depth, he said, and the only way forward was for the creation of an autonomous professional black theatre. It was some letter. In response, the Ford Foundation stepped forward with a three-year grant worth $1.2 million and in 1967 the Negro Ensemble Company was born. As well as being an employer of fully fledged creative talent, Ward and his co-founders wanted the St Marks Playhouse-based group to offer something for the next generation. Tuition-free workshops and a general atmosphere of inclusion and aspiration went a long way to fostering these goals.

Success for a project like this can often be judged by the number of feathers it ruffles. The NEC caused controversy on both sides of the Atlantic and on both sides of the racial divide. Just in case anyone thought that America was the only country with an inherent discrimination problem, a 1967 London performance of the company's first production, *Song of the Lusitanian Bogey*, was peppered by heckling and abuse from right-wingers who resented its anti-colonial outlook. Back on its own doorstep, the criticism was more that the group was not black and extreme enough. Peter Bailey, writing in the *Negro Digest* in 1968, questioned whether the company had sold out by accepting the white dollar for its funding and employing white administration staff and producing white playwrights. How could the company truly reflect the Black Revolutionary outlook of the time when its hands were tied by financial obeisance to the very sector of society – white leaders – the movement was against. Under the headline 'Is the Negro Ensemble Company Really Black?' he wrote: 'It may be interesting theatre; it may be good theatre; but to call it black theatre would be considerably stretching the definition.'

Ward's response to the criticism came with the calibre of the work. Over the next decade the NEC premiered such landmark productions as *Ceremonies in Dark Old Men* by Lonnie Elder III, *The Dream on Monkey Mountain* by Derek Walcott, *The River Niger* by Joseph Walker and *The First Breeze of Summer* by Leslie Lee, all of them announced amidst a blaze of publicity that drew international attention to the developing black theatre traditions. Many of the shows were televised on PBS and some, including *The River Niger*, even transferred to Broadway where they played to packed houses of multi-racial audiences. That show went on to win the 1973 Tony Award for Best Play and in so doing guaranteed the financial future of the under-attack troupe.

Since its inception in 1967, the NEC has been responsible for producing more than two hundred new plays and offering a showcase for more than four thousand cast and crew members, among them Louis Gossett Jr, Sherman Hemsley, Phylicia Rashad – and Samuel L. Jackson. For it was here that, in 1976, he found his spiritual home when he arrived in NYC. It was also here, among the wise old voices at the NEC, that he was encouraged to hone his natural raw talent in the first step to becoming one of the most accomplished actors – black or white – of his generation. Some of the lessons he learned then, he still employs to this day.

The main Jackson trick, taught by the NEC's Lloyd Richards and Douglas Turner Ward, is to flesh out a full biography for any character he plays, regardless of the size of the role. Background influences everything, he says, and context is all so ask the right questions and you can devise a whole history for anyone. You might only have a couple of lines, but they could be said in any number of ways, depending on the type of person your character is. And if it doesn't say in the script, then find out. Make it up. This, after all, is the business of make-believe.

'You can make up a birthday,' Jackson says. 'You can make up a birthplace, a family background; educated, not educated; poor, rich, middle class? What kind of friends? That's the process.'

Putting the hours in to develop his talent was no sacrifice for Sam. He lived and breathed his work; it was, after all, his obsession. He took advantage of every free workshop, every training initiative and every opportunity just to hang around other theatre folk. There were readings with new writers, directors to meet, auditions to prepare for with other actors. Always something going on.

'I was in New York for nineteen years and it was an exciting time in my life,' Jackson recounts. 'You don't necessarily have to be on Broadway, you can be off, off Broadway, and be involved with good projects.'

And with good people. Although there was no shortage of competition for work, it was not 'dog eat dog' like in LA. Friends watched each other's auditions, wished each other good luck. And meant it.

Of course, although keen just to be involved, if there was an actual job to be done – however minor – all the better. Any role Sam could get he would take.

'They tell you when you enter the theatre: there are no small parts, only small actors,' he explained to the *Voice*. 'You don't go in there and just half do something because, "Hey, I'm not the third lead." '

That approach would pay dividends – dividends he is still collecting today.

Sam and LaTanya did not move to New York to hide from Hollywood but to prepare for it. Although geographically they could not have been further away, they both knew that LA was a hungry town and unless you were one of the lucky few it would chew you up and spit you out just for being there. Acting was what Sam was put on this earth to do. Not waiting on tables, however much it improved your networking connections.

'I always said I would never go to LA until they sent for me,' he recalls. 'I had too many friends who went there looking for work and kind of disappeared.' Life in LA seemed to involve a lot of sitting around waiting for agents to call. If Sam was going to wait, he would do it in New York where he could busy himself in the meantime. (The move would eventually happen, but more for LaTanya's career chances than his.)

So it was not as an alternative to movie-making that Sam ended up in NYC, rather as something to do while he waited for that call. He reasoned that if a producer is looking for a black actor and has the choice of someone with years of stage experience or someone who hasn't, who are they going to choose? He would take whatever he could, part-wise, in order to fulfil his movie-star ambition. But what he would not do is stop trying; and if you stopped acting, he thought, you were giving up.

At least waiting tables in Beverly Hills would have put some money in Sam's pocket, though, and to most people this might have seemed a preferred option. For the first few years, Harlem life was tough. Sure, they were both learning, picking up knowledge and experience, new friends and new skills here and there. But financially, it was a further sign of Sam's dedication to his Hollywood dream – or his obsession with it – that he pulled through. Even when he did have work in 1976, he was often poorer at the end of it than before he turned up. 'There were times when they only paid me $35 for the whole run,' he says. 'You'd spend that getting the train to the theatre.'

But things improved. They had to. Sam was getting better and better with every performance, making more and more contacts through his incessant theatre networking. It was only a matter of time before he was noticed. Unfortunately, it was not by Hollywood, but once he took time to appreciate the difference, he was just as excited.

'At a certain point I focused on the work,' he says, 'and I lost sight of career goals that I had. I started doing plays that were winning Pulitzer Prizes and ended up with a good reputation.' Which, in itself was a good thing, just not the thing he had set out to achieve.

It would come though if he plugged away long and hard enough. It would come for him, just as it would come for the best of his contemporaries working the same route through and around Broadway: his friends Morgan Freeman, Denzel Washington, Wesley Snipes and Laurence Fishburne. 'There are so many people who came out of that time who have viable careers, as opposed to guys who graduated from college and went to LA and you never hear of them again.'

Of course, when Jackson says he started doing Pulitzer prize-winning plays, it did not happen overnight. But it did happen eventually. In fact, his total body of theatre work during those New York years makes impressive reading, give or take the odd early years experiment. There were Shakespeare in the Park plays every season that he and LaTanya participated in, as well as various things for The Public Theatre. As he says, some of these were not the biggest productions. Some of them were so far off Broadway, in fact, they were virtually New Jersey. But when the highlights came they stood out.

While LaTanya won a place on Broadway with her role in Ntozake Shange's *For Colored Girls Who Have Considered Suicide/When the Rainbow is Enuf*, Sam had his share of the big time too. In 1981, the NEC had probably their biggest success, and he was part of it. Written by Charles Fuller, *A Soldier's Play* recounts how African-American forces were first allowed to participate in combat in a non-segregated army during World War II. The play follows a unit of African-Americans and their African-American sergeant and the racial tensions that their very existence throws up as they are deployed to dig ditches and take part in training sessions rather than be trusted with actual combat. The racism comes from within the group as they question each other's regional and class distinctions. A murder within provides the dramatic climax.

Under Fuller's subtle hand, there are no stereotypical white villains. Everything that happens, good and bad, does so as a result of the dynamics of any particular group of individuals. And he lets the audience devise its own message. If you can spot the irony that the unit of soldiers are about to fight for freedom abroad while still facing segregation at home, then that is fine. But if you don't, enjoy the play and see you next time.

The success of *A Soldier's Play* in the Ensemble's fifteenth season blew the minds of everyone involved and before long it had transferred to Broadway before embarking on a national tour. It won the Critics' Circle Best Play Award and the Pulitzer prize as a play, followed by three Academy Award nominations when it was later made into a movie (as *A Soldier's Story*). Night after night, then, at Theatre Four on West 55th Street, Sam Jackson was involved in a hit production. And it felt good. You did not have to have an addictive personality to want this feeling to last for ever.

There was only one downside to the whole experience, and that had nothing to do with Sam's work. *The Soldier's Play* tour took the cast to Topeka, scene of the landmark 1954 education trial. Topeka, as it happens, is close to Kansas City. Kansas City, by coincidence, happens to be where Jackson's paternal grandparents live. 'My father's mother lived there,' he says. 'She'd always sent me Christmas cards and birthday cards to make sure I knew I had another set of grandparents.' He decided to take Zoe and LaTanya on a visit. When they arrived in Kansas City, however, there was another member of the family already there: his father. The pair talked for a while about his not paying for Sam when he was a child. 'He was pretty flippant about it,' Jackson Jr says. Matters worsened when Sam was taken to meet a sixteen-year-old neighbour – and her baby. 'He's like, introducing this baby to me as my sister!' Sam says. 'I'm looking at him, thinking, "This is stupid, it's crazy."'

After a short while, Jackson could bear it no more and left, taking his real family with him. The next he heard of his father was when a doctor called to inform the dutiful son that Daddy was dying. Did Jackson want to have him put on life support? 'I said, "He has a sister in Kansas City," ' he recalled with bitterness to *Premiere*. ' "Call her and see if she wants him kept alive." '

That sorry interlude aside, *A Soldier's Play* hadn't finished with him yet. One night in Manhattan a young NYU film school student came backstage to meet Sam and tell him how much he'd enjoyed his performance. It transpired that the student was a graduate from Sam's old alma mater, Morehouse. He said his name was Spike Lee and that he was going to be a famous film director one day. Sam was impressed.

'I went to NYU and looked at his student film and saw that he was serious,' he recalls. 'He said when he got ready to make a film, he was going to call me.' It was working; Sam had made a contact through his theatre work. Now he had to hope that it came off.

But there was more from the stage. Sam also originated the roles of Boy Willie and Wolf in the premiere performances of August Wilson's *The Piano Lesson* and *Two Trains Running* which brought his face and name to a new audience. If either of these plays ever transferred to the silver screen, the critics were agreed that he would have to take the step up with them. He was that good. But what were the odds on any studio picking them up? Pretty good, as it transpired, but not just yet . . .

Samm-Art Williams's *Home*, directed by actress and director Billie Allen, proved almost as successful during its lengthy off-Broadway run in 1979 before transferring to the big league with Sam as an integral member of its cast. Even the *New York Times* was impressed: 'A play that all theatregoers should embrace,' it raved. It centred around draft dodger Cephus Miles who loses his land during a stay in college and is forced to build a new life in a big city in the face of temptations from drugs and prostitution. Given Sam's taste for narcotics and fine living and the fact that he had elected not to go to Vietnam – 'I wasn't anti-war, I just didn't want to die' – the play could not have found a more empathetic cast member. Whether its producers knew it or not.

In truth, Sam's drink and drug problem was one of the best-kept secrets in town, for the time being anyway. Certainly LaTanya was in the dark about the extent of it. She had to be. Why else would he have returned to their house one day in 1980 to be handed an invitation to his own nuptials. 'I came home and she handed me a wedding invitation and told me to make sure I was at the church on that day,' Jackson remembers. If he had any qualms himself, he has never mentioned them.

The impetus had originally come from LaTanya's grandfather who wanted her to stop living in sin after ten years and marry before he died.

The ceremony took place in Atlanta, where LaTanya grew up. On the back of their stage success, she knew how to put on a show. Still, with seventeen bridesmaids, seven candle-lighters and two thousand guests, things seemed a little extravagant, so much so the whole production was actually reviewed in the local rag, the *Atlanta Constitution*. Now that's fame. But, if Sam was any judge, this was just the beginning. The 1980s would be their time, he just knew it. How could Hollywood resist?

5. I WAS GANG MEMBER NUMBER THREE

Hollywood. A factory of dreams in a city of angels. Creator of illusion, purveyor of magic, dealer of the winning hand. Recognise the picture? You should. It is the one that the movie business has been carefully crafting over the last century.

And yet . . .

And yet, hidden in its past, not very far and not too well hidden, some might say, there is another Hollywood. One that doesn't conform to the vision created by the PR fluff. One that is actually more endemic of life in mainland America. One that actually reflects the times around it. While the USA struggled with racism in the 1900s, what was Hollywood's position? One would hope it was the vanguard of those trying to break down those segregated barriers, using its massive influence for good. Unfortunately, one would be wrong. Hollywood has always been a mirror of society; by offering what the public wants – and what the public wants is generally something close to its own tastes – the movie business makes the most money. The avant-garde, the controversial, the off-the-wall ideas – these do not make the cash register sing like a good old-fashioned homespun yarn featuring real people and places and situations that audiences can identify with. The image of America that Hollywood reflected in the early 1900s is not one to be proud of.

The fact that one of the first pictures even to feature a black character was called *The Wooing and Wedding of a Coon* gives some indication of the thought processes at work back in 1905. For the earliest decades of motion picture history, in particular during the silent era, black society was either ignored or ridiculed. And when it was represented, as in *The Wooing*, or in others like *The Masher*, *The Nigger* or *The Octoroon*, it was always done so using white actors playing black characters, showing no advancement from Shakespeare's day when white men portrayed women and men of all ethnic backgrounds.

The first film about black society actually to employ black actors was the 1914 version of Harriet Beecher Stowe's *Uncle Tom's Cabin*. The 1903 and 1909 versions utilised white actors under heavy make-up. It was a turning point of sorts, as Peter Noble, in *The Negro in Films* realised: 'Thus for the first time, a film about Negroes actually used coloured actors and thenceforth with notable exceptions, the practice of using burnt-corked whites to play Negro parts gradually fell into disuse.'

The talkie era of motion pictures saw a slight improvement in black representation on celluloid. Showcasing the natural singing talents among many black actors was one of the notable areas of improvement. But still the tendency was to marginalise the black part of society, both in American and European films. By World War II, by which time black troops had been fully integrated in the American fighting machine (as pinpointed in Charles Fuller's *A Soldier's Play*), the editorial bent on any film set was one of exclusion: if at all possible, the black contingent was not shown. When this proved controversial (and only for reasons of 'realism' rather than racism), a compromise solution of adding a token black character to any given film found widespread popularity. Wesley Epps cropped up in *Bataan*, Ben Carter put in an appearance in *Crash Drive* and Rex Ingram appeared in *Sahara*, all films of massive contemporary exposure. Without exception, however, each character was relegated to background scenes, rarely given centre stage. Notably, when Epps did get a central role in one scene, it was in a subservient manner (he cups water in his hands so that his white colleagues may drink).

By 1944, Lawrence Reddick had compiled a seemingly definitive list of nineteen occasions on which you might spot a black character in a major movie. As a compilation of generally negative stereotypes, it takes some beating: the savage African; the happy slave; the devoted servant; the corrupt politician; the irresponsible citizen; the petty thief; the social delinquent; the vicious criminal; the sexual superman; the superior athlete; the unhappy non-white; the natural-born cook; the natural-born musician; the perfect entertainer; the superstitious churchgoer; the chicken and watermelon eater; the razor and knife toter; the uninhibited expressionist; the mental inferior.

While we may have lost the more offensive of these two-dimensional representations – the 'mammy' or village idiot – some have been harder to shake off over the last sixty years. *Heat of the Night*, for example, painted the sublime Sidney Poitier as almost deified in his perfection. *Casablanca* had Dooley Wilson as the fabled ivory-tinkling 'Sam' as little more than Humphrey Bogart's cipher. The 'superior athlete' stereotype is still redolent, to the extent that it was wonderfully spoofed by Wesley Snipes in *White Men Can't Jump*. While it's true that the average Arnold Schwarzenegger part or Clint Eastwood's *Dirty Harry* character attract the same depth, both are selected from a broader base of roles for white actors. In a minority environment, every punch has to land.

Given the small percentage of black talent ushered onto the large screen, it's no surprise to learn that black actresses fare even worse than their male counterparts. For most of the 1900s, major black movie stars won their audience in other media – Diana Ross and Diahann Carroll for example. Other names, such as Gloria Foster or Lola Falana would find mainstream audiences almost nonplussed at their mention. Significantly, Foster's most landmark work, and the project which propelled her to millions of households as a talent to behold, was *The Matrix* and its sequel *Matrix Reloaded*. Her role as the cookie-baking Oracle brought her fame and appreciation undreamed of throughout the previous fifty years of professional struggle against a system stacked against her. Sadly, she died before work was completed on the final part of the trilogy, *Matrix Revolutions*. Who would be black and a woman in Hollywood?

By 1971, of course, the Black Revolution was in full swing and nowhere more prominently than in the guise of John Shaft, the ball-breaking, head-busting, pussy-sniffing 'private dick' played by Richard Roundtree. He went up against the corrupt NYPD, against the white ruling class of New York and against every prediction of what makes good box office. And, what's more, he beat them all. Black characters had started to get their head in films like John Wayne's *100 Rifles* (Jim Brown's character was on a par with that of the man christened Marion Morrison) and *For Love of Ivy* (Abbey Lincoln famously went nose to nose with white screen goddess Doris Day). Now they were not only getting the parts, but they were being allowed a run at the audience. Minority films will always win minority audiences if the budget reflects the difference. But if enough faith – and enough money – is put into a project, then wonders can happen. Black films can make large profits. And that, as anyone who has stood in the shade of the giant letters on Hollywood Hill will tell you, is what the town is all about.

Of course, putting a black man in front of the camera because he will make you money is no further a step towards racial equality in film-making than hiring another actor (of whatever colour) because they have big feet or red hair. In 2003, of the black stars making the most money – certainly the ones making the most noise – the majority have been fast-tracked onto the silver screen from some other medium where they already have an audience. That audience, it is hoped, will be transferable. Comedians like Chris Rock and Martin Lawrence, rappers such as Ice Cube, TV stars like Will Smith, have all taken the step up. In no case, however, could it really be called a victory for the brotherhood.

As Samuel L. Jackson says, 'Why are they looking for the next Brad Pitt or Tom Cruise when they should be looking for the next me?' The answer is that black talent will always be a minority interest in Hollywood while there is a superfluity of white decision-makers. If black talent sells, then black talent will be put on the screen. But for black talent to truly flourish, for it to stand a real chance in the carnivorous Hollywood bear-pit, then there has to be parity of black talent behind the camera too. Forget the giant pay-packets for the actors in *Coming to America* or *Independence Day*. Real power is wielded from behind the scenes, by directors, writers, producers, agents. With white men casting for films written by white men, the chances for black actors – unless they fall into one of Reddick's nineteen categories – will always be slim.

In the late 1960s, companies like The Third World Cinema Corporation sprung up, with famous faces like James Earl Jones, Ossie Davis and Rita Moreno as their figureheads. Their aim was to promote full participation of black talent in all aspects of film production. Years later, Spike Lee leads a small band of black producers continuing the tradition. As with the Negro Ensemble Company in New York's theatre district, Lee and his colleagues realise that black roles for black actors have to be sought by black producers; there is no point waiting to be a white writer's afterthought or, worse, part of a professional dowry next time the 'ethnic' look becomes fashionable. And through this realisation, just as through its enactment, comes power. Power to create, power to perform, power to have a say. And in Hollywood, having a say does not come cheap.

For all his good work in epoch-defining black theatre, Sam Jackson was honest enough with himself to admit that he was still awaiting the Hollywood call. Theatre was great as far as it went, but just as his mother acknowledged his career as soon as she saw him on TV, so he knew that true recognition as an actor could only come from a successful movie career. A solid stage CV behind him could only improve both his technique and his chances. It was the NEC's Douglas Turner Ward who had taught him that luck was the confluence of preparation and opportunity. In 1980, after four years of solid NY theatre work and various small screen bit parts, he felt ready to take The Call when it came. Unfortunately, when the phone rang, it turned out to be a wrong number.

After almost five years in development hell, one of Broadway's big hitters was finally being given the silver screen treatment. Helming *Ragtime* in 1980 was Milos Forman, and Sam had been given the nod by his agent that a part was his. The truth was slightly different, as the 32-year-old actor found out.

'My first big film where I mistakenly thought I was off and running on my way to Hollywood was *Ragtime*,' he recalls. 'I was Gang Member Number Three.'

The experience proved a rude awakening, not least because of the way Sam found the movie business treated some of his heroes. At that time, it was customary for actors to attend an interview stage before they were invited to audition. While Sam was waiting to meet Milos Forman, he was joined by James Earl Jones, at the time the most famous black actor in America. Obviously the great man was there to fine-tune his role as Booker T. Washington or some other prominent role in the script. The truth was slightly different. He was there for an interview too. 'I was like: "Wait a minute, you're James Earl Jones. You did *The Great White Hope*." Yet there he was doing the same thing as I was doing.'

The moment was epiphanic for the fledgling actor. Whatever happened as a result of that audition, he resolved that he would never rest on his laurels. He would never take 'the next job' for granted. Being an actor is a flaky enough business without having the concomitant trials of race to contend with so he would take what work he could get. If the great James Earl Jones – the voice of Darth Vader in Sam's beloved *Star Wars*, after all – had to scrabble around for work, what hope was there for everyone else? 'That's the reality of it. You'll be fighting the same battle for ever.'

That show business is a hit-and-miss venture cannot be doubted. Even the original director of *Ragtime* had been thrown off the picture. According to the *Hollywood Reporter*, in September 1976 – when Sam was just putting down roots in Harlem – Robert Altman was taken off the project by producer Dino De Laurentiis. It was nothing to do with the *M*A*S*H* director's take on *Ragtime*, either. Unfortunately he and De Laurentiis had fallen out over the edit of Altman's *Buffalo Bill and the Indians* and, rather than go through that again, the producer had removed Altman from the next project. E.L. Doctorow, author of the *Ragtime* book, was one of many said to be against the decision, even beseeching Forman by letter not to take the job – thus allowing a return route for Altman. It was not to be.

In many ways, *Ragtime* was everything that Sam had been waiting for: a big budget, grand scale movie with black people at its core. That his character was a 'social delinquent' in a cast of 'perfect entertainers' might mean that Reddick's 1944 list was still relevant almost half a century later, but there were more positives than not. And Gang Member Number Three was one of them.

Ragtime was given a nominal release in November 1981, the same month as the Oscar-friendly *On Golden Pond*, before hitting four hundred US screens the following month. The *Hollywood Reporter* called it 'a triumph in all areas', from James Cagney's return from retirement to Forman's sharp direction. 'It would be difficult to imagine a movie more richly textured, more opulently mounted or more ambitiously themed,' it said.

Variety was equally glowing but spotted a cynical opportunity. 'The film does have one unexpected card up its sleeve: a strong, dignified theme of frustrated black American strivings that, properly exploited, could signal some crossover into black markets.'

Within a fortnight of *Variety* noting this marketing window, Paramount Pictures had responded. In the first event of its kind, the studio launched a second strand publicity campaign which appealed directly and specifically to black audiences. Where the general (read 'white') poster advertisement had comprised a silhouette of white star Elizabeth McGovern against a patriotic rendering of the stars and stripes, the new series of billboards featured *Ragtime*'s newly discovered talent, Howard E. Rollins, and an assembly of most of his black co-stars. There was even a new hard-hitting, controversial tagline: 'A black man said, "Respect me or kill me!" They took away Coalhouse's wife, child and pride. He made them pay in a way America will never forget. It was a tough time. It was Ragtime.' Contrast this with the lily-livered romanticism of the master campaign's slogan: 'Young, beautiful, passionate and scandalous. She was America in the time of Ragtime.'

It may have been gauche, it may have been heavy-handed, but the second campaign certainly worked. The Coronet picture house at 59th and 3rd in NYC's predominantly white East Side, reported a 25 per cent black audience – way up on normal statistics in that area. The Loews State cinema in Times Square attracted a 30 per cent black audience, again, up on its usual quotient for most mainstream – that is, white – films.

When it comes to profit, every group, large or small, whether divided by gender or religion or age, is a 'market'. The fact that a major movie studio was pandering to the black dollar with *Ragtime* could only have been good news. Except . . . except that this was only 1981. As recently as just over twenty years ago, Hollywood still had a ghettoised approach to black audiences. But at least with *Ragtime*, the tide was beginning to turn. It may have been driven by a craving for further profits but very few things are not. And, if it had the result of opening doors of opportunity to black and ethnic talent, then it would be worthwhile.

Sam Jackson certainly thought so. Watching himself on the Loews theatre screen that November, he was convinced that this was the start of the Big Time for him as an actor. He may not have won major billing in the film – the mighty James Earl Jones had not even won a part – but not only was it a step in the right direction, this was a film that was going to presage a new era in black entertainment. And Sam was ready to take advantage of it.

'Joyous, happy and free,' are Jackson's chosen words to describe the period of making *Ragtime*. He had a chance to shoot a major Hollywood picture for Paramount without leaving his beloved New York and he had turned in good work. The ball was starting to roll in his favour and he was ready for the movies to come his way. Now he had a bona fide major picture on his CV, it was only a matter of time.

* * *

If someone had told Sam Jackson in 1981 that he would not step onto another movie set until 1987, he would never have believed it. Not after his good, if brief, work on *Ragtime*. Not after his impressive stage notices. Not with the talent he possessed.

But it was true. Seven years between engagements. Seven long years after filming *Ragtime* and eleven since arriving in New York to earn his fame and fortune. Of course, he never found that out, not really. No one actually told him he was washed up. No one actually said, 'Give up on the film thing because you're not going to get another job for almost a decade.' No one did that; in fact, no one did anything, and that was the point. No one rang him, no one booked him, no one put him forward for parts.

In many ways, the uncertainty, the not knowing if today would be the day, was worse than the actual disappointment that it hadn't happened so far. Even for someone with Sam's healthy confidence, the gradual chipping away at his ambitions, the erosion of his hopes, was a painful and undignified process. For LaTanya it was almost like watching a loved one deteriorate in hospital. As Sam says, 'At a certain point I focused on the work and I lost sight of career goals that I had.' Unfortunately, to get him through that time, the 'work' was not the only thing to gain his renewed attention. What was the phrase? When the going got tough, the tough got . . . stoned.

6. WHAT, YOU A PIMP?

Over the years since he cleaned up his life, Samuel L. Jackson has had plenty of time to ponder the variables of what could have been, of what might have happened had he stayed on the hedonistic path to hell. One thing is sure: if he hadn't stopped when he did, that is to say, before his income hit stratospheric levels, then he may not have survived the trip. He is not that kind of guy, and he knows it. 'If I was making the kind of money I'm making now, with the kind of appetite I had then, you would not be sitting here talking to me now,' he told the *Guardian* newspaper in 1998. 'You'd have written my obituary years ago.'

Money to Sam Jackson in the early 1980s was a means to an end. And the end was drugs. 'I was working every day, doing what I did, and nobody else knew,' he says. 'But the job never stopped. I mean, how else was I going to pay for my drugs if I didn't have a job?

'You make it, I abused it,' he says. And how. This, don't forget, was a man with an addictive personality. 'If I bought a six-pack of beer, I drank the whole thing. I can't have just one of anything.'

He is also competitive. 'If the guy next to me was doing one or two lines of coke, I was doing six,' he says.

Frustrations at the lack of follow-up to his appearance in *Ragtime* meant that the start of the 1980s was not the healthiest time for Sam. There was no bad mood that could not be treated by another pill, no bout of jealousy that could not be tempered by another drink. At least he was getting regular good work on the stage. Even this, though, would soon not be enough. Even this, his greatest thrill, would drive his chemical dependency higher.

'I was watching people do things I thought I should be doing and torturing myself for it,' Jackson recalls. One particular production particularly sticks in his mind: understudying for Charles Dutton on Broadway in *The Piano Lesson*. 'I was watching the show every night and being like, "Oh my God, I want to do this play!" ' By the time Jackson did get his chance, Dutton had been nominated for a Tony for that role. 'I was like, "Aaargh!" Bugged.'

The relief at being given his own run in the show didn't get him through those early months, however. That was the job of the beer. And the drugs. And – as a result – the women. The unholy trinity was complete, as he shamefacedly recalls: 'They all go together. They all join forces at some point.

'I was staying out, not coming home, drinking, drugging, womanising.' In short, doing anything to make himself feel better – everything that is, except the one thing that would work. 'I should have been putting myself in a healthier acting situation by getting my own job.'

The extent of Sam's philandering was revealed in an interview in 1997 when he admitted how much he fancied his *Jackie Brown* co-star Pam Grier. For a lot of men, the woman who put the 'foxy' into *Foxy Brown* was the stuff of fantasy in her early Blaxploitation movies; nowhere better proven, as far as Sam was concerned, than in her 1972 picture *Women in Cages*. 'I came out of that movie wondering where I could find myself a woman like that,' he revealed in the *Calgary Sun*. 'I found me some good substitutes over the years but I never got me the real thing.' Considering that he had been living with LaTanya all his adult life, and certainly in 1972 when that movie was shown, it's obvious that any success in Sam's quest for his own Pam would have to have been at an adulterous level.

It's also obvious that his various demons were responsible for each infidelity as one drunken spur-of-the-moment act followed another. Interestingly, it is the only aspect of his 70s and 80s behaviour for which he shows any real remorse today. 'I remember the old days when I would get with somebody and when the sex was over, it was like, "Now what?" ' Jackson told *Essence*. The prospect these days of paying for one mistake for the rest of his life is enough to guarantee an end to such behaviour.

His wife, LaTanya, is equally open to discussing the subject. 'With the affairs you end up saying, "Did they have a stopping point?" I think they did. But he's had to forgive me, too,' she suggests. 'I've had to learn the importance of guarding my tongue.' I think most people would agree who was more deserving of forgiveness in this relationship.

By 1982, there was another reason for Sam to try to stay on the straight and narrow: the arrival of their daughter, Zoe. In truth, it just gave him more cause to celebrate and more justification in feeling aggrieved that other actors had got his parts – parts he needed more than ever now he had a family. In other words, more reasons to lose himself in drink and narcotics. Before she was eight years old, Zoe was sharing her mother's suffering. LaTanya, in fact, refers to a period in the marriage as 'the Villa in Hell' – because that's where she felt she was living during her husband's wildest times.

'I was mad,' Jackson says. 'I was crazed. I was not happy with who I was. As a result, she and our daughter paid a lot of taxes for me doing crazed things to myself that transferred to them.' Only LaTanya's willingness to fight kept the family together.

As the 1980s wore on and Sam put in more and more hours on his craft, his professional frustrations simply got worse. Everywhere he seemed to look, there were others getting what he felt he deserved. While he was in a hurry to get back to a new play, his contemporaries were moving on. 'All of a sudden, one of them would disappear,' he admitted to *Film Review*. 'Like Denzel would disappear, Morgan disappeared, Wesley disappeared and I kept doing the plays.'

Towards the end of the decade, LaTanya began to become suspicious about the extent of her husband's partying. The affairs would become less discreet; the drinking seemed to start a little earlier in the day; the dope he occasionally liked to take a drag on seemed to have a wilder effect on him. But for the first years of their daughter's life, all she saw was her man trying to get by in the capricious world of acting; a man having the odd drink and maybe a bit of blow. Nothing heavy. In her heart, though, she knew that his work could only be improved if he was completely sober – whose work wouldn't benefit? She had never seen anyone act like her Sam. No one could move her on stage like he could. But all the same, she sensed there was latent potential going untapped and that was the worst thing about living with him. Seeing him not get the parts he wanted and yet not going the extra mile in his performance.

The truth was that, apart from the fact that he had never acted sober, Sam knew that he was good. He was very good. He could take a script and work with it, get the best from it – but, according to LaTanya, without ever really getting the best from himself.

'My wife had been telling me for a long time that I was this kind of bloodless actor,' he says. That he was talented enough to read a script and deliver the words perfectly. 'But she said there was nothing coming out of my heart. I was only acting at people and not for them.'

Not only did he not act for them, there would be times when Sam could barely contain his contempt for the paying customers the other side of the footlights. 'I used to stand on stage and watch the audience,' he says. 'I would say, "Fuck them." And I eventually reached a point where the audience was not a concern of mine.'

Looking back, he knows that everything LaTanya said of him was true. At the time though, he was in no position to take it in. Not on a cerebral or a visceral level. 'I used drugs to keep folks away from me because I didn't want them in my space,' he says. 'And that included my wife. I would go on stage and do what I had to do and it was easy for me.'

It says a lot for Sam's talent that, for all his attitude problems, for all his feelings of being passed over for others, for all his extra-curricular activities, he managed to hold down a string of decent theatre jobs. And when one engagement came to an end, he seemed to have few problems winning the next role – despite everything. 'When I went to auditions I reeked of beer, and my eyes were red because I'd been smoking reefers all day mixed with a little crack here and there,' he says.

For all the disdain for his audiences, and even taking on board his pent-up envy at the successes being achieved by his contemporaries, Sam never lost his enthusiasm for learning his trade. Some of the bits of non-theatre work he was starting to pick up would have driven many a man to drink, but as long as there was something to gain professionally, Sam didn't mind. 'I used to go to Boston once a year and get beat up in *Spencer for Hire*,' he reminisces about one regular TV highlight.

It is hard for the outside viewer to fathom what benefits Sam could have plucked from another TV contract, but justify it he does. The job in question was understudying Bill Cosby on his ratings-topping TV show. Sam would pitch up and run through the once-great comedian's lines with the rest of the cast, allowing the technical crew to measure their shots for the main event. Surprisingly, Sam does not consider the two years spent on this project a complete waste of time – there's always something to learn. 'Back then I'd never done a three-camera set, so I could watch them move the cameras around, watch the director call shots,' he says. 'It was like being paid to be in class.'

This thirst for learning took Sam further afield in his quest for stagework. Apart from New York Shakespeare Festival appearances in plays like *Mother Courage and her Children*, *Spell F Sharp* and *The Mighty Gents*, and NEC parts in *Sally/Prince* and *The District Line*, Sam also took increasingly leading roles in *Ohio Tip-Off* and *Native Speech* at the Baltimore Centre Stage. And as well as August Wilson's *The Piano Lesson* and *Two Trains Running* at Yale Rep, Sam also appeared as Lyons in the playwright's *Fences* at the Seattle Repertory Theatre. Immersed in Pulitzer prize-winning plays and working with challenging directors enabled Sam to grow as an actor – and forget his original goals. 'For ten, twelve years, I totally lost sight of that Hollywood thing,' he says.

Well, maybe not totally.

In 1986, the biggest black star in the USA was Eddie Murphy. *Beverly Hills Cop* had made him the hottest ticket in town and, like any zeitgeist celebrity, for a time he appeared able to do no wrong. Murphy had originally made his name, and his dollars, as a comedian in the Richard Pryor mould, although many of his fans would never have seen his act. As a consequence, a feature film production of one of his stand-up shows was planned. In an odd innovation, it was decided to top and tail the live scatological routines with sketches of Eddie relaxing at home. Guess who won the part of the comedian's uncle in the three minute skit? Damn right.

It may have taken seven years, but by Christmas 1987, Sam's follow-up to *Ragtime* was finally up and running and hitting cinema screens all over the world. The fact that Murphy cut such a controversial figure could not hurt either of their careers. The fact that the end result, *Raw*, was so well received confirmed it. Even for such a minority-interest production up against the likes of *Good Morning Vietnam* and *Batteries Not Included*, it was obvious to Sam that this was one guy worth staying in touch with.

After six years of nothing, however, it wasn't just Eddie Murphy offering a big screen try-out. On 4 November 1986, shooting started on a German-backed film called *Magic Sticks*. Filming was done entirely on location in New York and one of the city's finest actors had a part. He even had a character name.

The plot concerned a young drummer, Felix (played by George Kantz), who obtains a pair of – you guessed it – magic sticks from a street peddler. When he drums with them, he discovers that all genuine New Yorkers become hypnotised by his beat, responding with jerky, Kraftwerk-style dance moves. Armed with this dubious ability to turn the whole city into a Lionel Richie video, Felix sets about doing what any self-respecting movie character would do – he uses his rhythmic power to woo a girl, music student Kelly Curtis.

Given that the film soon descends into standard hiding-the-sticks-from-the-local-hoods territory, it's refreshing to see that Sam's part in the picture is slightly less stereotypical. Not that he would have turned down the part if it hadn't been. But for the first time in his fledgling movie career, *Magic Sticks* offered him a more integral role and even some decent lines. Despite being laboured with the name 'Bum', it is Sam who starts things rolling by handing over the drumsticks in the first place – pretty decent behaviour considering Felix has just crashed his bike into Sam's pavement stall. When he notes Felix eyeing up a record in his collection, Bum says: 'You got a good eye, boy. What's your line?'

'I play the skins.'

'What, you a pimp?'

Boom boom.

Maybe it's not Murphy-style hilarious, but unlike his bit parts in things like *Spencer for Hire*, at least it was intentional humour. Compared to Sam's other big project of the year, it was also, refreshingly lightweight.

Considering Harriet Beecher Stowe's original book, *Uncle Tom's Cabin*, has been credited in part with kicking off the American Civil War, no production of her powerful text can ever exactly be a barrel of laughs. The Showtime Original Movie production broadcast on the cable channel in June 1987 was no exception.

Away from his family for the shoot in and around the plantations of Natchez, Sam was glad to be joined on the set by a couple of familiar faces, *Spencer for Hire*'s Avery Brooks and *The Cosby Show*'s Phylicia Rashad.

Weighing in with his particular brand of stage-trained pathos, Sam plays George, the husband of heroine Eliza (Rashad) and father of Jimmy (not quite the name Stowe originally gave the character). When slave trader Haley takes a shining to Jimmy and Uncle Tom, the family is split up as Eliza flees with her son to a Quaker sanctuary. While Rashad and Brooks quite rightly won the plaudits, Sam's measured fury and understated sorrow come flooding through his performance. When the family is reunited, his emotion makes uncomfortable viewing.

Not bad for an actor only capable of putting in a 'bloodless' performance.

After the years of waiting for the call that never came, Sam had long become uninterested in the unique charms of filmed work. In fact, thanks to the way he had turned to an endless spiral of drinking and smoking to mask his original disappointment, he was emotionally unfazed by the sudden upswing in his fortunes. The damage to his ego had been done a year or two earlier; at the same time, his chosen 'cure' had all but blunted his ability to give a damn now that things looked like improving.

There were other factors too, that meant he didn't start doing cartwheels at the thought of three major-ish releases in one year. One of those, of course, was his honest love of his stage work. Combined with his natural propensity to obsess on a subject, his booze-fuelled enthusiasms meant that Hollywood would have to work a lot harder in 1987 to impress him.

'I had totally lost my great Hollywood plan at that point because I was getting better as an artist and able to do the kind of acting I wanted to do,' Sam says.

There was also the feeling that, in order to conquer the movie business, he would have to start again, with all the hassles of lower-level auditions, smaller parts and fewer successes. Compare this to his burgeoning respect levels as a stage actor and Sam's late 1980s predicament is similar to the problems faced by famous English pop stars who want to 'crack America'. Years of hard graft, small tours and embarrassing media antics finally get them to a position of greatness in one country. But to make it across the pond they have to start again, playing in sweaty venues, pressing the flesh of various industry players and generally turning the clock back a few years to the humiliations of their youth. Very few seem prepared to give up the Rolls-Royce lifestyle in one territory to return to the tour-bus hell in another.

For Sam, it was a similar call, albeit on a different scale. There was no doubt he had become a sizeable fish in the Broadway pond. Did he really want to trade down his personal size for a shot at a larger potential return? He weighed up the options: 'I had this great theatre reputation,' he says. 'I was working with people that I really respected and who appreciated me, and my craft as an actor was growing.'

On the other hand there was the knowledge that Morgan Freeman had just filmed *Street Smart* with Christopher Reeve, and Denzel Washington had just won a part in leading docusoap, *St Elsewhere*. Even in his fuggiest mental state, Sam felt he had no choice.

7. IF YOU'RE GONNA GET SHOT IN THE HEAD, GET SHOT IN THE HEAD BY SCORSESE

Look out for anyone who says that school days are the best days of your life. They tend to be people who have amounted to very little in adult years. The type of people who can't cope with making their own decisions or taking their own road. Or they have Alzheimer's. But in the case of Sam Jackson, they might just have a point.

When Spike Lee had swung by Sam's dressing room back in 1981 to say that they would work together one day, there was more than a pinch of wishful thinking on both men's sides. Sam, of course, had nothing to lose by cultivating a friendship. He was already earning a living from acting; he had done his schooling and was putting it into practice. But, he realised, in this business it never hurts to be nice to people who might be able to help you. And there was another thing: this huge-rim-spectacled film student was all right. A bit intense, maybe; even a bit arrogant for someone who has achieved nothing so far, but basically a good kid. And he liked to party too.

Spike Lee did go on to fulfil his dream. In 1986 he shot *She's Gotta Have It*, a ribald look at black youth, for Island Pictures. In the vast publicity that followed its release, Lee came across as a man on a mission to rebalance the black and white agenda. His work was unashamedly black and unashamedly loud. So, coincidentally, was he. He gave good quote, he was provocative and he also wielded no mean talent. He was one for the future.

But what about Sam Jackson's future? Despite those early promises, a script with Sam's part in the film never arrived. Fair enough, he thought. This sort of thing happens all the time. But then Sam heard about Lee's next film, a musical paean to the college of his youth. And then he knew he had to get involved.

Morehouse College holds mixed memories for Spike Lee and Samuel L. Jackson. On the face of it, Lee was never moved to confront a governing body in order to protest his views, so theoretically he probably enjoyed his time there more. However, not only did Sam discover the hardcore joys of narcotics at Morehouse, the college was also responsible for introducing him to the two most long-term influences on his life: LaTanya and acting. Without Morehouse, his life could well have taken a more mundane route. Without Morehouse, this book would probably not exist.

Lee had his own fondness for Morehouse, however, and purposely planned to film his second movie, *School Daze*, in its grounds. Unfortunately, Morehouse had different ideas. 'Three weeks into the shoot, we were asked to leave the campus,' Lee recalled in *American Film*. The then president of Morehouse, Hugh M. Gloster, feared that the film would have a 'negative' impact on the college's enrolment policy – what parent would want to send their child to a school that was seen on the cinema screen to encourage 'cursing, drinking or doing the nasty'? Lee had, after all, dared to show nudity in his first work, and Gloster feared the worst.

Fortunately for the production, Morehouse is only one of the colleges under the Atlanta University Centre umbrella (Spelman, where Mrs Jackson attended, is another). Agreeing not to include Morehouse in any shot, Lee was allowed to proceed on the other campuses. In March 1987, he and his cast of 500 – made by the camera wizardry of Ernest Dickerson to look occasionally like 5,000 – began work. Among the 500 was Sam, just as Spike had promised six years earlier.

'He said when he got ready to make a film, he would call me,' Jackson says. 'And sure enough he did. And sure enough I still had to audition for him.' The point about auditioning would later lead to a rift between the two men, but for now Sam accepted it as both people doing their jobs. Even so, the role he won was not exactly prominent – even Lee's own part as Half-Pint was larger. Billed as an Adidas-heavy local yokel called Leeds, most often seen in group scenes, it was hardly the kind of kudos Sam might have been expecting, especially with fellow New York board-treaders Ossie Davis and Laurence Fishburne taking the leads. Considering that Jackson and 'Fish' are mistaken today for each other, even by studio bosses who should know better, and considering that Jackson's talent is every bit the equal of his good friend's, it was little wonder the tequila and cocaine was required to ameliorate the sense of professional injustice.

For all Spike Lee's idiosyncrasies, he was certainly a man cut from the same cloth as Sam as far as his place in society went. Or, more importantly, his place in a society dominated by white culture. No sooner had *She's Gotta Have It* made headlines than Lee was being compared to the only thing white reviewers knew: other white film-makers. 'One thing I hope *School Daze* does is knock all this goddamn "Black Woody Allen" shit out the window,' Lee said in 1988. A lot of people would take that as a compliment. 'Fuck dat,' was Lee's opinion. To his mind, white entertainers – like Al Jolson, Benny Goodman, Jerry Lee Lewis, Pat Boone, Bing Crosby, Elvis Presley, The Beatles, Janis Joplin, Mick Jagger and even The Blues Brothers – had stolen so much from black culture that comparing him to any white director was an insult.

More than anything Woody Allen could have – or has – done, *School Daze* goes all out to tackle class and colour at the fictitious Mission College. Replacing many of the classic 'negro role' stereotypes with 'normal' people with normal, boring lives, the film reveals for white audiences – if they care to view it – that black communities can have their own problems with racism and class; that not all black people fall neatly into boxes marked 'superman' or 'social delinquent'.

On the positive side, then, Sam was working for the first time with a similarly outspoken idealist as himself. More than the personal acclaim, he felt proud to be participating in a landmark piece of black culture – an off-beat musical at that. More than anything, he saw the movie as a statement of intent; not just for himself, but for all black people in the creative industries. This was a black film starring black actors made by a black auteur. It could be the start of something big.

One white man thought so. When Island Pictures balked at the required budget for *School Daze*, despite earning $7 million from Lee's first film, Englishman David Puttnam was quick to snap up rights to the second film for his company, Columbia. Once again, Sam was involved in a big budget picture from a major studio. By the end of the year there would be others.

The Eddie Murphy contact had paid off. *Raw* had been an altogether smaller scale production, but now, following the oriental mishmash which was *The Golden Child*, Murphy was returning to larger productions. Remembered for his part as Murphy's 'uncle', Sam confidently won an audition to play the part of a 'hold-up guy' in *Coming to America*. It was his second Paramount picture and his second with Murphy, so things were definitely looking up for his career. But again, he was reduced to a minor, unnamed role in a movie starring a former comedian and a chat show host (Arsenio Hall). At least the inclusion of Jackson's idol, James Earl Jones, playing Murphy's African king father, gave Sam hope that 'proper' actors did have a place in the movies. If he plugged away, he felt, he would get there. And if he didn't get there, he had his cocaine. And his tequila. And his beer.

If Sam had felt himself underused in *School Daze*, his experience on the Michael J. Fox film *Bright Lights, Big City* left him totally bemused. Towards the end of 1987, Sam won an audition and signed a contract to appear in the James Bridges project. Then his role was written out. In a rare moment of Hollywood morality, he was paid in full for his non-participation. There were days when this sort of behaviour would have suited him fine. The more money for the less work, the better. But other days, he just wanted to act; to be seen; to be given a chance to show what he could do. When Spike Lee came calling the next time, he would get that chance.

After yet another round of auditions for his friend, Sam began shooting in Brooklyn for *Do the Right Thing* in July 1988, alongside another Morehouse old boy, Bill Nunn (Raheem) and *School Daze* pal Ossie Davis. Finally Sam had a chance to prove something of his range. Dressed in a fisherman's hat, Bermuda shirt and shorts, his Mr Senor Love Daddy carves up the screen as the irresponsible entertainer at the heart of the movie. It is a virtuoso performance and one in which Sam is given free reign to be as loud as his character's clothes. Also, as the innovative linking device for the movie's action, he operates in the same holding-it-together territory as Steven Wright's 'DJ' in *Reservoir Dogs*.

Sam's colourful character apart, the rest of the movie veers into high propane territory. Lee's use of a quote from Malcolm X prior to the end credits – 'the use of violence in self-defence is a sign of intelligence' – and the movie's top-and-tail chants of 'Fight the power, fight the power!' throw a stick in the wheel of the racial harmony that is prevalent in just about every other Hollywood film. The movie centres around Lee's Mookie's friendship with a couple of white kids. Almost out of nowhere, the happy-go-lucky first hour of the picture distorts into a near race riot, culminating in Nunn's character getting killed by an overenthusiastic cop – an overenthusiastic white cop.

The film doesn't always make easy watching and some of Lee's early techniques are as clumsy as his writing can be cartoonish, but the overall result of *Do the Right Thing* was achieved. It was an interesting piece of film-making; as the *Hollywood Reporter* says, 'There are numerous cross-signals here and so many possible interpretations that it will invite post-screening discussions well into the night. Controversy has, after all, always been known to be an asset to the box office.' A domestic return of $28 million, double that of *School Daze*, seemed to prove the point.

Given the nature of the movie industry, in particular the sloth's pace of its production, any new trends or new faces can take a year or two to spot. Films shot one year can often not see the light of day for another twelve, 24 or even 36 months, depending on things like post-production, personnel changes at the studios or even just finding a release window. Towards the end of 2002, for example, audiences were treated to a double helping of Leo DiCaprio as he took the lead in two major blockbusters: Steven Spielberg's *Catch Me if You Can* and Martin Scorsese's *Gangs of New York*. The films were shot a year apart; other factors contributed to the end result of DiCaprio competing against himself at the box office.

On a smaller scale, it means that at the same time Sam was putting the finishing touches to a major career advancement like Mr Senor Love Daddy, he was still signing up for smaller parts in other pictures: anything to keep working; and any work to keep smoking.

Consequently, when filming for an Al Pacino movie became an option in 1988, Sam was onto it. Who wouldn't be? Apart from the chance to work with the *Godfather* star and even Ellen Barkin, it was hardly a step forward. Blink and you'll miss his duplicitous role as 'Black guy' in *Sea of Love*, but he's there. (Other highlights of the film include a bar-band reggae version of 'Another One Bites the Dust'.) A role as voice-over artist ADR in three-pronged TV movie *Mystery Train*, a wistful project charting the decline of Memphis, followed. As with *Sea of Love*, it was a good project to be involved with, even if his part was small. 'Rarely does something dull happen on screen,' said the *Hollywood Reporter*, 'and writer–director Jim Jarmusch knows how to fill a frame simply and wittily.' His next role, as Calvin Fredericks in the Danny Glover vehicle *Dead Man Out*, gave him greater screen time than the previous two, but the end result – in terms of quality and success – was less convincing. In fact, the net result of his filming work in 1988, *Do the Right Thing* aside, proved little more than unchallenging disappointment.

It was all in stark contrast to the quality of his work on the New York stage, but it was more lucrative and, he felt, better for his career in the long run. It's funny how he 'lost sight of the Hollywood thing' during those fallow years when he couldn't buy a movie role. Now, however, with minor roles coming thick and fast, he was beginning to readdress the area. Typically, he did so in his usual obsessive-compulsive style.

In 1989, Sam Jackson signed up for seven big-budget motion pictures of varying quality. The only consistent factor was him and his talent; how the director deployed it, of course, varied wildly.

From the year low of playing the character 'Dream Blind Man' in the quite unnecessary *Exorcist III* to yet another great part – Madlock – in another Spike Lee production, *Mo' Better Blues*, Sam really reached new heights in the diversity of his character playing. He may not have been threatening the leading-man appeal of *Blues* star Denzel Washington (he certainly wasn't threatening his screen time, in this almost-backwards step), but the years of creating mini biographies for every role he undertook on stage were paying off. Time after time on one movie after another, Sam's NEC discipline was helping his myriad cameos threaten to steal the show from bigger, more exposed actors.

'I don't short-change people just because I'm only going to be around for four minutes as opposed to two hours,' Jackson says. He still asks the same questions of his character, regardless of number of lines. For example, imagine playing a robber: is he robbing because he's on drugs? Is he robbing to feed his family? Where is he going once he gets the money? The answers provide the backbone of the part: 'You take the stereotypical roles and you fix them so that when somebody sees them you are not a stereotype, you are a person, you are a character.'

A couple of highlights from 1989 prove the point. As Minister Garth in *Def by Temptation*, Sam got to try something a little different in this surprisingly stylish horror flick from debut writer–producer–director James Bond III. As father of Bond's lead character, he swaps his pulpit-thumping for all-out humping as he is tempted into bed by a man-crazy demon – and pays for his sins with his life. For all its 'marvellous dialogue' (*Sight and Sound*), what attracted Jackson to the part was the fact that, like Lee's movies, it had an all-black agenda.

For sheer contrast, turning up as Mickey the taxi dispatcher in Alan Alda's soft-soap comedy of manners, *Betsy's Wedding*, was hard to beat. Despite Jackson's well-rounded, if brief, performance, it was still a shame to learn that, at $20 million, *Betsy's Wedding* took ten times that of the better-thought-out, but ultimately niche and less expensive, *Def by Temptation* at the US box office.

Expectations were not so high, then, for the Blaxploitation sequel *Return of Superfly*. Despite a strong performance from Jackson as Nate Cabot, the movie would eventually sink without trace with barely half a million dollars to its credit. If Sam was worried about such things as takings, his next movie, *Shock to the System*, began to address the slide. Just how much his erratic character Ulysses contributed to the film's $3 million domestic earnings is difficult to quantify. What is far easier to work out, however, is how much of his following project's £90 million box-office action was down to him. The answer is nothing. In a New York gangster movie by Martin Scorsese starring Robert De Niro, very little else gets a look in. Certainly, the part of victim-waiting-to-happen Stacks Edwards in *GoodFellas* was never going to set his career on fire, considering he is on screen barely long enough to say any lines before he takes a bullet and goes down. But as far as experience of a massive production, working with major stars, and just working in his hometown, it was irreplaceable. As the man says, 'If you're going to get shot in the head in a movie, then make sure you're gonna get shot in the head by Scorsese!'

As part of a larger plan, Jackson threw himself into trying to break away from theatre and into the more lucrative movies. He was as prepared on Scorsese's New York locations as he had been on any stage. Not only did he not feel any sense of intimidation at seeing some of the great names of cinema at work, but he felt he deserved a little more respect than he was afforded. If not as an actor, then at least as a human being. Despite being in his adopted home town, the shoot was not one that Sam cares to remember with fondness. 'The only people who talked to me in six weeks were Ray Liotta, Joe Pesci and a guy named Johnny No-Speak,' he says. If Sam knows the reason, he's not telling. At least one of the stars of that film would have the chance to make amends a decade later.

While part of him was raging hard against the iniquities of a business that could see him always passed over for the lead role, another part – the part driven by his pure, obsessive love of acting – saw it as just par for the course. He simply needed to remember that definition of luck and make sure he was prepared. In his moments of sobriety, Sam had no doubts that the good things would come as a result of all these bit-part appearances in such a motley ensemble of work.

'They were learning experiences for me, they were stepping stones,' he avers. 'I always think that everything leads to something else. The more film roles I did, the more comfortable I became in front of a camera.' For a predominantly stage actor, the different, more laid-back environment of the film set did take more getting used to. For a start there was the weird luxury of being able to do more than one take – anathema to a stage thespian. And then there was the general richness of everything to do with each picture. Coming from a stage background where grants and public handouts provided the backbone of many productions' existence, this was an eye-opener for Sam, as indeed it was for his friend Denzel Washington when he made his first movie.

'I was on location for the first time and they gave me this giant Winnebago,' he recalls. 'It had everything in it, including a fully stocked refrigerator. The contents of that refrigerator were worth more than I had ever earned.'

But for Sam, getting his face known was the most important thing at the time. Not only did audiences watch films (hopefully), but so did casting directors and producers – the very people who could make a significant impact on his career. 'The more people saw me, the better known I became to people who were making those kinds of decisions on who to hire,' he explains. A small part here could lead to greater exposure there.

All success, of course, is relative. When Sam and LaTanya had first pitched camp in Harlem more than ten years earlier, they had been grateful for parts that paid enough to cover the subway fare to the theatre. Running a family home on $35 a week took some doing, even in the 1970s. A decade of increasing success and acclaim later, however, and even the ambitious Sam knew he was well off.

'I was a successful actor,' he admits. 'I was doing a couple of films a year. I was doing plays with Pulitzer prize-winning playwrights. I was making $800 to $900 a week. I was successful.'

And so he was. He was reading the lines, getting inside his characters' heads, turning up on time and playing the part. But, according to LaTanya, it was still 'bloodless'. She knew he had more to give, she just didn't know why he couldn't do it. But then, she, like everyone else, was oblivious to the double life Sam was leading at the time.

'They had no idea I was this fucked-up person doing all this other stuff,' Jackson admits.

'I started rehearsals fucked up. I did plays fucked up. It never occurred to me that I shouldn't be fucked up.' Although cocaine was Sam's drug of choice at this stage, there was nothing he had not tried. The results were not pretty, he has admitted in hindsight: 'Things were a real fucking mess. I can wholeheartedly assure you of that.'

After 23 years 'in control' of his addictions, Sam sensed that a crossroads was approaching. With the greater demands of his increased work schedule and the need to be seen by more people, he was finding it harder on a daily basis to maintain his abstemious appearance. The red-eyed auditions were becoming more and more frequent and for the first time he began to question whether his drug use was the problem when the parts did not become his.

One of the tell-tale signs of cocaine use, however, is increased paranoia. By the late 1980s, Sam Jackson had a pretty good line in blaming others for his shortcomings. As far as he was concerned, all of the problems with his career were the fault of other people. He had also reached the point where being as far off his face as possible was the answer to almost any given situation. When, through drunkenness, he did not win a part, his first reaction was to have another drink. On the other hand, as the work did start to come in and more and more pressures were put on him, he found himself reaching for the white powder even more. For those around him, it was not a pretty sight, and by 1989, even LaTanya was aware of a change in her man.

'I was drinking heavily, doing crack, I was cheating on my wife, basically becoming a living terror to everyone around me,' Jackson admits. At the heart of it, if he was honest, was still this sense of injustice that, however much he had, he could have more if it weren't for other people. 'I was one angry black motherfucker.'

Apart from the increase in his film workload and having to balance this against his theatre work, the deterioration in Sam's grip on his behaviour – his façade was slipping every day – was also down to the change in his drug use. After too much cocaine-snorting left his septum ruptured (he refuses to have it fixed to this day as a reminder of the dark past), he simply switched to smoking it. It does not matter if you are a hardened cokehead or a wide-eyed beginner looking to step up, no one wins when it comes to smoking cocaine. The day Sam lit his first crack pipe was the beginning of the end.

'There's no way you can smoke cocaine for a prolonged period without coming to your knees,' he says. Despite what large swathes of the UK media scene think, you can't function normally on cocaine and, more importantly, you can't mask its effects. 'It's not a social drug,' he says. 'It's antisocial.'

It is an interesting quirk of Sam's addictions that throughout his long usage, he generally seemed in control enough to put his pleasure and health – relatively speaking – ahead of any extreme dependency. There are few people who would deny that heroin is an antisocial drug as well. It is also renowned for its addictive qualities. And yet, when he first encountered the drug during his Morehouse days, Sam instinctively knew that the potential pleasures could not justify the equally potential perils. Considering his propensity for compulsive behaviour, it is quite remarkable how he was able simply to walk away from this most moreish of narcotics.

'I OD'd a few times while doing heroin,' he recalls. He still remembers watching a guy pound his chest while someone else tried to keep him conscious by talking to him. He remembers being put into a bath of cold water to try to wake him up. And he remembers the feeling of being outside his own body, watching to see if he would live or die. Most importantly, he remembers giving up. 'The third time I OD'd on heroin I quit that drug completely,' he says. 'It's too dangerous.'

Twenty years later, however, some of Sam's spirit had been crushed by his relentless substance abuse. Now, in 1989, it did not seem to matter to him that he was freebasing cocaine and overdosing. Each time he got over it. And then he would start again.

At home, LaTanya and Zoe were firmly ensconced in Villa from Hell. When Zoe was born, LaTanya had put her career on hold to take care of their daughter. In its way, this placed more responsibility on Sam to succeed – and drove him further into the arms of depravity as he tried to cope. He was not easy to live with, as he admits. LaTanya would leave in the mornings with Sam promising to clean the house and wash the dishes. On her return, she would find the house as she left it and Sam just where she had last seen him – only now sporting an uncomprehending sort of spaced-out look. When he wasn't just annoying towards her, he was occasionally quick to become argumentative and LaTanya was quick to fire back. The situation was becoming untenable and LaTanya was only just beginning to surmise the reason why. It wasn't long before her fears were confirmed.

The contributing factors to Sam Jackson's eventual implosion are impossible to pin down precisely. But two things are definitely attributable: one is that Sam's paranoia about his own relative lack of success in the movie business eventually swung round to examining his own role. The other is even more direct: LaTanya found out.

If anyone had done anything to advance the career of playwright August Wilson it was Sam. Having acted – with decent credits – in three of his dramas, he had certainly brought to life some of the writer's characters, enervating their scripted dialogue and bestowing upon them real, three-dimensional lives that were never there on the written page. Why then, when he had created the character of Boy Willie in *The Piano Lesson*, was he passed over when the play was turned into a film? Other cast members made the leap and, until he turned up to audition, he was considered a dead cert. Was there something about his eau de beer aroma that put the casting director off?

Then there were the plain old stupid 'accidents'. Mishaps that could befall anyone. Anyone, that is, off his head on cocaine and beer. Three days before his 41st birthday, Sam suffered the ignominy of being dragged along a station platform with his foot caught in the door of a subway train. This was a man who had had audiences eating out of the palm of his hand the night before. This was a man who had acted in at least seven big-budget film productions that year. This was a man at risk of killing himself on drugs and alcohol dependency. Today, Sam dismisses the event: 'That had nothing to do with anything else other than stupidity,' he says. Perhaps so, but it was that certain brand of stupidity that always seems to afflict those not totally in control of their actions. Despite being consigned to crutches for a while, the physical bruises from that escapade healed soon enough. Its effect on Sam's family was longer lasting. LaTanya's suspicions were fully aroused about his bad-boy behaviour. At last she was no longer swayed by his defence of being stressed by work – plenty of their friends were in the same boat but didn't act in the same way as Sam. Home life had deteriorated to little more than a series of arguments. It had to come to a head. And it did.

When LaTanya Jackson came home one day to find her husband slumped over the kitchen table, crack pipe in his hand, she had all the evidence she needed. When her initial panic had subsided, she got angry. Very angry. So angry, in fact, that she woke Sam up, not only from the cocaine-induced slumber he had fallen into that morning, but from the decades of believing that he could only exist with chemical help. The years of believing that he was in control of his powdery pastimes were wiped away. The delusions that he was under, the arrogant assumptions that he was master of his own destiny with drugs and drink, were destroyed. Sam Jackson was a cipher, a husk. He was a hollow man. He was no longer a drug user; drugs used him.

There was only one way that the Jackson marriage would survive. In LaTanya's opinion, there was only one way that Sam would survive.

Rehab.

Part 2

CALL ME MR JACKSON

8. SAM JACKSON WAS DEAD

Samuel L. Jackson is buzzing. He is Mr Life And Soul. He is the party. Check this guy out, he is connecting with everyone. Everyone knows him. High fives, low fives, the looks and the moves. This dude has it all. And the threads. So sharp they should cut him. Look at the way he operates, look at the way he is everything to everyone. But the eyes. Look into the eyes. The smile says 'vacant' but the eyes say 'engaged'. He stares back at you like a man possessed. Like a man possessed by cocaine.

But how? Sam has been clean for a year. He stopped doing drugs months ago. Why in 1991, is he in front of us, clearly off his head, being shot by his dad? How is this possible?

When the Negro Ensemble Company's Douglas Turner Ward told Sam that luck was the coming together of opportunity and preparation, he had no idea of how thoroughly his pupil's life would bear this out. The 21st century is littered with careers in ruins, talents lost to other temptations. How sad that Oliver Reed had barely completed work on his comeback picture, *Gladiator*, when his decades of self-abuse caught up with him, just at the point he had rediscovered his thirst – and huge ability – for acting. Sadly he is not the only unfulfilled talent. While Dudley Moore was making his fortune playing drunks in Hollywood, comedy partner Peter Cook was living the life for real in north London, content to let his career fall fallow. Others are more fortunate; they get the help they need in time. Rarely, though, do people live the wrong life for more than twenty years then go on to have greater success sober. Rarely – but not never.

Six weeks in a New York drying-out clinic was all it took for Sam Jackson to put his demons behind him. For good. As he says, 'I met people in rehab who had been in eight times, I only needed to do it once.' The likes of Reed, Cook, Richard Burton and countless others never stood a chance because they didn't want it enough. Not really. Others, like *Hannibal* villain and early Burton contemporary, Anthony Hopkins, were more successful in their battles. And so was Sam Jackson, for one very good reason. It was his own decision.

LaTanya's discovery of her inert husband may have lit the fuse, but the powder keg had been primed for some time. In his own heart, Sam knew that his life was coming to another crossroads: one path would be hazardous and full of early trials; the other would seem easier for a while but would be shorter, a lot shorter. He was convinced of that. He also realised that only one of those paths could bring him what he wanted professionally. After a lifetime spent using alcohol and drugs as a performance crutch, the time had come to stand up for himself. By himself.

'There are people who do drugs and work every day and never get tired of doing it,' Jackson says. He was not one of those. 'I was kind of burned out and miserable.' Burned out through years of living a double life; miserable due to the increasing realisation that all his problems were his own doing. For the first time he could see what was holding him back: himself. 'I wasn't as crisp as my mind told me I was,' he admitted to the *NME*. 'When I realised that, it was easy to make a change.'

Telling LaTanya he wanted help was the easy part. Now he had to see it through. Apart from the obvious hand-holding that led to his withdrawal from addictions, the rehab sessions opened Sam's eyes to wider issues, ones which would never have occurred to the drug-addled actor of a few months earlier.

'Recovery is all about introspection and questioning yourself,' he says. Of all the questions he was encouraged to ask himself, one struck home: when did you last do something to please yourself? In Sam's mind, he was 'the great pleaser', out to make friends, make them like him, put others first. But there was another way to make others happy, he learned. 'Today I feel I'm a much better person now that I've focused on pleasing myself, which in turn pleases others around me.'

While it may be odd hearing that from someone previously in the notoriously selfish grip of drug dependency, there is a deeper meaning. The beers, the tequilas, the marijuana, the coke – they were all ways of coping. Yes he indulged in them intentionally and sure he enjoyed it all. But the consequences – the adultery, the lying, the self-obsession – these were by-products. Until the day he admitted he had a problem he was as much of a victim as his wife and daughter. He just didn't realise it.

Ironically, a large part of Sam's logic for drying out was that same logic that kept him bombed in the first place: his career. He had never acted sober and it had never occurred to him to try. But with the movie parts coming in thick and fast and the stage parts becoming more taxing – everything he had ever wanted, in other words – he realised that he was struggling to keep up.

Eventually, he surmised, the red eyes and beer breath that accompanied him to auditions were beginning to count against him. Parts that should have been certain were mysteriously given to others. Directors who had actually requested he come along were suddenly showing him the door. The final straw came when he confidently strolled along to screen test for the movie part of Boy Willie in *The Piano Lesson* – the role he had created on the Broadway stage and made his own. He was devastated to be told that the part wouldn't be going to him. No specific reason was given, but it set Sam thinking.

After a lot of soul-searching he concluded what was obvious to others: 'I used to make $150 a week, now I make $8 million a picture,' he states. 'I was in my own way for a long time.'

Even though he suspected it was for the best, entering rehab would still take Sam's career into the unknown. He was learning that he couldn't perform on drugs as well as he thought he could – but could he perform at all without them?

'All of a sudden I was clean and wondering about the aspects of my performance,' he admits. 'It was like, "Can I still do this?" Because I had never done it without it.' The answer was an emphatic 'yes'. By his own calculations, his performances were up to 110 per cent better. 'I thought, "Oh, so this is what my wife meant," ' he says.

For an actor proud of his technical skills and the degree of commitment invested into every part, the dawning sense that maybe his potential had been underutilised was sickening. Nobody likes to hear the words 'what could have been' said about them, and Sam was no exception. 'You start thinking about all the years you've wasted,' he says. 'I said to myself, "Jesus, I could probably have been here ten years ago." ' For a man stoically unfamiliar with regrets, this is as close as it gets. Typically, though, he takes the phlegmatic – and the religious – view: every experience shapes us; what doesn't, kills us.

'You go through things for a reason and, if you are lucky, God doesn't let anything bad happen to you.' A lot of bad things could have happened during the drugs years; his marriage could have broken up, he could have died. But he pulled through and, according to Jackson, emerged better for the experiences. 'I couldn't have cleaned up before – it just wasn't the right time for me to be in this state,' he says.

Without question, the first onslaught of acclaim that would come Sam's way relied more on his shaky personal history than anything he had picked up in drama class. Once again, it was Shelton 'Spike' Lee who made it happen, as he revealed to the *Financial Times*.

'He rang me up and said, "Sam, *Jungle Fever*, next summer, part for you." Click. Spike is not into heavy discussion of roles.'

At the time he made the call, Lee was oblivious to his castee's epiphany. But he soon learned.

'I had to keep calling Spike from rehab and telling him, "I'm in rehab but I'll be there. I've done the research," ' Jackson says. 'It was a funny kind of thing. By the time I was out of rehab, about a week or so later I was on set and we were ready to start shooting.'

Filming on *Jungle Fever* started in New York on 20 August 1990. The movie was another abrasive take on the race question from a writer/ director growing in confidence. Wesley Snipes was Flipper, a smart, happily married business man. He has a problem with hiring an Italian as his company secretary; her family has a problem with her working for a black employer. The inevitable happens and an interracial affair starts. For whatever reason, Lee is not interested in the couple's actual miscegenation after that point. What drives the director is the effect on each family and social circle when one of its own introduces their partner. As Flipper's brother says when he hears about the relationship, 'You always do things the hard way.'

The same could be said of Flipper's brother himself. His name is Gator Purify and he's a loudmouth, show-off, user, abuser – and crack addict. And guess who was to play him? Having walked the audition, Sam arrived at the set virtually straight from rehab. In truth, coming so soon after his treatment, there weren't many parts that he could have handled physically at that time (his body was still showing signs of 'purifying' itself), but this was the coincidence of fortune he had been waiting for. If Sam couldn't play this one, he couldn't do anything.

'I basically didn't need any make-up because I was still detoxing,' he recalls. Uniquely, when the opportunity to do *Jungle Fever* came along, Jackson didn't have to create a biography for his character: he was – or had been – that person. 'I could step into that character and make him breathe, live and be somebody real that audiences could actually look at and go, "Oh my god, I know who that is, that's my brother, or my cousin." '

Fresh from the recovery programme of rehab, Sam also had a personal take on how the character should be. Enough actors have played addicts for audiences to know the basic signs. There is a checklist that subconsciously needs to be gone through in order for us to realise that, yes, this character on the screen is a junkie. It's the same for drunks: if an actor can bring even an approximation of Sue Ellen in *Dallas*, for example, then audiences will consider it a job well done. But every so often, an actor comes along who is able to subvert that accepted view. The tell-tale signals are still there, but so is a lot more. A whole lot more. In Sam's case, he was bringing personal baggage that no one had ever seen before. It was painful but, he felt, that is how crack addicts behave. And he should know.

'The easy part was doing the drug part of the role,' he says. But there was another aspect that few actors could have picked up on. Part of Jackson's rehab programme had involved a study of how addicts destroy their relationships, and how they manipulate the people around them. That was the aspect that Jackson recognised from his own life; that was what he knew he had to bring to the part of Gator. He discussed it with his director who told him to follow his instincts.

'I've abused people and abused their trust,' Jackson admits. 'But that was the human element that was needed to make the character totally believable and not a cartoon junkie.' Gator's subsequent treatment of the characters played by Snipes, Ossie Davis, Ruby Dee and Halle Berry shaped him as a tangible and rounded addict far more than any physical moves could.

Although it hurt him personally to invest Gator with so many of the qualities he was still trying to excise from his own life, Sam was glad he did it. The feedback at grass-roots level was amazing. 'The wonderful thing about the role was that people came up to me and said that I was their brother, their father, their husband, cousin, somebody. Everyone's lives have been touched by a character like Gator and they all found it very real and very close to themselves.'

In fact, taking on the role in the first place had been something of a tonic for Sam. Ever his own man, even when signing on for clinical treatment for addictions, he totally disagreed with the advice given by his doctors when the Gator role came through. To a man, they all agreed that no good would come of it. Guess who won the argument? And guess who has been proved right? With typical brutality of thought, Sam has no time for those naysayers now. 'Counsellors?' he says. 'My attitude was, 'If I never see you people again for the rest of my life, it'll be too soon.'

One can see where they were coming from. Perhaps for their average client – the ones who needed seven or eight visits to come to terms with their problems – it was sound advice. On the face of it, immersing yourself into the life of a crack addict so soon after living the part could only end in tears. But this was Elizabeth Jackson's boy they were talking about. He may be compulsive, he may be obsessive. But if he puts his mind to something, there isn't a force in this world that will slow him down. And anyway – why shouldn't he now become compulsively obsessive about staying clean?

One of Gator's stand-out scenes in the movie is where he has to dance. A lot of directors would have had an opinion on this but Spike Lee, for all the accusations of being too hands-on, knew when to let his actor have his head. The first thing Sam did on receiving the *Jungle Fever* script, in fact, was to cross out the non-verbal instructions. 'Some writers can write, but most of them can't act, so why are they giving me stage directions?' he says, showing an ego as healthy post-rehab as before. Lee is renowned for letting his cast work out the finer details of a part – 'he doesn't sit down and have long conversations about characters' – which suits Jackson just fine. So when Lee's script said Gator 'dances' it was down to the actor to find out how. The end result, then, was pure Jackson.

In *Jungle Fever*, Gator swans around the movie trying his luck with every character going – friends, strangers and family. His foul-mouthed pothead girlfriend, played by amazing newcomer Berry (who had great difficulties mastering the swearing, Jackson is amused to recall), suffers particularly, although it is how Gator destroys his parents' trust (with tragic consequences) that really defines his character's emotional vacuum. There is only one motivation in his life and that is feeding his habit. Sam plays it with more orthodoxy than any other actor before or since. As if his life depended on it. And, in a way, it did.

Far from hiding from his earlier problems, Jackson wanted everyone on the production to benefit from his experiences. For the sake of reality, Jackson took it upon himself to open his co-star Berry's eyes to the sort of depths to which her character would be exposed and the emotions she would feel. Despite having put that life behind him, Jackson gave her a guided tour of the drug dens, the backstreet boozers and the various iniquitous haunts of his past. It was an eye-opener for the young actress, but it gave her the perfect ammunition to shape her role. For Jackson, it was testament to how far his recovery had come in such a short space of time that he could expose himself to the scenes of his earlier problems – and walk away.

Had the 'Gator experiment' backfired and audiences turned their noses up at his character, then Jackson still would have profited from the role. As it was, he became the most admired performer in the piece. Without exception, it was Gator who caught the public and the press's eye. Oprah Winfrey asked, 'How did they get this cocaine addict to turn up on set long enough to shoot the movie?' However, she was watching Sam Jackson up there playing an addict, not being one. And strangely enough, it actually helped him. Not only to release a few demons but, in particular at the point where Gator's father, played by Ossie Davis, kills him, to achieve some sort of resolution within his own life.

'It was a catharsis,' Jackson says, explaining that when Gator died, so did the actor's former personality. 'Sam Jackson was dead. From then on, I would no longer answer to the name Sam. It was Samuel L. Jackson or nothing at all.'

As well as denoting the official birth of his new, improved persona, *Jungle Fever* also marked the start of the world's love affair with Sam – sorry, Samuel L. – Jackson. Although Spike Lee movies are less about actors than about themes – and the theme of this one was the spicy topic of interracial relationships – occasionally the odd person's name gets a mention in reviews. Oprah was not alone in getting worked up by Jackson's performance after the movie's 1991 release. *Empire* singled him out for special attention: 'In the space of a few minutes, Flipper's crackhead brother Gator – an inspired creation from Samuel L. Jackson – suddenly takes centre stage where previously he had merely shuffled around.' The *New York Times* concurred, showing the office crystal ball is still fully functioning: ' . . . Samuel L. Jackson, whose performance as a crack addict is also worthy of an award.'

No sooner had the film started doing the rounds than talk began of Jackson being in line for some proper recognition – from his peers. The first big awards competition to come along, however, did not even include a 'Best Supporting Actor' category in its script. That didn't stop some people banging the drum anyway.

The night before Spike left for the Cannes Festival he was still insisting to his friend, 'You're gonna win something.'

'Spike, they don't give supporting actor awards at the Cannes Film Festival,' Jackson replied, and for the next few days, continued with business as usual: audition after audition. Then one afternoon he checked in with his agent to see if there were any callbacks.

'I think people from the Associated Press are looking for you,' his agent said. 'You won some award at the Cannes Festival.'

Jackson could have been forgiven for thinking he was having another bout of hallucinations, but it was absolutely true. The jury at Cannes had been so bowled over by his performance in *Jungle Fever* that, for the first time in their history, they had created a 'Best Supporting Actor' category: and Samuel L. Jackson had won it. What's more, when the film was released to a wider public, he also picked up the New York Film Critics Circle Award for the same category.

With success in the air, there was a certain amount of expectation as the year's Oscar nominees were announced. For the first time in his career, Jackson felt the kick of rejection that arguably comes as much from colour as talent. Despite the press hype and build-up, he did not even make the short-list of nominations. Welcome to the wonderful world – the wonderful white world – of the Academy.

The experience would have a scarring effect on him. 'After *Jungle Fever* I kind of let it go with the Oscars,' he says. He had turned in the performance of his life, probably one of the greatest ever portrayals of an addict; he had received the unique Cannes prize and won the New York Film Critics award. But come the Big One, he was overlooked. In his place on the nominations short-list, it seemed, was the entire cast of *Bugsy*. In disbelief at missing out, Jackson took LaTanya to see the Barry Levinson movie on the day of the nominations to see the standard necessary to impress the Oscar voters. He wishes now he hadn't bothered. 'My wife came out and she was crying and saying, "It's so unfair." And, like, Harvey [Keitel] and Ben [Kingsley] are great actors, but they didn't do anything in that movie.'

When he wasn't fuming about the iniquities of his profession, Jackson was spending more and more time getting to know a new 'addiction'. It was called golf and, for some reason, he seemed to have the mentality to enjoy its peculiar demands. 'I'm an only child so I like solitary kinds of things to do,' he says. It's not a team sport, not even a group participation one. No matter how many people you're playing with on the greens, in reality you play golf by yourself. 'It's you, the ball and the golf course,' he says. 'You can't blame anybody else for your mistakes, and you take all the credit.'

If that didn't sum up Jackson's approach to life, nothing would. Especially the psychological side. 'The sport is played 80 per cent in the head and 20 per cent physically,' he explains. 'It's just an awesome, awesome thought game, and golf courses are cool places to hang out.' We'll take his word on the last part, but at least he was honest about his priorities. He, personally, had to be enthused by something for it to be worthwhile. All the agents and managers in the world could not compete against his own opinion. For example, while his counsellors and therapists were warning him away from the role of Gator, he could think of nothing more logical. That's the kind of man he is. In every area.

He also takes a personal view of the kind of support groups people like him are 'supposed' to need. While he is not averse to putting in an appearance at the odd Narcotics Anonymous meeting, Jackson will not attend Alcoholics Anonymous gatherings. 'Everybody there's pissed off because they can't have a drink,' he said in the *Guardian* in 1998.

Two things came of Jackson's participation in *Jungle Fever*. The first was that he discovered that acting sober wasn't so bad after all. 'The one thing that happened to me once I got clean was that I was able to make a personal investment and not just the exterior bit,' he told *Time Out*. He had always been able to get the right facial expression, the right vocal inflection and the right interpretation of what the relationships were. But, as LaTanya had pointed out, there was no heart to his performance. 'Until I got clean I was not able to personally go in and project what the character felt to an audience so they could have the experience with me.'

The second bonus to come from the movie was what he had always wanted: 'All of a sudden I was having lunch in Hollywood,' he says. 'It just kind of happened.'

The call had come and there was no way he was going to miss the opportunity to make it stick. Samuel L. Jackson was on his way to Hollywood.

9. I AIN'T WORKING NO TEN WEEKS FOR $150,000

In August 1990, just a couple of weeks before *Jungle Fever* commenced its New York shoot, Jeffrey Katzenberg, then chairman of Walt Disney Studios (he is currently a third of the private studio Dreamworks SKG) put in an appearance at the fifteenth annual convention of the National Association of Black Journalists in America. His statement was simple: 'The studios and networks must take it upon ourselves to create opportunities for blacks. The responsibility for advancement must rest with those who have the power, the money and those who, if they have the will, can make it happen.'

To his credit, Katzenberg was already putting his company's money where his mouth was. In addition to committing $2.5 million for a fiscal 1991 training–hiring programme for minorities, Disney had made it a policy that every intern hired during the summer of 1990 had to be a minority.

Interestingly, black star Louis Gossett Jr (Oscar winner for *An Officer and a Gentleman*) and director Keenan Ivory Wayans said that it wasn't the business of companies like Disney to make improvements. 'Why don't the likes of Sidney Poitier, Bill Cosby and Eddie Murphy start our own studio?' asked Gossett. The whole black artistic community should come up with its own money, he reasoned. 'We have to prove that, business-wise, we represent the money-spending public.'

Wayans was more blunt: 'I don't think it's fair to rely on the studios to represent blacks. Corporate black America should support the arts just like corporate white America does.'

Ignoring the salient fact that the country's leading black drama group, New York's Negro Ensemble Collective, was originally funded by 'corporate white American' company Ford for the propagation of black culture, there was sense to be heard here. It was, after all, the same message that Spike Lee had been advocating from his first picture, *She's Gotta Have It*. Ironically, however, Lee himself was proving far from immune to charges of racism. Despite the obvious pro-blackness of his movies, various groups in the early 1990s were becoming increasingly disturbed by the perceived antagonism towards other minorities. *Jungle Fever* took a pop at white oppression – that was OK, but *Mo' Better Blues*, according to some commentators, was little more than a thinly veiled anti-Jewish attack. According to Abe Foxman of the Anti-Defamation League of B'nai B'rith, the movie's portrayal of club owners Moe and Josh Flatbush 'as greedy and unscrupulous, dredges up an age-old and highly dangerous form of anti-Semitic stereotyping'. He accused the director of hypocrisy: 'Lee has employed the same kind of tactics that he supposedly deplores.' (In years to come, Lee would counter a racist argument with another high-profile film-maker by bemoaning how it would be inappropriate for him to litter his movies with words like 'kike', so he was obviously alert to the danger.)

Lee's defence, if that is the word, was that by promoting blacks there would always be other groups who felt targeted – this is exactly how black people have been treated for years. It was a view shared by Samuel L. Jackson. Fifteen years after he had arrived in Harlem from Atlanta, the debate stirred by Lee's very existence meant that there was the first glimmer of Hollywood acknowledging its weaknesses. And nowhere was it weaker, either by design or coincidence, than in its racial inclusion policy.

As yet another black actor in a much-talked about movie to have been passed over by the Academy of Motion Picture Arts and Sciences, Jackson knew better than most the extent of the changes required. Until now, however, he was hardly in a position to make much impression on society's wider consciousness – his 'Hate Whiteys' theatre group aside. What had changed in 1991 to make him reconsider his opportunities? He had received the call from Hollywood. At last.

'I waited until I had an offer,' he says. 'And it came from Spike Lee.' Suddenly Jackson was shuttling over to LA on the redeye to have meetings, lunches and auditions. He was moving up in the world. His name was beginning to mean something, to carry a certain weight. Even movies that had already been and gone were suddenly deemed worthy of revisiting, just to catch his performance. As a sign of his growing success, the US box office charts for the week that *Jungle Fever* started shooting showed no fewer than three 'Sam' films in the Top 50: *Mo' Better Blues*, *Betsy's Wedding* and *Def by Temptation*. Three hits, three different roles in three very different movies. If this was anything to go by, Samuel L. Jackson would prove to be difficult to pigeonhole. A sign of things to come? (In the same week's chart there were healthy showings from Morgan Freeman's *Driving Miss Daisy*, Eddie Murphy's *Another 48 Hours* and Whoopi Goldberg's *Ghost* – bringing the total of even vaguely 'black' titles (discounting *Betsy's* 'white' *Wedding*) to five.)

As had occurred a couple of years earlier when he first started to make an impression as a cameo player, the peculiar schedules of movie making meant that Jackson's diary for 1991 was pretty full. Arguably, too full. Nineteen-ninety had proved a busy year for him and *Jungle Fever* had been just one of his projects. When they all started to emerge the following year, there was a distinct danger of his newly established 'brand' being diluted. Apart from the Lee movie, there was nothing else that really grabbed an audience's attention, although each project deserved consideration on its own merits.

Any early chance to work again with rising star Halle Berry in March was snapped up. *Go Natalie* was a romantic comedy centring on how Joseph Phillip's real estate man with everything to lose falls for Natalie – and decides she is worth losing everything for. In a totally black acted/written production, the tone of the film is less *She's Gotta Have It* than *The Cosby Show*, in that colour is merely incidental to the plot. Jackson's role as Monroe is ever so slightly more significant, however, although at least he felt more secure in his role than Berry who only joined the cast on the first day of shooting (original Natalie, A.J. Johnson was replaced at the last minute). If they could fuss over the lead casting, imagine what a mess the producers could make of coming up with a title. 'The film was originally called *Go Beverly*, but they had some problems with someone who claimed to be Beverly and wanted to sue for all this money,' Berry reveals. Before they came up with Natalie, there was the idea that *Go Halle* might be the answer. Their new star was less than keen. 'I got freaked out and said, "No, I don't want to be 'Go Halle' for the rest of my life!" '

In the event, *Go Natalie* was dumped altogether in America, where it plied its wares under the more pedestrian moniker *Strictly Business* (*Natalie* lived in Europe). Seven million dollars represented a healthy US box office for the picture, and the reviews were supportive, especially of Berry and the writing. But no one picked up on Jackson and it was little surprise. The role was too insignificant to notice, however good he personally was. Unfortunately, it would be a criticism that would dog his entire career.

Just as Jackson was often the spectator, watching as friends and contemporaries Morgan Freeman, Denzel Washington and Wesley Snipes left New York for The Call, he could have felt the same during his early movie career. No sooner had he spotted Berry's talent than he watched her go on to become the leading black actress in the world, with roles in *X-Men*, Bond films and her Oscar-winning *Monster's Ball*. It was the same with his next two pictures. Both *Johnny Suede* and *Jumpin' in the Boneyard* were decent films, and he had interesting, if small parts (as B-bop and Mr Simpson respectively). But after these films, what happened to his career? Compared to a certain Brad Pitt and a certain Tim Roth, both of whom springboarded from their individual lead roles to greater things, not a lot. It wasn't that Jackson was picking bad projects – his next job, the ABC movie of the week, *Dead and Alive*, opposite *Taxi* star Tony Danza, was very well received, but the review in the *Hollywood Reporter* could have been talking about his own career trajectory when it said: '*Dead and Alive* is a surprisingly potent, incredibly well shot and directed film that deserves more attention than it is probably going to get.' Somehow he needed to make that step up, and as soon as the post-*Fever* rush settled, he would put his energies into making it.

No sooner had he thought this than the perfect vehicle came along. In theory. Unfortunately, all was not what it seemed. After the worldwide acclaim for *Jungle Fever*, Spike Lee was reaching a lot further with his next project. The racial question so artfully skirted round in his last film would be promoted to centre stage in his next movie: a biography of the radical activist Malcolm X. After four seasons at 'Spike's summer camp', there would be a part for Sam, everyone assumed. When filming of *Malcolm X* started in New York on 16 September 1991, however, Jackson was nowhere to be found.

'There's only one star in a Spike Lee movie and that's Spike,' he says bitterly. After two major awards for his role as Gator, Jackson had naturally assumed that a couple of things would change for the next picture. One, he didn't expect to have to audition any more; two, it was time to look at his salary. He was no longer a nobody prepared to work for 'scale' – the minimum fee set by the actors' union – as he had done previously. It was some time before he discovered how wrong he was.

'Denzel had got the part of Malcolm but he wasn't around for the casting of the other characters,' Jackson explains. In Washington's absence, Jackson agreed to read with the various auditionees. Only at the end of the process did Lee announce it was Jackson's turn to try out – despite seeing him work as various characters already. Maybe this crass insensitivity could have been overlooked if there was an offer on the table worth swallowing your pride for.

'Most of the actors who've passed through Spike's films actually outgrow him,' Jackson reveals. 'We won't work for nothing any more.' Jackson was even less inclined to do it when he took a glance at Lee's property portfolio: a townhouse and an office in New York and a new house in Martha's Vineyard. Lee has always been an evangelical type of film-maker, insisting he has a social message that needs to be heard. The implication has always been that it should be the duty of every 'brother' to help him realise that message; if this means working cheaply, it's a sacrifice for the cause. Jackson refused to be swayed by that argument when it came to signing on for *Malcolm X*. 'I said, "If this is about uplifting the race then let me share some of the profits because you'll be uplifting the race by helping me."'

Tact, it seems, is not Lee's strong point. Take for example his 'brave' decision to make a film about miscegenation. Considering the whole point of *Jungle Fever* is to see Snipes' decent family man engage in an affair with a Caucasian, one would have considered that the writer had some sympathies, if not for his character, then for the actress playing opposite him. Public comments along the lines of 'I am solely attracted to black women' meant that Annabella Sciorra, playing Italian Angie, seemed isolated to begin with. With her going on record as finding the idea of a white woman going with a black man purely out of sexual curiosity far fetched, the pair soon reached non-speaking level. Tricky when you're trying to make a picture. 'We didn't get along that great,' Lee admits. 'And now we don't talk. But I must say, she was the best person we auditioned and I think her performance in the film is great.'

Dumping Lee was a risk for Jackson, but this was a clean man of principle taking it, not a crackhead chancer desperate for cash for his next fix. There would be other work and, in fact, by the time the buzz of *Jungle Fever* started to get around, there was a noticeable upturn in his offers – maybe not in the quality, but certainly in the budget. In 1991, after successes with the *Indiana Jones* and *Star Wars* series, there was no greater star than Harrison Ford. Already building an audience for the Tom Clancy *Jack Ryan* strand, Ford was about to embark on the next instalment. And along for an audition in LA was Samuel L.

If you are going to appear in implausible spy romps, then the quality of your character will matter. From what Jackson could see as he read for the part of military man LCDR Robbie Jackson in *Patriot Games*, this could be the role to take him to the next level fame-wise – assuming he won the part.

He needn't have worried. Producer Mace Neufeld and director Phillip Noyce were as impressed by him as everyone else. The part was his: here's the script, see you on 2 November for shooting. For the first time, Jackson was in with a shout at making a real impression, and not just in this film. As *Premiere* magazine pointed out in May 1992, *Patriot Games* was scheduled to be just the first of three sequels to Clancy's *The Hunt for Red October*. Best of all, Jackson's character was slated to feature in them all. The potential financial rewards were frightening. After years of scraping by, he was attached to a project that had 'money spinner' written all over it. And he was happy. Zoe was going to get some serious spoiling. The brownstone in Harlem that he and LaTanya had been renovating on and off could finally get some attention. This being sober lark could prove to be very lucrative – and the Jackson family were in just the mood to enjoy it.

Fast forward six months, however, and Jackson encountered another rude awakening, Hollywood style. The standard practice on this type of film of rewrites and more rewrites meant that, as far as the actor could tell, his role had dwindled to little more than a 'glorified extra'. Unfortunately, he only discovered this when he turned up to shoot. His first mistake was to care – there was no drop in salary, after all, and many would have been content to take any size part in the trilogy. His second error was to mention it in public. Still a novice in the political aspect of the movie business, Jackson saw no reason not to be honest when a journalist at a press junket for the movie asked how the big picture experience was, so he replied that he wished he'd been able to earn the money that they paid him, rather than just kind of showing up. 'The producer, Mace Neufeld, thought I was an ungrateful son of a bitch,' Jackson claimed later in *Premiere*. 'I had a three-picture deal, and he had me written out of all of them.'

Welcome to Hollywood.

Almost sixty years after Lawrence Reddick devised his list of nineteen stereotypical roles for black actors, Samuel L. Jackson was in danger of being the living proof. By the age of 44 he had clocked up more than twenty feature films and certainly played his fair share of criminals. If it weren't for the money on offer each time, there was a good chance that one or two of those roles would never have made it past his innate sense of race inequality. It has never bothered him as an actor to play a part – but what does worry him is the association audiences might make between his colour and his role.

'There are criminals in our society and somebody's got to play them,' Jackson told *Premiere*. 'But it's a shame that a lot of people think that all criminals in the world are black.' It's a debate that he has always had at home with LaTanya. On this subject, though, she is adamant that the quality of the role is of more importance than its message to the paying public. 'My wife made me understand that James Cagney and Humphrey Bogart made very good careers out of playing criminals.'

At the same time as the Jacksons were having this discussion, *New Jack City* and John Singleton's *Boyz N the Hood* were helping to compound the stereotypes. Unfortunately, each film was attracting criticism for glamorising violence – with the result that there had been a massive increase in gang warfare in Los Angeles' Compton district since the two releases. In March 1991, Jackson had himself taken part in such a gang movie, *Juice*, featuring latest rapper with attitude, Tupac Shakur. Directed by Spike Lee's trusty cinematographer, Ernest Dickerson, it was a hardcore take on the problems facing young black men raised on gang culture. When the movie was prepped for release in 1992, there was a furore over its marketing. In the light of the current climate, it was felt irresponsible to have posters of four hooded gang kids, one brandishing a gun, with the tag line: 'If you want respect you have to earn it. You have to be willing to stand up and die for it.'

For all the uproar, Dickerson actually delivered a sound movie, and Jackson turned in an equally solid performance as Trip. As *Variety* noted, there was more to this film than controversy: '*Juice* demonstrates the black community's untapped talent waiting for opportunities on both sides of the camera.'

If anyone was untapped, it was Jackson. But while he busied himself on fulfilling contracts on the smaller fry of pre-*Jungle Fever* projects, the word among casting directors was that this guy had potential, or 'legs' as they call it, in terms of longevity. On the back of a decent pay packet for his inchoate performance alongside Harrison Ford, Jackson was aware that his star was rising. When scripts started coming to him – rather than him chasing them – the point really hit home. One of the first was for a project starring Willem Dafoe, Mary Elizabeth Mastrantonio and wild man of celluloid, Mickey Rourke.

It was flattering that he was being pre-selected for a part in *White Sands* but, considering his recommendation was coming on the back of Gator, he was resigned to the type of character the producers had him pencilled in for. As soon as his eyes fell on the name 'Lennox' in the script's Dramatis Personae, he realised that this, as the obvious black character, must be the part they wanted him to study.

He was wrong.

Lennox is the bad guy played by Rourke. If Jackson wanted it, it was the part of Greg Meeker, an FBI agent, that they wanted him to consider. 'I had to go back and read the script again,' Jackson admits. 'I like Meeker a lot. He's not obviously bad or obviously good.' In particular, he liked the fact that, as a stretch from Gator, he got to show a range of ability.

Credit for the bold casting choice goes ultimately to *White Sands* director Roger Donaldson. In Jackson he recognised all the component attributes that Meeker needed – and then some. 'He's got enormous resources as an actor,' he says. 'He's extremely talented technically. Sam can do something in one take, then go back and build on it. He's spontaneous but he's well trained. And he's a nice guy.'

After a lifetime of being chosen for a part as much for his skin colour as his talent – doing justice to a succession of screenwriters' visions of their criminals or down-and-outs being black – Jackson was at last being given a shot at proving his acting chops despite his race. It's true: Meeker was never written as a 'black' character. But the producers realised that if the right actor came along, he came along. If he happened to be black, so what?

This example of casting colour-blindness is not as common as one would hope. The fact that it happened relatively early in Jackson's career would seem to indicate that his reputation was capable of overriding the concerns of colour on screen. And so it would, but with nothing like the regularity that you would expect, even for an actor of the standing that he would acquire.

'Sometimes when executives read a script and it doesn't say "African-American", they take some convincing that I'm the guy who can do that,' he expounds. 'When my name comes up, it's, "Oh my God, I hadn't thought of him." '

As if proof were needed, there would be plenty of times over the following years when he would go for parts – as Samuel L. Jackson, household name and gen-u-ine movie star – only to be told, 'Sorry, we don't know if we're going that way, Sam.'

That way. Two short words, but together they expose the latent racism redolent in the thought processes and business decisions of myriad mainstream producers and major Hollywood influencers. Without even discussing it, the unspoken perception is that white films have white leads, black films have black leads and you mix at your commercial peril. Money comes from targeting an audience and reaching that audience; you earn nothing by preaching mixed messages. The proof, the theory goes, is in movies like the audience-polarising work of Spike Lee. His pictures do not appeal as broadly as other pictures because they are 'black' works. In fact, when *Mo' Better Blues* first opened, many a theatre reported viewer horror when heart-throb Denzel Washington becomes involved with a non-black girl. Even Lee refrained from devoting too much screen time to Flipper and Angie's cross-race relationship in *Jungle Fever*.

Lee has never shied away from 'statement' movie-making. He has a point to get across about decades of black culture being overlooked by mainstream cinema, and he makes no bones about it. In widescreen with Dolby sound. But while Lee is overtly scoring political points with his pro-black polemics, there is a more moderate view. It is one of social inclusion. As Samuel L. Jackson says, 'The world does have people like us in it. We do almost every job that's out there.' By which he means, there should be no such thing as a 'white man's occupation' or a 'black man's career'. And, by extension, this should be reflected in movies. An office guy is an office guy is an office guy, regardless of being black, white, Hispanic or Asian. Can he push the buttons, work the computer, make the calls? Then he can do the job.

And yet, for all its noises and for all the statements made by Disney executives, mainstream Hollywood remains ridiculously simplistic in its desires and decision-making. There is a real fear that a film with a black star would be treated as a 'black movie'. Reviewers and audiences would treat it as a statement rather than a piece of entertainment. It would be making a stand and judged on different criteria to the one originally intended. And, most important of all, it would not make as much money.

The ineluctable logic is that even an actor of Samuel L. Jackson's calibre could be considered more trouble than he was worth by casting directors – just because of his colour. Which is why, when the role of Meeker was adjusted to fit him, it mattered so much. He was being judged for his abilities in front of a camera. The blueprint of Meeker never mentioned he was black; but then it never said he wasn't either. And as for being worried about the baggage of having a black actor involved? How could signing up the award-winning star of *Jungle Fever* for your movie ever be seen as a bad move?

Not only did *White Sands* prove a refreshing eye-opener for Jackson as far as his favourable treatment went, but it also marked the first time that he made serious money. Big money. Considering that he had just lost out on the *Patriot Games* series, he felt more than compensated by his fee for this picture: $75,000 for ten weeks' work. He could buy his brownstone home for that. The good news didn't stop there. As with *Patriot Games*, *White Sands* marked the first stage of a new three-picture deal he had just signed with Paramount. And, get this: for taking part in the second movie his salary would double. If you had told Samuel L. Jackson a couple of years earlier that he would soon be earning $150,000 a picture, he would have looked accusingly at his crack pipe. But it was true. He had a contract. He was a success.

Except . . .

'Making it is a very relative thing,' Jackson says. A starving man will eat anything you offer him; but a discerning diner is likely to be harder to please. As soon as Jackson got used to the idea that someone thought he merited $75,000 for ten weeks' work, then so did he. 'At first it was like, yeah, wow!' he says. 'I was going to make $150,000 for the second movie.' Unfortunately, once he got to Hollywood he realised this fee was near the bottom end of the scale. 'By the time they offered me the next movie I was like, "I ain't working no ten weeks for $150,000." '

What had been his wildest dreams come true had turned into another example of Hollywood exploitation. And, regardless of the amount of noughts on his cheque, he was the one feeling exploited. He was being taken for the starving man when he felt he was the discerning diner. As a man of principle, Jackson had to make the stand, even though he admits today that it was foolhardy. 'It was crazy for us,' he agrees, 'because we'd been living in New York, sneaking on the subway, barely making $30,000 a year.'

It would not be the last time that Jackson made a stand about the salary system in Hollywood. Pay him an amount equal to those of similar talent and experience and he'll be content. Value him less than the next kid off the block booked in for his fifteen minutes of movie fame and watch the feathers fly . . .

Jungle Fever may have been the catalyst, but it was *White Sands* that altered Jackson's thinking about his future more significantly. Spike Lee may have provided the call from Hollywood (at least from his parent studio's part of it), but it was Roger Donaldson that provided the call *to* Hollywood. 'I used to go to my agent's office and say, "Hollywood call?" "No, Sam, not today," ' he recalls. 'Then after I got that special prize at Cannes, I said, "Hollywood call?" and my agent said, "Yes, they did." It was *White Sands*.'

Still feeling the guilt of having put his family through enough for his selfish pleasures, it did not occur to Jackson even to raise the subject of transposing his clan westwards in order to help his burgeoning movie career. Fortunately, he didn't have to.

While he was setting about crafting a new career based on his stage foundations, LaTanya was in a transitional period of her own. Having put her ambitions on hold to have and raise Zoe (and be occasional nanny to her errant husband), she was once again working. TV appealed to her and she appealed to it. Unfortunately, where many of Jackson's television jobs had been local, the first serious part LaTanya won was far from it. It was a great job on great money with great people. But it was in LA. They discussed it as a family but there was no way that she could commute and neither wanted to spend time apart and meet at weekends. Decision made: the Jacksons were going to Hollywood.

Sadly for LaTanya, the family had no sooner put down west coast roots than the reason they had relocated disappeared. 'Unfortunately the series was cancelled very soon after we got settled,' Jackson says. 'My daughter was already in school and we weren't going to jerk her around by going back to New York so we ended up staying.' Just like that. On the plus side, there are worse places to find yourself living than a spacious Tudor style, four-bedroom home in Encino, California.

Although he didn't want it to be for him, the move was a positive one for Jackson's career. With a multi-picture Paramount deal in his pocket, he needed to be more local, more visible on the scene, more available for all the extraneous demands that are associated with making big-budget productions.

What he needed to do now, however, was consolidate his worth by picking vehicles for his talents. There was no point being on a decent contract with a major studio if he didn't show what he could do. As usual, he adopted the approach that he had always had on stage once he was in a position to choose. Since the only thing in a production Jackson could control was his own personal performance, he would pick his parts on the strength of his character's opportunities, regardless of what was going on in the rest of the picture. Why waste energy trying to second-guess the outcomes of the numerous variables that go into making the average movie? 'Even if the film's not great, I'm always trying to pick an interesting character that I haven't played before,' he says matter-of-factly.

It's an interesting policy and one guaranteed to test the patience of movie fans or professional critics. What is the world coming to if you can't pigeonhole your actors? But that has never been Jackson's intention. His aims are somewhat loftier; or at least, his role models are. When Sir Laurence Olivier died, the Oscars paid tribute by running a film montage of his various characters. As one great characterisation morphed into another, Jackson was awestruck at the range. 'That's the ambition,' he says. 'To have this body of work that people could look at and be moved by.' And to date, he wasn't doing badly.

Picking projects for the character rather than the piece as a whole, though, can throw up problems. Joining up with the great Children's Television Workshop for the *Ghostwriter* TV series may have been worthy education-wise, but it wouldn't do much for Jackson's long-term future – unless he fancied linking up with Big Bird. He shouldn't have worried. The CTW project was just a stopgap till his next job. And his next job just happened to be a lead role in a movie opposite Nicolas Cage, nephew of Francis Ford Coppola and Oscar-winner designate. Unfortunately, this happened to be during Cage's screwball period. And their joint film, *Amos and Andrew*, more than qualified.

While not quite as 'excruciating' as *Sight and Sound* claimed, *Amos and Andrew* was never going to take Jackson's career to new heights. At best, it is farce; at worst, it is failed farce. When Pulitzer Prize-winning playwright Andrew Sterling is seen carrying a stereo inside a posh house in an exclusive New England holiday resort, neighbours assume he must be a thief: he is black, after all. It is only after cops come shooting and turn Sterling's house into a siege zone that the mistake is revealed – it is Sterling's home, bought and paid for. Not wanting to blow his chances of political office, the police chief hatches a plan to plant a convicted villain in the house, then claim he was holding Sterling hostage, thus producing heroes of the force. Obviously it all goes wrong as Cage and Jackson's characters bond.

Somewhere beneath E. Max Frye's $750,000 script, is a sentiment that Jackson was able to grab hold of as he built up his character biography. In particular, Sterling's appearance as the epitome of internalised anger. 'I have that, yeah,' Jackson says. Growing up during segregation in the South had taught him to turn the other cheek when he most dearly would have loved to strike out against his oppressors.

Unfortunately, for all the glory the lead role won him, the film failed to win over critics, with many citing Cage as the only saving grace. On the plus side, an audience worth $10 million domestically meant that several thousand people had seen him carry a lead role – and there had to be a few casting chiefs among them. It wasn't his fault, after all, if the script stank.

For the next part of his studio deal, Jackson was able to repeat the double-header co-starring set-up with another member of one of Hollywood's great families – only this time the laughs were intentional. If you are going to try something new, and comedy really was new to Jackson, then there was no better place to start than *National Lampoon's Loaded Weapon I*. Taking Shane Black's *Lethal Weapon* series and spinning it on its head, *NLLW* cast Jackson in the wet Danny Glover role opposite Emilio Estevez's big-haired Mel Gibson spoof. With nods to dozens of other buddy movies, cop series and, of course, the entire Leslie Nielsen back catalogue, the film fired enough bullets for some to hit home. And, what do you know? It worked. Jackson could do comedy, just like he could do everything else. Straight.

The fun starts from the opening sequence. The boys' mission: to recover a microfilm containing a formula by which cocaine can be turned into cookies. Featuring wonderful cameos and larger roles from the likes of William Shatner, Tim Curry, Whoopie Goldberg and an uncredited Bruce Willis, it wore its tongue firmly in its cheek. Bizarrely, that wasn't enough for all reviewers. 'It's not always as funny as it might be, but in this kind of comedy, tirelessness is an end to itself,' said the *New York Times*. 'Some gags are really funny,' condescended the *Hollywood Reporter*, citing Jackson's schoolmarmish command for no giggling in the ranks, which leads to police officer Phil Hartman doing a couple of stand-up jokes at an incongruous microphone. *Sight and Sound* threw up an opinion that managed to criticise both *Loaded Weapon* and its source: 'How do you parody the already parodic?' The answer, they decided, was you couldn't. Not very well, anyway. *Empire* was more even handed: 'There may not be a laugh every minute, but there are enough to satisfy most devotees of the relentlessly silly, tasteless school of parody.' The one word of outright criticism came from *Variety* who didn't get what Jackson was up to. 'He plays straight, doesn't even come close to raising a smile and merely proves he would have been miscast opposite Mel Gibson in the first place,' it railed.

Regardless of the critics, *Loaded Weapon* found a solid audience. At the US box office alone, it took $30 million; doubled internationally. Sitting in his new home, Samuel Jackson was beside himself. It may not be rocket science up there on screen, but a film with him as one of its two stars had just earned more than $50 million. And that felt good. Very good.

Of course, the portents for success with a *National Lampoon* movie were always going to be good. Filming started in June 1992, but Jackson wouldn't know anything about its success until its release in April the following year. In the meantime he had plenty of other projects that were nowhere near as certain of hitting the big league, although his first showed potential.

His next project was another comic hero project, but slightly less mainstream for a couple of reasons: one, it was another black movie; two, it was too honest to be a proper spoof. *Meteor Man* was the brainchild of Robert Townsend, who had directed Jackson in *Raw*, and it was a project that arose from serious thoughts. 'I wanted to make a movie for kids,' he says. 'Kids don't get enough people to look up to.' His idea was to have a second grade teacher get hit by a meteor which then gives him super-powers. The teacher's mother convinces him to go out on the streets and close down the crack dens. It was hoped *Meteor Man* would be the first of a series of black heroes, with Damon Wayan's *Blackman* and Wesley Snipes' *The Black Panther* in the pipeline at the time.

Unfortunately, despite a community spirit to the $20 million picture that saw stars like James Earl Jones cut their fees to appear – multi-zillionaire Bill Cosby took part for just $100 per day – and despite another believable performance from Jackson, the whole was wide of the mark, at least audience-wise. Townsend had been intending to make a movie to appeal to a mainstream audience despite its black cast, in the same way that Cosby's own show did. 'I don't believe in separate cinema,' he says. 'I want to show the human side of Afro-American people. None of *Meteor Man*'s commercials were about "that jiving superhero, baby".' That crossover failed to materialise and the movie received only limited exposure. *Variety*, which had already exposed its lack of a funny bone on *Loaded Weapon*, was not surprised. '*Meteor Man* is a comedy with a true paucity of humour,' it concluded. *Sight and Sound* were more baffled: 'Why hasn't Townsend received the recognition given to John Singleton and the Hughes brothers?'

Jackson would soon be in a position to suggest a few answers to that question as he signed up for the brothers' new project, *Menace II Society*, in October. For a start, it seemed Albert and Allen Hughes don't take any crap from anyone. 'We were never going to bend over backward to do just any project,' Allen says. 'People tried to throw us anything and salivate over it.' His brother agrees. 'Certain studios said, "You'll take this and you'll do this because you have nothing else," ' he recalls. 'We said, "See ya." ' What they wanted to do, and what they ended up doing, was taking the mean streets of *Jungle Fever* and *Juice* and turning them up a notch. The celebrated video directors' new film was going to be 'about cycles of violence in the black community,' Allen explained at the time. 'It takes place in Watts and moves from the '65 riots to what they bred: victim/criminals or hustlers. I don't think of them as criminals because they're living under desperate conditions.'

Ready to engage in the maelstrom of *Menace* after two comedies, Jackson plays Tat Lawson. It was appreciated. 'The acting is like a whiplash, hard and gritty,' said *Empire*. 'The Hughes brothers pack more punch into their raw 97 minutes than a catalogue of Spike Lee or John Singleton movies.' 'While commercial prospects don't compare to *Boyz N the Hood*, *Menace* should readily escape the ghetto of specialised minority films and play well in urban areas,' *Variety* said. 'A very flashy debut,' said the *New York Times*.

Given the movie's explicit language and prominence of gun culture, it ran a risk of being censored out of the marketplace. In particular, when the movie should have been released in the UK on video in summer 1994, it didn't actually make it into shops until a year later. The reason? The BBFC refused to grant it a certificate. That altered in 1995, leaving *Reservoir Dogs* and *Dirty Weekend* as the only videos at the time still pending a release.

Ironically, another picture Jackson worked on at that time also fell foul of the censors' scissors. For some reason, when Tony Scott presented his finished film to America's Motion Picture Arts Authority, they had a problem reconciling Samuel L. Jackson and *Dracula* star, Gary Oldman, discussing oral sex at length with the director's aim of winning a fifteen certificate. Cuts were ordered, condensing the scene from twelve minutes to just under two, much to Jackson's disappointment. 'They were not gonna let us sit around and have an oral sex conversation,' he reflects. 'It just wasn't happening.' Which is a shame, because his character, Big Don, proved one of the quirkiest and, therefore, more interesting of the actor's career to date. The option, which the Hughes brothers refused to take, was to tone down and maybe get a restricted release.

The film was *True Romance*, starring Christian Slater, Patricia Arquette and Dennis Hopper at the head of a cast of cameo players ranging from Brad Pitt to Christopher Walken. A road movie on paper, in reality it was a darker, more distorted version of the brand. And it was funny. Full of great dialogue, jaw-dropping non sequiturs and obscure discussions, it appeared to be saying something new. Quite what, nobody knew; but there was a feeling. Tony Scott had brought the film to life, but credit for many of its qualities went to its original writer, a 25-year-old video store clerk from Knoxville. From what he had seen, Jackson liked the man's work, in particular his way with words. If only he had got a chance to say a few more of them, he was sure he could make them come alive.

Just because he was in California now and not New York, Jackson saw no obvious reason to change his working methods. Years of ill-paid stage acting had taught him the value of The Work. As conscious as he was of his own self-worth in the relative marketplace, he never set out to get rich at the expense of his Art. If the part was interesting, he was interested. Sticking to his guns, he saw no problem in opting out of his movie career for a couple of weeks to take part in a TV film called *Simple Justice*. There was a very good reason for his decision, however: the subject meant a lot to him.

The first feature-length drama for the PBS series, *The American Experience*, *Simple Justice* was a two-and-a-half hour film spanning the twenty years that led to the famous 1954 Brown vs Board of Education decision in Topeka; it also serves as a pretty good bio-pic of Thurgood Marshall, America's first black Supreme Court Justice. Among a cast of thousands, it was difficult to stand out, but Jackson was happy to take the minor part of a steward just to be involved in this landmark feature.

Simple Justice aired on US television in January 1993. By then Jackson was well into a punishing schedule of film-making which he hoped could take his career to the next level. While there was an obvious contender for 'big hit of the year' among the five projects he was hoping to tie down, he had no idea that another film, one with barely an $8 million budget, would be the one to change his life.

His movie of March 1993, *A New Age*, sadly was not the one, although it had potential. Written by *The Player* screenwriter Michael Tolkin, the movie was a dark comedy (another one) about a former Hollywood agent and his wife who open a Melrose Avenue boutique to raise money so they can afford to divorce. 'In *The Player*, they would call this "a cross between *Carnal Knowledge* and *Shampoo*",' Tolkin said. Without Robert Altman to marshal Tolkin's script, the movie flagged a little, but Jackson shone as swindler Dale Deveaux, as the *New York Times* confirmed. 'Another of the film's more down-to-earth characters is the huckster played by Samuel L. Jackson, a ball of fire as he teaches how to swindle strangers by making telephone sales.' Overall, though, 'a film all dressed up but with nowhere to go' – *Variety*. It was a similar story for *The Search for One-Eyed Jimmy*, a movie that wouldn't get released until 1996 – a huge gap even by

Hollywood standards. Surely quality had nothing to do with it? 'No member of this talented ensemble registers strongly,' was *Variety*'s bored opinion.

For the next step in Jackson's plan for stardom, he went back to a smaller project, but one which might cover him in more glory. Imaginatively cast as Sam, Jackson plays an errant father who tries to keep his son on the straight and narrow through the power of chess in Boaz Yakin's *Fresh*. Sidestepping his initial fears that this New York-based film could offer him yet another stereotype given a human face, Jackson felt that not only was there room for him to work, but the whole script made a refreshing attempt at a statement, one that was close to his heart. 'Nobody else since, in my opinion, has written a film about the ghetto that is as sensitive and touching as that one,' he says of the (relatively) obscure 1993 picture. 'If it's the story you want to tell and you tell it from the heart and invest it with the right cast, you have a right to do so, whoever you are.' In the tricky situation of trying to impose values on a son he didn't live with, Sam uses chess to communicate. His son, a drug runner called Fresh, soon uses the skills he picked up from the chessboard to checkmate the drug barons who were responsible for his girlfriend's death.

Although a small film which would earn a relatively low $8 million at the US box office, *Fresh* gave Jackson some of his best personal reviews to date. 'People like Jackson could put black cinema where it belongs, on the leading edge of American movie-making,' said *New Yorker* magazine. The *New York Times* agreed, saying, 'Delicate and sympathetic work from Mr Jackson says a lot about the originality of this film's vision.' *Variety* concurred. 'Although forbidden to see him, Fresh surreptitiously meets his father, Sam (the excellent Samuel L. Jackson), in Washington Square for sessions of speed chess.' On top of the glorious reviews, *Fresh* shared joint honours at the 1994 Sundance Film Festival, pleasing its producer, Lawrence Bender, no end.

Praise indeed. And, were it to be followed up by equally worthy 'statement' film-making, then probably true. But at the same time Samuel was shooting *Fresh*, he also managed to fit in four days' work on another picture. When it opened in 1993 it would become the biggest film of all time. But Samuel L. Jackson didn't know that when he signed up for it. All he knew was that it was being directed by Steven Spielberg and that it would, when the CGI boys had finished, be about dinosaurs. It was *Jurassic Park*.

As Ray Arnold, one of the fated computer workers on crackpot scientist Richard Attenborough's DNA-tastic island, Jackson's character spends most of his time on a swivel chair trying to squeeze into the same frame as felonious *Seinfeld* stalwart Wayne Knight. It's another solid rather than spectacular turn, however, not that Jackson cares. 'I did a good job considering,' he says. 'And you won't find three kids on the planet who noticed any of the actors in that movie anyway.' Point taken.

As a way to end the year, *Jurassic Park* provided a billion dollars-worth of reasons to remain an actor. But, as Jackson is the first to admit, there were other reasons to see that particular film. As far as his people were concerned, however, it was the sort of job that paid the bills; and their commission. Other times, however, he had to follow his heart – and his art – as he had proved.

'Occasionally there have been things to do that my agents haven't wanted me to,' Jackson says. 'I ended up doing them and they realised that I saw something there that they didn't. Like in *Fresh* and *Menace II Society*. Those are enjoyable little things that don't even put gas in the Mercedes.'

There was another movie to end 1993 which wasn't the most financially sensible, but heck – what a character. New acquaintance Lawrence Bender had recommended him for a part; all Jackson had to do now was win it.

10. I LOVE YOUR WORK, MR FISHBURNE

No one likes a boaster. Somehow, though, Samuel L. Jackson gets away with it. Is he a pretty good actor? Yes. Does he think he is? Yes – but then most actors do. The difference is that very few of them actually admit to thinking it, much less come out with the sort of self-congragulatory comments guaranteed to rile a certain section of the media. 'Back when I was doing theatre, I used to wish I could watch the play that I was doing,' he said with disarming immodesty to the *Observer*. 'But I wanted to watch them with me in them. Now I have the opportunity to do that.'

Jackson, then, has a very healthy ego. He knows he can act and, what's more, he has proved it, night after night on the gruelling treadmill that is the Broadway stage. More than his experience, though, he knows that he is technically adroit with the principles and techniques behind the profession. He has, after all, been studying or plying the thespian trade since the 1960s. In short, he has done the time and now he is reaping the rewards.

New York was the perfect place for Jackson's type of talent. Here was a city bursting with opportunities to learn, watch and take part in every aspect of stage craft. He was surrounded by hundreds of like-minded individuals all intent on getting the chance to give the performance of their lives in front of a row of footlights night after night. This is what acting was about. This is what being an actor was about.

Imagine his shock, then, when he pitched up in Los Angeles the first time. And the second time. And the next, and so on. Imagine how long it took him, in fact, to get to grips with the one chasm-like difference between the City of Angels and Manhattan which had never occurred to him: LA is about movies and television and moving image and film. It is the centre of the world's entertainment industry, the hub of its multi-billion-dollar empire. And yet it has no theatre culture.

If it has no theatre culture, where do its actors act?

The day that question occurred to Samuel Jackson ranks as probably one of the most depressing of his life. The answer, of course, is they don't. Not most of them. The majority of actors who 'make it' in Hollywood have little or no formal training outside of modelling school and acting classes. Even fewer have any experience of maintaining a whole script in their brain and delivering their lines, without breaks, over a two-hour period. If Marlon Brando can memorise each line before each scene, and shoot an entire movie in that piecemeal fashion, why can't everyone? And many of them do.

'LA is the only city I've been where you meet actors who've never done theatre,' Jackson says ruefully. 'We're surrounded by people who, let's face it, have never even been in a play.' More times than he'd like to consider, he has had conversations along the following lines:

'Where did you learn to act?'

'I'm learning!'/'I did X number of television shows.'/'I've done two movies already.'

'Yeah, but where did you learn to act?'

'Everybody can act.'

'No, they can't.'

He might sound condescending – and he means to – but he has a point. He also has an advantage. A background in TV-only work will provide you with certain rudimentary abilities. Theatre experience, however, is the thespian equivalent of an army boot camp. It's hardcore, it's unforgiving but you come out of it with talents you never knew you had and the wherewithal to utilise them fully, as Jackson explains.

'A lot of LA actors ask me how I did that monologue,' he says. 'All of them actors who've never done a play.' To be fair, plenty of actors who have done plays have been impressed by the man's achievements in 'that monologue', so powerfully was it delivered. What monologue, you ask?

When *Reservoir Dogs* received its world premiere at the 1991 Sundance Film Festival, it made a lot of people's stomachs churn. 'I was at the first public screening of *Dogs* at the Sundance Festival and all these auteurs were running up the aisle saying, "Oh, this is sick!" ' Samuel Jackson laughs. At the time, though, watching in the dark as Michael Madsen cut off the cop's ear to a Stealer's Wheel soundtrack, Jackson felt his own wave of something like nausea. But it wasn't in response to the bloodletting on the screen. Not directly. It was envy. And a sense of frustration. Samuel L. Jackson had auditioned for *Reservoir Dogs* and not got the part.

There was nothing new in that, of course. His theatre life had been one round of unsuccessful try-outs after another. It was the same in movies: right place, wrong face. Or right face, wrong race. But he had never missed out on working on something that was so different, so challenging and – that rarest of all Hollywood attributes – so new. And realising how good first-time writer/director Quentin Tarantino's end result was hurt.

'Quentin gives people something new and unique, so they felt refreshed by it,' Jackson says. 'We're fed the same thing so much by the Hollywood machine that when something like this comes along, it's engaging.' It doesn't hurt that Tarantino is, as Jackson puts it, the 'consummate thief' – no one else in Hollywood has his talent for remembering specific scenes from so many movies, and then using them in his own mix 'n' match style so you think you're watching them for the first time.

'I was still in New York at the time and I went to a casting call – on a Sunday!' Jackson recalls. 'I read the script and it was amazing to hear these guys just talking about everyday stuff, guys who had a very unique outlook on life. It was pretty intense stuff. So I went to the audition, and naturally I didn't get the job.

'I was supposed to read with Harvey Keitel. Harvey wasn't there and I ended up reading with Quentin and Lawrence Bender and I was like, Who are these guys? Consequently my audition was not so great.'

The job in question, the contact for Tim Roth's undercover agent, ultimately went to Randy Brooks and Jackson moved on. (George Clooney famously failed to win the role eventually taken by Madsen.) But some people just do not know when to quit – especially those with compulsive–obsessive leanings. Fired by the freshness he found in Tarantino's script, Jackson had no hesitation in chasing the part of Big Don in *True Romance*. He also read for Oliver Stone's treatment of Tarantino's early script, *Natural Born Killers*. With two strikes and a part cut down to nothing in a non-Quentin-directed film, however, it was time to face facts: he and Tarantino were destined not to work together.

That realisation seemed to bother one of the men more than the other. When Jackson approached the director at Sundance, he was knocked back by Tarantino's lack of tact. Burbling in his typical, gregarious, post-modern hippy-love-peace manner, he was quick to ask Jackson what he had thought of Brooks's performance. Rub it in, why don't you.

'I went up to Quentin at Sundance to tell him how much I liked the film,' Jackson recalls. Impressively, the director remembered the failed auditionee. 'Hey, how do you like the guy who got your part?' he said.

'You made a mistake, but no big deal.'

And so the two men moved on. Jackson to his roles in *Patriot Games* and *White Sands*, Tarantino to grabbing the movie world by the throat and announcing his own arrival. As just one of the dozens of well-wishers swamping the new auteur at the festival, Jackson would not have been surprised to have been forgotten the minute the two men had shaken hands and separated.

The plot of *Reservoir Dogs* had originally come about during a planning session for another project. As a wannabe actor, Quentin Tarantino had encountered nothing but knock-backs despite five years of lessons. The next best thing, he reasoned, was to try to make it as a writer/director. Working in a video store – Video Archives (formerly Video Outtakes) for ten years had fed his phenomenal appetite for movies of all genres. An adrenalin-powered motormouth, his enthusiasm and knowledge of his subject convinced a few others that he might be worth backing. One of them, Lawrence Bender, had just produced a slasher flick for $100,000. Ever the chancer, Tarantino said that if Bender would produce him, he would write a script that could be directed – by him – for $50,000. Bender agreed. And then, just three-and-a-half weeks later, he saw the script.

'I read it and thought it was amazing,' he says. 'I said to Quentin, if you give me some time, I can raise some real money for this and we can do it properly.' Tarantino, wrapped up in the need for speed, wasn't convinced and gave his friend a deadline. In the end, both were glad he did.

The script was for *Reservoir Dogs* and it came about when Tarantino was mulling over how to break into movies. He figured the short film route to be favourite. Make a short, tour it at the festivals, build a reputation and – to quote Mia Wallace – 'disco'. Rather than waste any time on an elaborate one-trick calling card, however, he came up with the idea of writing a series of short stories that he could make individually at little expense, and then compile at the end to produce one long-format picture. With his friend Roger Avary, he embarked on a hunt for hackneyed genre stories, 'the oldest chestnuts in the book', that they could distort. Avary came up with the tale of Butch, a fighter who refuses to throw a bout. Tarantino devised a scenario involving a hired gun taking the local Mr Big's wife out on a date. A third instalment featured a robbery gone wrong. The more he considered it, however, the more the latter episode appeared to have a life of its own. Lifting it from its short-story framework, he made sure the action could all be shot in an affordable indoor garage shoot and presented it to Bender. And the rest . . .

Not quite. With *Reservoir Dogs* up and running and shocking the blue-rinse brigade and *Daily Mail* reader equivalents the world over, Tarantino went back to his short story collection. There was a noticeable *Dogs*-sized hole. And then he had the inspiration of two assassins. Not only would he film their 'hit', but he'd show them before and after as they went about their day. And he would use them to link the other two stories, rather than have three discrete pieces. And he would call it *Pulp Fiction*.

Samuel L. Jackson heard about the new project when he was in New York working on *Fresh* in summer 1993. It was no coincidence that *Fresh* happened to be produced by Lawrence Bender. If Jackson had had to compile a list of the last things he expected, a brand new script from a guy he'd met briefly at a film festival the year before featuring a bespoke part – written with him in mind – would probably have featured near the top. He could not believe his luck.

'Two years after auditioning for *Reservoir Dogs*, Quentin called me and spoke about this new script and this character he was writing with me in mind,' he says. A short while later a script arrived from Danny DeVito, whose Jersey Films would be making the picture with Miramax, bearing the note: 'If you tell anybody about this, three guys from Jersey Films will show up and kill you.' As it transpired, once Jackson actually looked at the package, he nearly died anyway. 'The script killed me,' he says. 'I was blown away. To know that somebody had written something like Jules for me. I was overwhelmed, thankful, arrogant – this whole combination of things that you could be, knowing that somebody's going to give you an opportunity like that.'

There was still a moment of doubt, however, based on previous experiences. 'I had done *True Romance*, read *Natural Born Killers* and auditioned for that and when I heard he had me in mind when he wrote this part, I wasn't too excited. But when I got the script, I was like, God, this is amazing.'

'I wrote the role of Jules for Sam Jackson,' Tarantino says. 'I've always been a fan of his. I knew he exuded an incredible feeling of power and that, given the opportunity, he could express this Richard III side he has in the movie.' Who else, Tarantino reasoned, could dominate a scene and move people around a room like pieces on a chessboard while remaining seated, as Jackson does in the final scenes of *Pulp Fiction*?

'The first time I sat down to read it, I couldn't believe it,' Jackson says. 'I had to read it twice to make sure I wasn't fooling myself into thinking this is a pretty brilliant thing.' He wasn't. It was a part that would not only define an actor's career, but it would become a standard text for all film students and critics and movie makers. It was, in short, a Big Deal.

Building on his work on *Reservoir Dogs*, the new script was saying something fresh. For a start, it was using dialogue to move its action forwards. 'Theatre is a "tell me" medium and film is a "show me" medium,' Jackson explains, 'but Quentin found a way to marry the two.

'He has a great ability for writing natural dialogue. Even though these people are killers and misfits in society in a certain kind of way, they have real conversational things going on in their lives like normal guys, and that's just so unique.'

The part of Jules Winnfield, Bible-quoting hit man, leapt off the page as soon as Jackson read it. And, viewing the finished movie, it is easy to imagine it being written for him. By a quirk of fate that totally contradicts his normal head-down work ethic, however, he very nearly didn't get to play the part at all.

Being new to the 'having a script written specifically for you' business, Jackson assumed that it was a done deal – all he had to do was wait for a date to begin shooting. In the meantime he busied himself in New York with his chess grandmaster character in *Fresh*. When Tarantino asked him to come over to hear him read, he naturally assumed it was so they could hear the character's voice, nothing more.

Wrong.

'I didn't realise it was an audition,' Jackson admits. 'I just went in and kind of read it so they could hear how this guy sounded.' Unsurprisingly, it impressed nobody. The next thing he knew, another actor was being lined up for the prime part of Jules – someone who had cannily asked to read some of Jules's lines as an audition for his own character. In a burst of panic, Jackson 'went berserk'. His manager and agent were charged with hounding DeVito, Miramax bosses Harvey and Bob Weinstein, Bender and Tarantino himself to beg for a second chance. The industry paid off and a second reading was arranged, again for a Sunday. If needing to impress directly after jetting into LAX on the red-eye was bad enough, it got worse. Having originally been confronted by an empty room, Jackson's day got worse when Lawrence Bender introduced him to another member of their team. Taking one look at Jackson, he said, 'Oh no, you don't have to introduce me to this man. I know him. I love your work, Mr Fishburne.'

'I was like, Boom!' Jackson recalls. 'Oh my God – they don't even know who I am.'

The scene to be read was the film's closing dialogue between Jules and his colleague Vincent Vega, eventually played by John Travolta. Wordcount-wise it's 90 per cent Jules and 10 per cent Vincent – ideal to show off Jules's range. Like a good boy, Jackson was fully prepped for his second chance. But suddenly, when it came time to deliver, he baulked. Everything he was going to say, everything he was going to do, he changed.

'When I first read it, I had a totally different take on it,' he says. The obvious things to consider were how to most threaten Tim Roth's Pumpkin with his gun. During the audition process, another train of thought took over as he started to do that speech. 'Something happened and I did something totally different from what I had prepared to do,' he says, 'and that's what ended up in the film.'

Not only did he save his own skin with the performance, but Jackson also got Tarantino out of a fix. 'Lawrence Bender told me later that they didn't know what the end of the film would be until I did that audition,' he says, justifiably proud. And the moral of the story? 'If somebody tells me they're writing something for me, I know I cannot not do the things I've always done to make sure I get a job. Nothing can be taken for granted.'

Those things include constructing a fully formed biography for his character. He may not have signed it off until those moments at the audition, but it was something he worked on. By the time Jackson said his opening lines in *Pulp*, he would learn everything there was to learn about Jules Winnfield, from his obsession with coffee, to his loathing of dirty animals and his vegetarian marriage. He would bring parts of his own personality to the character where appropriate, and dwell on the natural links – their shared spirituality, for example, or their domestic bliss. Even Jackson's obsession with Hong Kong martial arts movies is winked at during Jules's closing speech where he says he wants to 'walk the earth', 'like Cain in *Kung Fu*'. There would be no line said by his character that did not reverberate through his secret history prepared by the man bringing him to life.

Just as instinct built on years of stage acting led him to change direction on a whim, another slice of fortune helped 'shape' Jules in another way. Tarantino had always pictured his garrulous hit man sporting an impressive afro hairstyle. When the wardrobe department ordered a suitable wig, however, something must have got lost in the translation because the wrong thing turned up. It was a tight-curled, wet-look Jheri style piece. The director was not impressed. 'No, no – afro!' he yelled. Having already grown the chiselled sideburns and moustache, an intrigued Jackson decided to give it a go. 'I put it on and started messing around with it and all of a sudden I looked at it and said, "This is it, man! This is the look!"'

With a killer look – for a killer's looks – and the challenging text nailed down ('I love doing two and three pages of dialogue'), Jackson was finally ready for the next phase in the movie's production. Moving back to LA as soon as his work on *Fresh* was completed in August, he was thrown in at the deep end work-wise, even though shooting on *Pulp* didn't start for several weeks. Once again, his background stood him in good stead as the entire cast was assembled weeks in advance of shooting to workshop and rehearse the script. For the work of an effervescent soul like Tarantino, enthusiasm, chemistry and the right dynamic between characters are crucial. In order to get everyone used to each other, the director arranged group dinner parties at local restaurants and hosted film nights at his house. 'We do full rehearsals so everyone gets to know each other,' Lawrence Bender says. 'Everyone feels like part of a big family.'

'It was like summer camp,' Rosanna Arquette, who plays Jordy, 'the one with all the shit on her face', reveals. 'It's how movies should be made.'

The camaraderie-building exercise had another benefit. With all the main players denuded of their paid acolytes for the bonding sessions, there was none of the sequestered wheeler-dealings with agents demanding script changes on their stars' behalf. Unlike in theatre where the printed word is god, movie scripts are there to be changed. The blue draft can always be superseded by the new version on pink paper, or the next on green. Where top-name actors are concerned, every script should be considered 'work in progress'. Bruce Willis, who plays boxer Butch, makes the link between Tarantino's methods and the 'tell me' medium: 'It's almost like doing stagework,' he says. 'Everyone respects Quentin's writing in a way that I haven't seen since I was on the New York stage.'

As an end result of the rehearsal process and, in particular, Jackson's thorough biography for his character, the film's writer was left open-mouthed (but not dumbstruck – this is Tarantino) in admiration. 'The way the actors gave life to the dialogues,' he says, 'they made a pretty damn good script an obsolete document.'

The fun didn't stop after rehearsals finished. Tarantino was walking past Jackson's trailer one day and was struck by the high-pitched caterwauling emanating from within. Sticking his head round the door, he found his leading man watching one of his beloved Hong Kong action flicks. As a huge martial arts fan himself, Tarantino made it part of his daily ritual to swing by the Jackson wagon. 'I used to watch a different movie every day,' the actor reveals. 'I've got hundreds of them, so Quentin used to come along every day just to see what movie I was watching.' In the years to come, he would find Zoe an equally ardent fan.

Apart from the fancy tonsorial trimming of his facial hair, the greatest tribute to Jackson's talent on *Pulp Fiction* was the fact that he did not become Jules until he was in costume. With the greatest respect, Bruce Willis's Butch did not provide Willis with any great leap character-wise; it was hardly new territory for either him or his fans. But watching Samuel Jackson pitch up for shooting every day in his oversized Spike Lee-style round spectacles, his casual slacks and jumpers and his evidently receding hair line, only increased the sensation of something special happening when he transformed into character. From a man dressed and carrying himself very much within the ballpark of his 44 years, to a sharp-suited, sharp-tongued, verbose assassin, the transformation was remarkable.

But, as Jackson says, he often picks projects on the strength of his character rather than the movie as a whole. Even if he got his work down perfectly, there was always a chance that others would let the side down in some way. On *Pulp Fiction*, no one did. 'I did my part and everybody did theirs,' Jackson reflects. The writer, though, takes the golden laurels. 'That film was 95 per cent all in the script. Quentin had that thing nailed. And there's some wonderful stuff that's not on the screen.

'I knew if the studio left us alone and let us do it the way it had to be done, then it would be awesome.'

And it was. It really was.

'Watching *Pulp Fiction*, you don't just get engrossed in what's happening on screen,' wrote Owen Glieberman in *Entertainment Weekly*, 'you get intoxicated by it.' No other film-maker apart from Tarantino, he confessed, could combine discipline and control with such large levels of 'sheer wild-ass joy'.

The *New York Times* was equally confounded: 'It must be hard to believe that Mr Tarantino, a mostly self-taught, mostly untested talent, has come up with a work of such depth, wit and blazing originality.'

Elizabeth Pincus in the *LA Weekly*: 'A pop-drenched dream reel, the film is both a reverential nod to the power of words and a stunning entertainment that more than lives up to its hype.' Roger Ebert of the *Chicago Sun-Times*: 'The screenplay is so well written in a scruffy, fanzine way that you want to rub noses in it – the noses of those zombie writers who take "screenwriting" classes that teach them the formulas of "hit films".'

When the picture opened the other side of the Atlantic, the feeling was the same. 'For all its violence, *Pulp Fiction* is a highly literate and even literary work,' said Alexander Walker in the London *Evening Standard*. He particularly cited the language: 'Tarantino mixes dialogue of structured formality rapped out by rococo characters with a vocabulary of a la carte choosiness. ("I'm gonna get mediaeval on your ass," says Marcellus.)'

Even the usually coruscating Julie Burchill was moved enough to stay until the movie's final reel before filing her copy: 'I really thought I was old enough to know better and that cinema in every shape and form had nothing left to show me,' she said in *The Times*. 'For once, I was wrong; and even better, I was happy to be so.'

Impressive stuff, then. And as each review came in, there was a palpable sense of the writer struggling to get all his or her words onto the page within their editor's word limit. Without the discipline of having to get their thoughts in order to meet a deadline, audiences could wallow in the sensation caused by the movie. Even so, there were too many things that caused viewers to sit up and take notice of *Pulp Fiction* to list. In fact, after years of trying to understand, Samuel Jackson is resigned to it being just one of those things that happen from time to time.

'*Pulp Fiction* was an aberration,' he shrugs. 'A phenomenon. I doubt Quentin could explain it. I know I can't.' But he can point to the combination of the non-linear plot, the music, the direction, the dialogue and the combination of talent that obviously combined to produce a work of timeless art.

In an age when numerous screenwriting books offer a step-by-step guide to creating the ultimate script, universities run degree courses in movie-making and there are even computer programs capable of devising so called 'perfect' storylines and plots, *Pulp Fiction* came like a welcome shot of adrenalin in the heart. Taking its three over-used storylines – the hit men, the date with Mr Big's missus and the bent boxer – it banked on audiences' over-familiarities with each genre to work against them. First, all the stories are linked. Second, they all take place in one day, which means you see how the killers' afternoon pans out after they have bumped their target. Third, it chops everything up chronologically and starts just before the conclusion of the third act before jumping back and forth between aspects of the first and second. Arriving at the height of the ossification of the American movie industry, it felt to many viewers just as *Star Wars* must have seemed to a stoned Sam Jackson back in 1977.

Tarantino's lines deservedly won many of the film's plaudits. Jules's opening dialogue with Vincent about the differences in fast food culture between America and Holland is funny in itself, but also a million miles away from the topic that audiences would have been expecting to be occupying their thoughts: namely, the fact that both men are on their way to carry out a mob execution. The dialogue triumphs again when, having reached their destination, the killers hang back outside for a while to continue their discussion about foot massages. While Vincent is oleaginous and oily, Jules is upright and uptight. His ego is pricked: 'I'm a foot fucking master,' he explodes, but the mood does not interfere with either man's professional sense. Inside the flat, diversions via more fast food comparisons and coffee tasting seem to affect each of the pair's imaginations more than their hideous occupation. And there, Tarantino achieves the undesirable – to make two cold-blooded murderers appear to be fully rounded, almost mundanely normal in their lives' ambitions and conversations. Killing is just a job. It's not a way of life.

Apart from the near canonisation of Tarantino, two other undeniable truths emerged from the success of *Pulp Fiction*. One is that John Travolta, whom Tarantino had loved in *Blow Out* but was more widely remembered in recent years for the saccharinely dire fare of *Look Who's Talking*, was suddenly a star again, immediately returned to the A list and able to command $20 million a picture. The other is that Samuel L. Jackson, as Jules, had just become the coolest man on Earth.

11. WHY'S THE CHINESE DUDE UP THERE?

Defining moments are, ironically, usually indefinable, and never more so than when in relation to a person's career. There is no scientific formula to the circumstances that lead to certain people at certain times attaining a sudden boost of career trajectory. There is no way of knowing when – or if – this hijacking moment might occur. All that we know is that it does happen to professionals in every form of public life.

Consider the moment Colin Firth strode from the Derbyshire lake in *Pride and Prejudice*. When Arnold Schwarzenegger junked the iron-pumping exploits of *Conan* and *Red Sonja* to become Terminator. When Elvis Presley appeared on *The Ed Sullivan Show*. When Robbie Williams released 'Angels' as a last-ditch attempt to salvage a solo career out of the dying embers of Take That. When Ursula Andress stepped out of the Caribbean in her white bikini in *Dr. No*. When Michael Jackson released *Thriller*. When Eric Cantona threw down the white shirt of Leeds and pulled on the red top of Manchester United. Or, when *Home Improvement* girl Pamela Anderson replaced Erica Eleniak for the second series of *Baywatch* – one red swimsuit switch later and David Hasselhoff suddenly had the most watched TV show on Earth on his hands. Nobody predicted it. Nobody planned it.

John Travolta's career was never the same from the moment he strutted down the New York streets as Tony Manero in *Saturday Night Fever*. The dance moves later in the movie captured the world's imagination and inspired myriad imitations, but it was the mood of the paint-carrying waster that captured hearts and fuelled his career through *Grease* and *Urban Cowboy* and *Blow Out*.

Bruce Willis's moment came years after he first appeared as the wise-cracking dick in *Moonlighting*. It came after he'd tried his hand attempting to emulate his onscreen persona in various lightweight comedies. It came when movie bosses had pretty much given up on his chances of making the step up. It came, let us be frank, when he was suddenly down to his vest in the first *Die Hard* movie. Cast out of type, this is when the public actually started to notice him – Bruce Willis – rather than another extension of his TV character.

Fellow *Pulp Fiction* star Samuel L. Jackson had tasted a certain amount of success by the time the film was released in 1994. He had turned the Cannes voting system on its head, after all, with his role in *Jungle Fever*. He had impressed in *Fresh* and *White Sands* and had made an impact in *Mo' Better Blues*. But honestly, he was nothing special. He was good, he was solid, he brought a certain depth to any role he took on. But he had no USP, as they say in marketing. No unique selling point. By 1994, he was one of those actors more in demand from studios and casting directors for his ability to do a job efficiently and without fuss rather than any belief that his presence would help sell tickets to the show. But by 1994, he hadn't had his Moment.

All that was about to change. When a Jheri-wigged Jules Winnfield first uttered the line 'The path of the righteous man is beset on all sides by the inequities of the selfish and the tyranny of evil men,' it was as though an entire movie-going generation was shaken out of its torpor. By the time the speech concluded with the words, 'You will know my name is the Lord when I lay my vengeance on you,' it was decided. Eyes blazing, nostrils flaring, mouth constricting around every word, Jules Winnfield had arrived. Suddenly Hollywood had a brand new (anti) hero to join its pantheon of icons alongside the likes of Dirty Harry, Travis Bickle and John Shaft.

Almost unnoticed, Samuel L. Jackson had just acquired a brand new career: as a superstar.

Apart from a bizarre review in the *New Yorker* which claimed John Travolta's Vincent 'held the movie together', the majority of the international press were agreed: Jackson as Jules took Tarantino's already sublime movie to another level.

London's *Evening Standard* got to the point: 'If the film has any single star outstanding in its ensemble company, it is Samuel L. Jackson. His magnificent basso voice carries the undertones of street rant modulated to pulpit sonority.'

Where Julie Birchill was more concise – 'Samuel L. Jackson – brilliant' – *Entertainment Weekly* waxed lyrical: 'As superb as Travolta, Willis and Keitel are, the actor who reigns over *Pulp Fiction* is Samuel L. Jackson. He just about lights fires with his gremlin eyes and he transforms his speeches into hypnotic bebop soliloquies.'

Even the *New York Times* was in agreement as to who was the genuine star of the show: 'Mr Jackson, never better, shows off a vibrant intelligence and an avenging stare that bores holes through the screen. He also engages in terrific comic teamwork with Mr Travolta.'

The first hint anyone had that *Pulp Fiction* would have the effect it did came at Cannes. A sucker for a good festival, like all genuine movie buffs, Tarantino has always felt confident enough of his material to give it an early run-out in the gala's competition. It has become such a tradition with him, in fact, that when the early rushes of his fourth feature, *Kill Bill*, failed to materialise at the 2003 show, the rumour mill cracked up a gear to spread the word that the production was clearly in trouble.

In May 1994, however, there were no such delays and *Pulp Fiction* was given its world debut at the Olympia Theatre in Cannes a full five months before it was due to be rolled out to an expectant public later that year. Keen to be a part of the hoop-la with the all-embracing Tarantino, rather than feeling like a spare limb out in New York while Spike Lee sucked up all the acclaim for *Jungle Fever*, Samuel Jackson flew in to soak up the atmosphere. As soon as the film was shown, he knew he had backed a winner.

'I knew people with my sensibility and sense of humour would like it, but I didn't think it would have a universal appeal,' he says. Proof that it was something special came when he saw the film at Cannes. The local audience enjoyed the film so much that it wasn't till halfway through that Jackson realised it was subtitled in French – people were reading it and still 'getting' it. 'That's when I realised we had something special,' he says. 'By the time it was over, I was so proud I was literally brought to tears.'

Those 'getting it' included one or two pretty powerful people. Rather than take the cowards' route of just allowing the picture to be shown, Tarantino and Miramax had gone all out and entered it into the main competition. At the end of the viewing at the final day of the festival, it was clear that the panel of judges had been as moved as Jackson. At the concluding awards ceremony, a white-dinner-jacketed Clint Eastwood, as the competition's president for the year, stood up to announce the winner: '*Pulp Fiction*,' he said.

Led by Tarantino, a 'bear' bearded Willis, a smartly shorn Travolta, Lawrence Bender, Maria de Medeiros (who plays Butch's French girlfriend, Fabienne) and Jackson trotted up onto the stage. Before he could speak, the director was waving a middle finger at the solitary heckler who was not so happy with the judges' verdict. But then he got into his stride, singling out his wonderful cast for transmuting his prose into movie gold. Standing alongside Bender, Jackson looked once again the bespectacled middle-aged man of his past rather than the very personification of fury and slickness seen on screen earlier. If that didn't rubber stamp his acting ability, nothing would.

Ironically, for all the acclaim he had been afforded previously in Cannes, Jackson was to miss out this time round in the personal section. Taking the Best Actor prize in 1994 was Ge You, an actor in the Chinese language picture *Life Times*. Did Jackson mind? Hell he did. And did he say so? Naturally. 'You know, six [out of ten] of those jurors told me I was brilliant,' he told the *Voice* newspaper shortly after the verdict at the festival. 'So I'm like, "Well, why's the Chinese dude up there?" '

He may not have looked the part, but without doubt there was a hint of Jules coursing through the actor's veins. It didn't last, however, and he regained his composure, leading co-star Bruce Willis, thankfully untroubled by the pressures of being nominated for acting trophies, to laugh: 'You're just sitting back and letting go of this whole thing.' On the outside he was. On the inside, Jackson was bracing himself for a new career of being in the shop window and being judged against his peers by strangers. He knew that when the movie was released on 7 October that year, he would be found a winner by millions of audience members. And that would do. For now.

For all its bombast and pyrotechnic delivery, the speech that proved the touchpaper to Jackson's ascent into the super-stratum had a curious origin. Ostensibly lifted from the Bible, Ezekiel 15:17 actually came to Tarantino's attention via less spiritual means. 'I first heard it in a kung fu movie, *The Bodyguard*, where it was featured in the prologue,' he admits. 'Then I found it in the Bible in a slightly different version.' There was also a Japanese ninja series called *Shadow Warriors* which used to be required TV viewing for the director and his friends. At the end of each episode there would be a lethal fight in which the Shadow Warrior chief would deliver an interminable speech about the necessity of exterminating evil. Whoever heard that speech could pretty much be sure that he was about to be executed. 'It's in that spirit that I used the Ezekiel quote in Jules's mouth,' Tarantino says. It's an epiphanic moment for Jules. 'For the first time, he recognises its true meaning. And that is the end of the movie.' And, of course, once he had heard Samuel Jackson say the words in his second audition, Tarantino knew he had got it right.

'Jules,' the director says, 'is the combination of a bad guy who projects absolute menace and danger and is also eloquent and intelligent – which makes him even scarier. Who else on earth could do that as well as Sam?'

Jackson is too self-aware to have let how good his rendition of Ezekiel is pass him by. 'When I did that speech at the end of *Pulp Fiction*,' he says, 'that was the moment that should have gotten me an Oscar. That's a crystal moment. That's a dynamic moment. That's a moment that people walk away with, and they go, "That was awesome." '

As with any sudden flare-up of new talent, there is always an element of dissent. At Cannes it was the lone heckler. In print it was the Mary Whitehouse brigade, up in arms about the level of violence in the film. Other news media wheeled out clergymen to decry the film's lack of a moral centre. Some even found fault with its supposed celebration of the lower echelons of society. Put on the spot, Samuel L. Jackson can respond to each and every one of these barbs.

'Violent?' he says. 'Actually they kill six more people in *Bullets Over Broadway* than we do in *Pulp Fiction*.' It celebrates creeps? 'It's just a story about people you don't normally get to spend time with, but you get to find out a little about them.' And no moral centre? 'The film is totally about redemption. Everyone in it whose life is spared is given another chance to do something with their lives.'

He speaks of course of his own character, Jules, who believes that God's intervention saved him from a hail of bullets early in the film. But also there is Mia, brought back to life by Vega's plunging needle after the heroin OD. And Butch, who fights his way out of the gimp's lair, saves his nemesis Marcellus and makes a getaway on a motorbike named 'Grace'. (He plans to flee to Knoxville, Tarantino's homeland.) And there's Pumpkin – not only spared by Jules desperately trying to be the shepherd, but also given his $1,500 in cash. Vincent, who markedly disputes Jules's interpretation of divine intervention saving his life, is graphically blown away by the born-again Butch with Marcellus's own gun (while the big man is out buying breakfast). Marcellus, on the other hand, finds it in his stony heart to forgive Butch for running him over and not throwing the fight in exchange for saving his ass from a fate worse than death. For him, anyway.

One of the delights of *Pulp Fiction* is its polarising take on the society under its microscope. Somehow, in living contradiction of the very idea of the movies being about make believe and suspending your disbelief for two hours, there was a section of the audience who did not drink in its words. Jackson has a take on these types, too. Scenes like the accidental in-car head splattering sequence, for example, seemed to cause a fuss.

'People were disturbed by the fact that they laughed at it,' he says, 'and reacted by saying they didn't like the movie.' Jackson actually thinks Tarantino wrote the *Pulp Fiction* scene because of the response to the ear-cutting scene in *Reservoir Dogs*. 'You can enjoy violence in a real and funny way, then realise what you're laughing at, then still not be able to stop laughing.'

The film also divides audiences, he reckons, because it goes against tradition. 'It's a "tell me" movie,' he says, 'and "tell me" movies are usually very boring.'

When the movie received its American debut at the Lincoln Theatre in New York on 23 September 1994, the full team was in attendance to witness first hand its effect on the US public. Whatever Bender and Tarantino's intentions were, they surpassed them. Never has a screening been met so warmly and yet with so many faces agog in befuddled admiration. And never has a screening actually caused a near fatality in response to one of its scenes. As Travolta's Vincent made to smack the hypodermic down into Mia's magic-markered chest, a scene quickly cut away to Rosanna Arquette's worshipful awe at this show of the mother of all piercings, a member of the Lincoln audience collapsed with some sort of heart seizure. While Lawrence Bender and Harvey Weinstein took the guy outside until medics supervised his full recovery, it had proved to the scene's creator how powerful the scene was: 'This scene fucking works!' he was thinking. 'It's too intense for human beings!'

By opening so late in the year despite being ready much earlier, *Pulp Fiction* stood a good chance of being *the* talked-about film by the time the imminent awards season kicked off a few weeks later. And that, everyone agreed, was no bad thing.

It was not a bad policy. On top of the $200 million it took at the box office, the film picked up Golden Globe nominations for Best Motion Picture, Actor (Travolta), Supporting Actor (Jackson), Supporting Actress (Thurman) and Screenplay. It won only Screenplay.

The British Academy of Film and Television Awards was slightly more generous, doling out BAFTAs for Best Original Screenplay and Best Supporting Actor for Jackson as the net result of the film's nine nominations.

The LA critics kept up the momentum, dishing out trinkets for Best Picture, Director, Actor (Travolta) and Screenplay. The New York Film Critics Circle and the National Board of Review each honoured the film with Best Picture and Best Director while the Independent Spirit Awards went further with Best Feature, Director, Screenplay and Actor – only this time, for Jackson, not Travolta.

If Jackson had been peeved by Miramax's outré campaigning for Travolta for the main actor category during the season, here was his justification. There was little he could do, however, when it came to the big one. Denzel Washington had famously resisted efforts to secure him a Supporting Actor nomination and had paid for his stance with having to watch co-star Hanks blub into his Best Actor award for *Philadelphia*.

Rightly or wrongly, the aggressive campaigning paid dividends and *Pulp Fiction* graciously accepted seven 1995 Academy Award nominations, including Travolta for Best Actor, Jackson for Best Supporting Actor, Bender for Best Picture, Thurman for Best Supporting Actress, Tarantino and Avary for Best Screenplay and Sally Menke, who had worked on *Reservoir Dogs*, for Best Film Editing. On the night, only Best Screenplay went the film's way. Famously, Tarantino omitted to thank a single person during his egregious acceptance speech, unlike in Cannes almost a year earlier. Just as famously, Jackson was not a happy bunny at missing out to 'a guy who did nothing other than lay in a coffin and be Dracula'.

'Why should I pretend I didn't want to win?' he asks. 'Everybody knows you're dying to win.' It didn't help when even daughter Zoe was reminding him that second place is the first loser. The fact that Oscar nominees are in a contest that they didn't volunteer to be in was also confusing. On the one hand Jackson was being told he was one of the best at his job. Then, as he found out, someone else is declared to be better. The result? 'As good as you feel, you don't feel as good as you might. I wouldn't trade the experience. It was great to be there, but it's always better to win.'

When Jackson came out and joked that the annual voting process involves all the ballots being shipped out to a Price Waterhouse that turns out to be nine little old guys sitting around pontificating on who they like that year, he made headline news. 'Everyone's talking about me hating the Academy but I didn't say it that way,' he insists. 'But all of a sudden it's "Jackson Says it's a Raw Deal!" '

While he admits that losing will never appeal to him – 'for every one person who leaves the ceremony happy, there's another four people really pissed off' – he prefers not to be entered in the race. 'My career is not going to be validated by me having a gold statue in my house for people to look at,' he insists. For Jackson, being stopped in the street by strangers telling him they like his films, or having lines from his films quoted at him in airports is proof enough of appreciation. 'That's a greater validation than one evening of joy that will probably turn to horror for a lot of others before the night's out.'

Depending on the mood you catch him in these days, then, Jackson can be either disarmingly laissez-faire about the goings on in the Academy's inner sanctum, or spitting feathers. Refreshingly, the more famous he becomes seems to have no bearing on what actually comes out of his mouth. More importantly, it sends out a signal that, for all his elevated influence since the morning Jules came into his life, he is the same guy who packed his bags and left New York. But that, after all, is what you would expect from a man who was 46 before he achieved his greatest success.

12. EVERYBODY WANTS TO BE A HERO

There are many facets to any actor's life that the ordinary guy in the street probably never truly comprehends. On the one hand there's the perceived lifestyle: glitzy, glam and ridiculously pampered. But beneath that spoilt veneer there is an industry that runs like a military exercise. A large reason why actors get chauffeured everywhere and why they have private planes is simply because they are on such a tight schedule and it is the only way the studio can guarantee the clockwork-running necessary to get things done on time – and to budget. They get put up in the best hotels and waited on hand and foot to keep them in the best mood possible – nobody wants a surly star to take out his irritation on a journalist sent to discuss the new multi-million dollar blockbuster.

There is another aspect that tends to be overlooked, too: the timing. An actor's participation in the production of the average movie falls midway in the entire schedule. The process kicks off with the script meetings, the financial arrangements and the production planning. Then comes actual shooting. Then comes post-production, by which time the cast have long since moved onto pictures new.

By the time the finished film is finally released, a year or two may have elapsed. It's at this point that the public pick up interest in the average picture – the odd piece of on-set gossip aside. It's at this point that the cast reassemble to complete the final stage of their contractual obligations: the promotion. By this time, the actors will be working on other projects. If you ever wondered why your favourite stars had odd hairstyles or 'interesting' facial hair during interviews for their latest film, it's because they are in the character of whichever part they are currently playing.

For the same reason, it's often fun to watch certain actors try to muster enthusiasm for a project you have long since heard that they did not enjoy making. (Pity poor George Clooney hawking *Batman & Robin* around the globe during Warners' most expensive press junket ever, knowing full well he was flogging a turkey – a fact that would be realised as soon as the first audiences were let anywhere near the finished result.)

The long gap between actors finishing their contributions and the movie's eventual release also leads to genuine forgetfulness during interviews. Most promotional interviews are vapid at best, but it is not just the actors being politically correct. It is possible they have worked on half a dozen new characters since the film in question's wrap party all those months ago – you try to remember amusing anecdotes about a job you did more than a year ago.

From the moment the *Pulp Fiction* roadshow started turning in May 1994, all of its actors bar Jimmie (played of course by Tarantino), were benefiting from their participation. Travolta's agents were rapidly cashing in on his return to the A list with headlining status in froth such as *Michael* and *Phenomenon*. Willis had staked a claim in the closest thing to an art-house movie he would ever come to doing, adding a touch of critical success to his rampaging box-office appeal. Thurman had put her life of odd characters in odder projects behind her, Ving Rhames had announced himself as any director's hard man of choice, and Harvey Keitel had chalked up yet another winning performance – all the while dressed as a waiter.

True to form, Samuel Jackson was not resting on his laurels during *Pulp*'s year of success. No sooner had he checked out of Hotel Tarantino than he was seen again on the small screen. Significantly, the colour-blindness from which he had benefited to win the part in *White Sands* was forgotten in his next role choices, at least for the projects of the next six months. As if for emphasis, his year started with a broadcast shown to coincide with Black America Month in the United States in February 1994. Filmed in Lexington, Staunton and Buena Vista Virginia, *Assault at West Point* gave the Showtime TV movie treatment to the true story of Johnson Whittacker's court-martial in the 1880s. Playing one of his two defence attorneys, the academic Richard Greener, Jackson injects his role with enough credibility for audiences to believe that he truly found his co-counsel racist. Given his own background, it was not too much of a stretch of acting talent.

An interesting point about *Variety*'s review of the film is their description of Jackson playing a 'black academic'. (It also says 'the acting is strong throughout'.) While there is an argument for the colour detail being relevant in the plot precis (although it is slightly tenuous), the main point to take from this is the fact that the magazine's editors did not rate Jackson's fame enough in February 1994 for his name to carry all the race information they needed. How that would soon change.

A month later the same magazine pulled a slightly subtler stunt in its description of the actor's role in another TV movie, *Against the Wall*. Based on another true story, this time the 1971 Attica rebellion, *Variety* notes how Jackson plays a 'Malcolm X-type activist' who befriends wet-behind-the-ears prison guard Kyle MacLachlan. Marking director John Frankenheimer's 'triumphant' return to the medium that catapulted his career forty years earlier, *Against the Wall* manages to pull out impressive performances, according to reviewer Ray Loynd – not least from Jackson who undertakes the first nude scene of his career during a prison strip search. 'Prominently co-starring and forging a bond of moral courage with MacLachlan is Samuel L. Jackson. [Both men] lurch from slam-bang-in-your-face confrontations to judiciously mixed, quietly tense stand-offs.' *Empire* magazine was slightly more detached in its review: 'About as sophisticated politically as 10cc's similarly themed hit "Rubber Bullets", but decently cast and directed with some grit.' *Against the Wall* was so powerfully told that Jackson was surprised and delighted to receive a Golden Globe nomination for his performance. So much for taking a risk by returning to television roles.

Ironically, the first project Jackson embarked upon following two such 'black' statement projects was in a similar vein, prompting the *New York Times* to remark how 'hot-button social issues are usually the province of television movies' – as the actor had just proved. Commencing shooting in Chicago at the end of March 1994, however, *Losing Isaiah* weighs in with enough decent performances from a stellar cast to take the result several notches above anything from HBO or Showtime. Yet again Jackson plays a lawyer ('acerbic and dignified' Kadar Lewis, according to *The Times*), this time charged with trying to win back a child from its adoptive parents now that its biological mother has come to her senses. The twist in the tale comes from the fact that the child is black (Marc John Jefferies) and the head of the foster family is white – Oscar-winner Jessica Lange.

Not only is Jackson seen once again firmly on the side of black oppression, even in this very localised sense, but there is also familiarity about his co-star. Isaiah's mother is played by Halle Berry, who reprises the tricks she learned from Jackson's guided tour of the drugs underworld for *Jungle Fever* to ham up a suitably crackhead performance here. Another co-star was from even closer to home: *Losing Isaiah* marked the first time that Mr and Mrs Jackson appeared in the same movie. It would, unfortunately, also be the last.

Despite good work from Berry and Lange, Jackson's character's tendency to trot out lines like 'black babies belong with black mothers' gives him little room to manoeuvre. *Variety* agrees: 'Jackson's one-dimensional lawyer is a disagreeable apparatchik of political correctness.'

Fortunately, there were more rounded characters in his repertoire, as the world was about to realise. *Losing Isaiah* was still being shot when its chip-on-his-shoulder lawyer disappeared for a week to the French town of Cannes. The rest, as they say . . .

When Samuel Jackson stepped onto the soundstage for his next film, it was as a different person. Not in his own mind, of course – his opinion of himself hadn't changed since he delivered his first lines in *The Threepenny Opera*. To the public and his peers, however, he was no longer Samuel L. Jackson, versatile character actor and safe pair of hands. He was The Man. More importantly, he was The Man Who Played Jules 'Foot Fucking Master' Winnfield. Even without the facial hair, and with the Jheri curls safe in storage, there was no mistaking the eyes that could drill for oil and the hovering presence of the character whose wallet contained the motif 'Bad Mother Fucker'.

Ironically, given Jules's cartoon-like Blaxploitation vibe, Jackson's first role post-Cannes' unveiling was his first non 'racial' role of the year. Swapping Chicago for his old stomping ground of New York, Jackson turned up alongside *Pulp* partner in grime Ving Rhames to add a small part to Barbet Shroeder's *Kiss of Death*. Playing the just-happens-to-be-black character of Detective Calvin, Jackson is responsible for giving some depth to *NYPD Blue* abscondee David Caruso's lead turn as Jimmy Kilmartin. The fact that Jackson was also reuniting with *Amos and Andrew*'s Nic Cage made it a shoot to remember for the brief time he was there. If he was sad to leave the Big Apple to go home, he needn't have worried: he would soon be back there.

Kiss of Death, with its tag line of 'whatever doesn't kill you makes you stronger', would go on to take nearly $14 million dollars at the US box office – just over twice the take of the more emotionally taxing (that is to say, depressing) *Losing Isaiah*. It was also a hit with critics. 'A sophisticated thriller with a tense, guarded style and brooding elegance,' said the *New York Times* on its release in April 1995. 'Pumps raw energy,' said *Playboy*. The UK's *The Face* noted how it 'lingers in the imagination long after you've seen it' while *Rolling Stone* said how 'Cage and Caruso strike sparks in this riveting piece of pulp fiction'. Revelling in the local scenery, the *New Yorker* magazine declared it 'the best crime movie since Scorsese's *GoodFellas*'.

Strictly speaking, *Kiss of Death* was not Jackson's first 'non-black-specific' character part of 1994. That honour went to his role in February of Rumbo – a streetwise dog in the dark made-for-kids MGM feature, *Fluke*. When Matthew Modine's character dies in a car crash, he wakes up as a mixed-breed mutt. Finding his (four) feet on the streets of another of Jackson's old patches, Atlanta, Georgia, Fluke is taken under the wing of Rumbo, who wisecracks his way through the classic mentoring role. While twelve golden retrievers were used to play Fluke, including celebrity dog Comet from ABC's *Full House*, Rumbo has no such body doubles. In fact, his time in the movie comes to an end when he takes a bullet for his new friend. Maybe there is something to be said for contributing your parts from the safety of a voice-over booth – it certainly saves on make-up time. Whatever the reason, the *New York Times* led the pack when it said Jackson's no-nonsense performance was guilty of 'stealing yet another movie'. For an actor whose physical presence carries such weight, the acclaim meant a lot to Jackson when it came on the film's release in June 1995. It made up for the slightly disappointing home box office of $4 million.

* * *

The mysteries of the Hollywood clock that sees actors promote films months after they have finished working on them has another knock-on effect for the stars of each picture. As Samuel Jackson had discovered a few years earlier after *Jungle Fever* and then *White Sands*, career progression in the movie business takes a while to seep out to the provinces of the viewing public. How many fans and movie-goers would be scratching their heads in 1995 as Jackson was seen to follow his epoch-defining role as Jules with throwaway lawyer in a chick flick weepy, a low-down-the-cast-list cop in a decent enough thriller and, most impressively, the voice of a dog in a too-dark-for-kids/too-daft-for-adults fantasy?

Given his penchant for the prolific, maybe Jackson would still have taken on all these roles. Maybe, but probably not. Yes, as an obsessive actor, the chances are that he would have worked on something, but the jobs would have been better, the parts stronger and more dominant, the films less throwaway. By August 1994, he was ready to start work on one such project deserving of his burgeoning status. 'Big' didn't begin to describe it.

'I think *Pulp Fiction* was very important in terms of the effect that I have on a story and on screen,' he reflects. The Academy Award nomination, in particular, was responsible for boosting the salary his agents could command. As far as international recognition goes, however, Jackson thinks *Die Hard: With a Vengeance* actually made a bigger difference to his career because, as the highest-grossing film in the world on its release, he was seen by millions of people all over the planet.

'I became a viable box office commodity to people because, prior to that, folks always said, "Oh, you know, black actors – there's Sidney Poitier, Will Smith and Eddie Murphy" – and then, all of a sudden, they knew who I was.'

Of course, nothing is certain in Hollywood and there were no cast-iron guarantees that the third movie in the John McClane series would recreate the magic of the first two (the first one, anyway). But reuniting Jackson with *Pulp* and *Loaded Weapon* alumnus, Willis, throwing in the latter's trademark dirty white vest, and shaping the action around a whole city rather than trying to emulate the claustrophobic tension of its predecessors' hotel and aeroplane, meant that the vibes were good.

Plot-wise, *Die Hard: With a Vengeance* reworked the old 'Simon Says' kids' parlour game with potentially catastrophic consequences. Introducing Jeremy Irons as the Aryan brother (once he'd applied the blue contact lenses and bleached his hair) of the first *Die Hard*'s Alan Rickman character – out for the 'vengeance' (and a bank-load of bullion) of the title – also provided the sort of linear connections guaranteed to hook movie-goers.

Despite the cards being stacked in the movie's favour, it still could have turned sour for its second lead. Unlike the first two films, this had 'buddy flick' written all over it, with Willis's character joined at Jackson's hip throughout. The fact that they fell into the 'black and white' category also threw up obvious comparisons, first with the *Dirty Harry* series (in which Callaghan's sidekicks always got wasted), then more recently with the *Lethal Weapon* franchise (and even Jackson's own *Loaded Weapon*). But whereas Danny Glover's character in *LW* had little to say of his blackness, Jackson's in *Die Hard* could not have been more verbose.

Manohla Dargis in *Sight and Sound*, explored the two relationships further, noting how, unlike Glover's character, Jackson isn't called on to curb Willis's character, but rather to serve as his captive audience. 'By the end of the film, Jackson's upright black man has learned the method of the white man's madness, turning from antagonist to helpmate, rising above his dislike of whites for the greater good.'

Part of this transformation comes from the closeness of the characters, in particular a segment where the two are actually handcuffed together. It's no coincidence that Jackson's hero, Sidney Poitier, suffered the same fate in *The Defiant Ones* when he was strapped to the ludicrously coiffured Tony Curtis.

Considering the fact that his skin colour in this picture was an issue, and considering that the movie's instincts have 'big budget blockbuster' written all over them, *Die Hard* actually provided Jackson with his first rounded character. Famously saving Willis's character from a fate worse than def in the film's opening sequence (McLane is wandering naked around the streets of Harlem wearing only a sandwich board declaring: 'I hate niggers'), his Zeus is the trademark 'straight man' of the picture.

'The person who went into the mish-mash with Bruce had to be square and staunch and righteous,' the film's director John McTiernan says. 'A republican, basically.'

Interestingly for such a slapstick adventure, Big Topics are discussed. Probably the biggest of them all in today's world, of course, is racism. In a move that would beach many 'serious' movies, *Die Hard* gamefully has both Zeus and McClane accusing each other of being racist, with the Willis character having far more ground for accuracy than his partner. Conducted between insults on many other levels, it works surprisingly well. Better, at least, than Jackson's 'racist' character in *Losing Isaiah*.

For all the film's cartoon-like subtleties, Jackson achieves a surprisingly fleshed-out end result in Zeus, his electronics repair guy plucked out of safe obscurity to save the city. At times the character's priggishness threatens to veer the picture into Glover vs Gibson territory, but it is saved by Jackson's trademark preparation. 'I still did a biography for Zeus,' he insists. 'I don't change the formula for making a character because it's an action movie.'

A year later, when the movie was released, the efforts would be appreciated, at least by *Sight and Sound*. 'One of Jackson's basic strategies is to infuse even the most potentially insulting scenes with a dose of ironic distance,' it said. That characteristic is, after all, what makes him such a good foil to Willis (and later Geena Davis in *The Long Kiss Goodnight*). 'It's also why he rises to the challenge of *Pulp Fiction* so gamely, delivering a far more complicated character than existed on paper.'

One of the reasons Jackson was able to make the character of Zeus work was respect. Not only in the sense that, since he was being paid, he should do the best job he could. But he never treated the movie as a popcorn throwaway exercise. The end result might be escapist nonsense – in the best possible way, of course – but it would only work if everyone treated the production of it as seriously as if they were working on *Schindler's List*. 'I wanted to break down stereotypes by showing Zeus as a great ordinary guy,' Jackson says. It didn't hurt too that he was a fan of the genre and the *Die Hard* series. As an owner of eight televisions at home, watching TV is something Jackson does a lot of.

'I've watched the original *Die Hard* thirty times,' he says. 'Why? Because it's *Die Hard*. If I'm channel surfing and I see John McClane, I'll stop and watch the whole film. I love that genre.'

Jackson also knew that there would be some serious fun to be had shooting the movie. Apart from working with Willis again, as soon as he saw the script he realised that, unless the computer-generated blue-screen boys were going to take over, there would be some major mayhem caused on the streets of New York. Major car chase set pieces around Wall Street, the Federal Bank and, in an audacious piece of planning, through Central Park, looked guaranteed to cause local city folk nightmares as the usual round of road closures and diversions swung into place at the behest of the fee-paying movie company. Remembering back to when he was a 'local', however, Jackson had no complaints other than envy.

'As a New Yorker, I'd always wanted to tear down those streets,' he says. 'Making the film was like going to an amusement park every day. It was like getting paid for the kids' games I used to play as a little boy.'

Like most amusement park rides, however, there was a downside to working with someone like John McTiernan. A lot of 'movie' actors might not have minded, but for someone with Jackson's theatre background, there were a couple of times when he felt underused.

'Some days it was really exhilarating but others were just tedious,' he says, 'because John had this film already edited in his mind.' It meant often Jackson was faced with instructions like: 'You pull up in this car and you look up in the sky because Bruce is there.' According to Jackson in *Empire*, that's not acting: 'That's reacting.'

Thespian gripes aside, by the time *Die Hard* hit cinemas and, more importantly, by the time its cast was thrown to the mercy of interviewers on the film's obligatory publicity circuit, Jackson was indelibly cast in people's minds as Jules Winnfield. It goes some way to describing the seismic effect of *Pulp Fiction* that even hard-nosed movie hacks became like normal movie-goers in its wake, even committing the cardinal 'fan' sin of imagining the characters on the screen are what the actors are like in real life. It happened with Travolta to some extent, but Jackson more so. He was Jules – end of story. Yet here he was, a year later, tearing through New York City in a costume consisting of user-friendly glasses and 'sensible' clothes. For many journalists there was only one conclusion: he did it for the money.

Not true. Not true one bit. Jackson had moved on from the principled wage demands of his *White Sands* days. For all its mega-budget and Willis's reputed $20 million salary, it wasn't exactly a name-your-price kind of gig. 'No way did I do it for the money,' Jackson insisted at the time. 'In any case, there wasn't much money. They paid it all to Bruce and Jeremy.' It was the thrill of being on the inside of a *Die Hard* movie, he claimed, that had attracted him, nothing else.

Said with all the zeal of a man plugging a movie. A few years later, when summing up his major films with Willis, Jackson was slightly more candid. '*Die Hard with a Vengeance* was fun,' he told *Empire* in 2002, 'but it was a money deal and I think we both knew that.' *Pulp Fiction*, on the other hand, was something both men would have crawled over the proverbial hot coals to be involved in. 'You read a script like that and whether you're Bruce Willis, Samuel L. Jackson or Pee-Wee Herman, you know that shit is like gold dust.'

Of course, not only was he a child getting to run amok in the toy factory, but Jackson was also keenly aware that this movie could become his new calling card – the platinum equivalent of his earlier work. The ensuing worldwide exposure would also strengthen his hand when it came to negotiating on future movies. And, as he was well aware, with Hollywood casting so few roles for black actors, it could not hurt to push his own name a little further up the list.

As if to prove it, by the midway point of 1994, 111 major studio movies had reached the production stage somewhere in the world. Less than 10 per cent of those pictures were either black movies or had black actors cast in the central roles. Allowing for the fact that the Malcolm X situation meant he was still ineligible for Spike Lee's annual celluloid adventure (this year it was *Clockers*), that left few obvious chances for an actor with lead aspirations like Jackson. Within a couple of weeks of his starting work in

New York on *Die Hard*, his old pal Denzel was pulling on his military uniform in Los Angeles and Washington for *Crimson Tide*. At the same time, Martin Lawrence and Will Smith were halfway through their Miami shoot of *Bad Boys* and Wesley was getting all glammed up in *To Wong Foo, Thanks for Everything! Julie Newmar*. But that was it for the summer of '94. Hardly rich pickings for actors, and certainly not for audiences looking for a little variation on a schedule beavering through projects like *First Knight, Mr Holland's Opus, The Brady Bunch Movie* and *Braveheart*.

All of which explains why Jackson puts so much industry into creating believable characters for every situation. In *Die Hard* it paid off. He thinks so – 'Bruce Willis was the star but people were interested in my character too.' So, when the film hit theatres as the most-anticipated release of 1995, were the critics.

As an 'entertainment first, plausibility second' blockbuster, *Die Hard* was always going to win more fans among movie-goers than critics, but whether the film itself hit the spot or not, everyone agreed that Jackson delivered.

Empire gave a rare five-star review and applauded the double-headed line-up for the movie's 18 August release. 'The relationship between the thrown-together Willis and Jackson is a treat throughout,' the magazine's Andrew Collins said. 'The latter's recurring racism-paranoia, though inherently funny, pointedly heading off any criticisms of a convenient black-and-white team-up.' The underlying tension between the two men never lets up, he said.

Starburst felt the 'snoozably predictable script' was 'retrieved by Samuel L. Jackson, a new sidekick for our lad, adding vitriolic wisecracks to the raw dynamite of the special effects'.

The American press had thumped home the same line when the movie opened there in May. 'Mr Jackson brings craftiness and pitch-perfect intensity to his role and here steals the movie from the ostensible hero and villain,' reckoned Caryn James in the *New York Times*. *Variety*'s Brian Lowry agreed: 'For his part, Jackson continues to impress, bringing ample humour to his character, who dives with remarkable speed and vigour into his life-threatening chores.' Considering both papers also reviewed *Johnny Mnemonic* and *Caspar* that issue, it's surprising that *Die Hard* didn't get a fairer crack.

Call it the *Pulp Fiction* factor, call it just being able to out-act Bruce Willis and a panto-villain-style Jeremy Irons (really that tricky?), but Samuel L. Jackson seemed to have won over enough of the traditionally snooty movie press to insure him against whatever up-in-flames project he was attached to – *Fluke* would be released just before *Die Hard*. For a short while at least, he was acting asbestos – inflammable. The question of how long the love affair would last would have to be seen.

13. I GET PAID LIKE A B-LIST WHITE ACTOR

Ever hear the phrase 'success begets success'? If you lived in Hollywood you would be hard pressed to avoid it on a daily basis. And if you didn't hear someone recite it like a holy mantra, you would certainly see people thinking it. There's only one thing Hollywood likes more than success and that's repeating success. Why waste expending R&D on new projects when you can dish up more of the same? In the Hollywood kitchen, you can reheat a soufflé.

Sequels, it reckons, are where the money is. Brand familiarity will win multiple audiences. At its best, this logic produces such wonderful episodic cinema as the *Lord of the Rings* trilogy and *The Godfather* saga. At its worst it gives us *Speed II* – containing all the elements of *Speed I* except Keanu Reeves; 2003's *Dumb and Dumberer*, starring neither Jim Carrey nor Jeff Daniels; and *Friday the 13th part 10*. It also gives us absolutely pointless remakes of classics like *The Italian Job* (no longer set in Rome), *Get Carter* (Stallone playing Caine) and *The Day of the Jackal* (that man Sly again).

On a smaller scale, Hollywood likes its actors to find a part they can play and stick to it. Comedy or action flick, you know what you get with Arnie – brawny hero with *Sound of Music* accent and no sense of humour. Hire Keanu Reeves and you're guaranteed a guy who, whether goofing as a daft sk8er boi or ripping into the Earth's mainframe reality in a fight for humanity's survival, will still say 'Woaah!' at any number of given script points. No sooner had *Pulp Fiction* exploded than Hollywood was crying out for more Jules Winnfield. Only one man could deliver what they wanted.

And he was saying no.

'I could easily have made a career out of playing Jules over the years,' Jackson says. 'Everybody's always sending me the script they think is the new *Pulp Fiction*.' His agents, however, are under strict instruction to vet anything involving a smooth-talking gangster, pointing to his theatre background as the reason for liking to try new parts. 'I won't allow myself to be typecast and neither will those people who take my 15 per cent and my 10 per cent,' he says.

Standing up to agents and reminding them who employs whom is one of the more pleasant tasks that a major star might have to undertake. At least the agents are – contractually speaking – on his side. But Hollywood is an insidious town and more than one decent talent has been snuffed out too early under the suffocating weight of the hangers-on, advisers and new best friends who suddenly appear from nowhere as soon as an actor achieves a certain degree of success in the movie business.

No sooner had Jules trotted off to 'walk the earth' than a host of strangers started knocking at Jackson's door, metaphorically and literally speaking. 'All of a sudden, everybody wants a piece of you,' he says. 'You're everybody's best friend.' The fact that his 'overnight success' materialised after several decades in 'the business' – he was 45 when he first pulled on Jules's wig – meant that Jackson was better equipped mentally to eschew sugar-coated appeals to his vanity. He knows others are not so lucky and succumb. Fortunately, his years of intoxication were well in the past. 'The most important thing is not to lose yourself in all that, not to let that particular moment validate the rest of your career,' he says. 'Don't change the work that you do so you can go back to the Oscars every year.' Pick work that is important for you, in other words, not something you think might just interest the Academy.

It also helps to cultivate those pre-fame associations. 'I have the same friends that I've had for the last thirty years,' he says. 'My level of success is a lot different from theirs, but I'm still the same guy to them, so it's cool.'

He's also the same guy at home. California life suited Zoe and she found schoolwork challenging and rewarding; her hope was to reach a college like Spelman or Vassar when she was older. When she wasn't overseeing the decoration of their African-influenced home, LaTanya was happy that work opportunities were more available in Los Angeles. Even if she never got another job, the man she called 'Pooh' was finally proving he was as good as she thought he was, and that gave her enormous satisfaction. On Jackson's part, the woman he credits with saving his life just carried on keeping him sane. 'I'm pleased that my life has been saved,' he says. 'I could have been nothing. Apparently, I was almost happy being nothing. But I'm here. I'm a survivor. This family has survived, and I'm grateful.'

A downside of Jackson's sudden worldwide fame post-*Pulp Fiction* and *Die Hard* was that LaTanya started to find herself having to compete with strangers for a piece of her husband. When an actor really connects with an audience, there is often some subliminal exchange that appears to run the other way. The end result is that fans often feel like they own their heroes, or at the very least that they know them. In reality, they only know their public persona. This can lead to all kinds of inconveniences on a daily basis.

Watching women hit on her husband is something that LaTanya had to get used to. She trusted him not to respond, but it didn't make it any easier to deal with when women pushed past her to get near him. She says it is

Early in his career Samuel L. Jackson appeared in a number of films by Spike Lee, a director with whom he would later have some disagreements. Two of these were *Do the Right Thing* (above) and *Jungle Fever*. In the second, he played a junkie – just after he himself had come off drugs for good.

A Hollywood star is born. As the Bible-quoting assassin Jules in Quentin Tarantino's *Pulp Fiction*, Samuel L. Jackson finally became a household name. He would go on to work with Tarantino again, both in *Jackie Brown* (below) and in *Kill Bill*.

Above As an action hero in a Hollywood blockbuster: across from his *Pulp Fiction* co-star Bruce Willis, Jackson enjoyed his work on *Die Hard: With a Vengeance.*

Right Jackson finally got a lead role – in *The Great White Hype* – in which he played the Reverend Fred Sultan.

Above Racism had never been too far away in Hollywood. Not only did *A Time to Kill* cover the subject in depth, but Jackson felt he should have been earning much more than co-star Matthew McConaughey by that stage in his career.

Left and below However, he was able to take roles in smaller films that he believed in: *Eve's Bayou*, which he also produced, and *Le Violon Rouge* (*The Red Violin*).

Samuel L. Jackson was finally acting with the big boys he could respect as his co-stars: with Kevin Spacey, who he had met during *A Time to Kill*, in *The Negotiator* and with Tommy Lee Jones in *Rules of Engagement*.

Left The King of Cool. Jackson had grown up admiring the Blaxploitation movies, especially *Shaft*. And here he was remaking the film – dressed in Armani.

Right Finally working with the director he had always wanted to – using a lightsaber in George Lucas's *Star Wars: Episode II – Attack of the Clones*.

Left Not many people can get away with a kilt – but Samuel L. Jackson did in *The 51st State*. Another producing job, but this time in Liverpool and with the only weapon of choice for Jackson – the golf club.

Right The old and the new in Hollywood. As Jackson becomes an old hand in the acting business, he is able to work with the up and coming talent, such as Vin Diesel in *xXx* and its sequel.

The women in his family: Jackson's wife LaTanya, who has helped him through the highs and lows of his life, and his daughter Zoe, his partner for watching his beloved Hong Kong action films.

usually the white girls who are the brazen ones, but one instance in Chicago saw a black girl grab hubby as the couple were walking. She lost her cool and shoved the amorous interloper away. 'The admiration, I can do without,' she says succinctly. 'But I do envy the inherent power people assign to him just because of who he is. Everyone just wants to kiss his butt.'

The combination of that butt-kissing and the sudden flood of scripts post-*Pulp Fiction* meant that 1995 was a year in which Samuel Jackson could have kicked back and taken his time to find another project. He could have done lots of things. What he did do, however, is sign up for another handful of pictures. Despite his new fame and, concomitantly, his new price tag, the deciding criterion stayed the same: 'Would I pay money to see this film?'

'I read a script to see if it's the kind of story I would pay $7.50 to go and see,' he explains. 'Secondly, I look at the character to see if it's someone that will present some kind of acting challenge.' What he doesn't do is check to see if he's the most important person in the script (beyond making sure he's on enough pages to justify turning up). Being the star is not why he does it.

'I could have been a gun-toting, Bible-spouting fool for the rest of my career,' he says, 'but luckily I was able to make some other choices.' The first of those choices (albeit one first discussed before Jules fever really kicked in) presented itself in March 1995, before the Oscars ceremony. It was actually two films – sort of. For reasons best known to producers Robert Jones and John Lyons, and to the Goldwyn studio, the movie that Jackson embarked upon in March 1995 was eventually released as *Hard Eight* in Europe and *Sydney* in the United States. Debut screenwriter and director Paul Thomas Anderson must have thought his chances of an international hit, and therefore his career, had died the day that decision was taken. Fortunately, he survived to go on to create hits like the singularly named *Boogie Nights*.

The film did not do any of its principle stars any harm either. Alongside Philip Baker Hall's eponymous (in America) Sydney were Jackson, a fledgling Gwyneth Paltrow and grizzled one-day gangmember of New York, John C. Reilly. Shot in Los Angeles, the picture drew comparisons of *Leaving Las Vegas* with its clever fixation on the gaming tables at Reno.

Cruising at altitude on a cloud-nine high from his Tarantino experience, Jackson was singled out for particular acclaim in the movie for his part as Jimmy, a vulgar Reno regular with a voracious sexual appetite and the bad influence on Reilly's John. In a so-so review, *Variety* raved how he 'steals every scene that isn't nailed down with a performance that occasionally recalls the flamboyant menace of his *Pulp Fiction* portrayal.' When the movie finally surfaced in the UK in 1997, a year after its alter ego had debuted in the States, Jackson's name had been promoted to the top of the cast list. Sadly, *Empire* found he couldn't save 'a slow, lumbering thriller'.

By the time filming started on Jackson's next picture, he found himself at the top of the cast list on merit. As *The Great White Hype*'s lead star, it was down to him to carry the movie – something he had never been expected to do before. Now though, riding on the crest of the *Pulp* wave, his name was perceived as being capable of putting bums on seats.

Speaking of which . . .

Despite playing some dozens of parts on stage and screen, by 1995 Samuel Jackson had never had to play a standard love scene. In fact, a brief scene in TV movie *Against the Wall* apart, there had been no cause to date for him to take his clothes off in front of a camera at all. That was about to change.

For his role as the Reverend Fred Sultan, a garish boxing promoter two parts Don King and a third Jimmy Savile, Jackson was facing his first proper nude scene. 'I stand up out of this whirlpool and say, "I am the American dream," ' he says. 'And I'm, like, totally naked.' Fortunately or unfortunately, depending on your taste, the final edit saves the actor's blushes, despite him finding it a 'liberating' experience. 'They don't let it all hang out on screen, but they do give me a great Mel Gibson butt shot,' he says.

As a satire on the corrupt boxing scene in America, and Don King's colourful life in particular, *The Great White Hype* pitches Jackson's Sultan against the easily corrupted characters of *LA Law*'s Corbin Bernsen and *Jurassic Park* alumnus Jeff Goldblum. There is also a decent turn from *Chicago Hope*'s Peter Berg, recently seen going up against Linda Fiorentino in *The Last Seduction*. ('I got more beat up doing sex scenes with her than during the boxing scenes in this film,' Berg admits.) A few stages short of highbrow entertainment, a lot of it is very funny. Jackson's colourful impresario, with his annoying catchphrases 'I love you' and 'You're my brother' is a wildly enervating turn from the man who last brought us out-and-out comedy in *Loaded Weapon*. (*One Eyed Jimmy* doesn't count.)

For all the glitzy razzmatazz behind Reginald Hudlin's production and its neat line in Mike Tyson jokes, *The Great White Hype* met with mixed reviews, oddly split between the UK and the US. It was the organs of the United States that found Jackson's latest racist character most agreeable. 'Jackson exudes a droll and charismatic joviality even though his character isn't taken much beyond the one-joke stage,' wrote *Variety* in May 1996 on the movie's release. The script though, it felt, did not match screenwriter Ron Shelton's early work on *Bull Durham* and *White Men Can't Jump*. The *New York Times* was more welcoming. Citing the movie's intention to be 'a race-conscious *Spinal Tap* for the world of sports', it concludes that the end result is uneven at best, 'raising benightedness to an art form'. The 'resplendent' Jackson, however, 'showing off Ruth Carter's wonderfully outlandish costumes, makes a delightfully sly presence'. While *Premiere* called it a 'hit and miss satire of race inside the sporting world', *Empire* came out punching. Even Jackson failed to dodge the flying gloves in its review: 'Jackson, normally the scene-stealer, spams it up to varying degrees and Goldblum is oddly dull.' It's an opinion . . .

Filming for *The Great White Hype* had kicked off in June 1995 in Fox's Los Angeles studios and Las Vegas – the latter location notably and ostentatiously plugging the MGM Grand in a piece of OTT product placement. At the same time, a dramatisation of a John Grisham novel called *The Juror* was getting under way in New York. Given how he intended to spend the latter part of his year, Jackson had good reason to track how this production went. While Goldblum flitted between *The Great White Hype* and his other commitments on the following year's anticipated summer blockbuster, *Independence Day* with man in black Will Smith, there was action from across the Fox yard on John Woo's *Broken Arrow* starring John Travolta. Popping over to each other's sets to catch up, it's a fair bet that the one thing that didn't come up was salary. Same studio, same headline status: Jackson wasn't sure, but he had a good idea that his former co-star was picking up an extra nought on the end of his wage. And that hurt.

Under Quentin Tarantino's knowing guidance, the role of the 'black man' in twentieth-century entertainment had been well and truly moved up the cultural agenda the day that he handed the part of Jules Winnfield to Samuel L. Jackson. With a grateful tip of the hat to the Blaxploitation movies of its inspiration, Tarantino had successfully produced a film that white audiences would claim as their own and yet would be dominated by its black characters and their language. With anyone else at the helm it could have been a tacky mess. But with the director's uncanny ear for dialect from all walks of life, *Pulp Fiction* became a virtual Linguaphone lesson for anyone wishing to speak 'street'.

Outside Tarantino's deliciously simplistic view of gangland LA, however, the real world sways to a different rhythm. Where Jules was Vincent's equal, if not his better, on screen, and where both men were beholden to the nefarious Marcellus, the dynamic was distinctly different for the two lead actors off screen. Despite both turning in star turns in the movie, with Jackson edging it in most people's opinions, it was Travolta whose star shot into the ascendancy as soon as word about the picture eked out. Within a couple of films his price had gone from 'just spell my name right on the credits' to $20 million a picture. Jackson, by contrast, was lucky to pick up a twentieth of such amounts. Why? One word: race. Says who? One guess.

'There's a big dollar disparity in Hollywood,' Samuel L. Jackson states. 'Had I been white with the same résumé, I'd be making a lot more money.' In fact, on pure skill levels, Jackson is convinced if he weren't black he would be picking up $20 million a movie. 'I get paid like a B-list white actor,' he says.

Over the years, Jackson has noticed the various excuses designed, he feels, to hold him back, even when it's a $100 million movie. 'They always tell me, "Come on, Sam, that was a Bruce Willis movie." Or, "That was a John Travolta movie," or "That's a dinosaur movie." That's how they keep you in place.'

In case Jackson's point is too subtle, it is this: as an A-list actor who happens to be black, he earns the equivalent of a B-list actor who happens to be white. Comparing like for like, his talent is not rewarded in the same manner as a white actor's would be. It's racism, pure and simple; it's market forces, say his detractors – deal with it. Whatever, it's a realisation designed to tax anyone's love affair with their industry. 'I know a lot of actors who dwell on that fact,' he says. 'They're pretty bitter. And it shows in their work.' Despite his comments, Jackson's obsession is not with money, it's with acting. Having wasted so many years being too drunk to realise fully his own talent, he doesn't want to get side-tracked again, certainly not by something as negative as anger – at least not if it affects his work. 'The iniquities of life are part of life,' he says simply. 'I'm making more money than I ever made before. And I know how to conserve it in such a way that I probably won't ever have to be broke again.'

If he were of a mind to let it bother him more, Jackson might find it awkward acting alongside those he knows are benefiting from his industry's secular view of his worth. He tries not to take any grudges to a personal level where his co-stars are concerned. 'It's not their fault,' he reasons. 'They can't say, "I want to take $8 million less so Sam can make more money."' And it's not as if Jackson can say to Travolta, 'So, John, next time you get a job, why don't you take $15 million so I can get, like, five of those millions?'

As an obvious counter to Jackson's argument, black star Denzel Washington happily trousers more than $10 million for his movies. Eddie Murphy, for a while one of the world's highest-paid entertainers, also commanded huge amounts during his peak. Unfortunately, they are the exceptions: one is the David Beckham of black cinema, guaranteed to punch above his weight as far as salaries are concerned, due to his status as a sought-after heart-throb and Oscar-friendly package. The other had established a career as a controversial comedian and could bring his comedy audiences across. By contrast, Wesley, Laurence and Morgan have spent most of their careers earning nothing like these sums. Considering they lead the way, along with Jackson, in terms of black movie clout, it seems to support the race-related view.

As if to prove it, Jackson's final project of 1995 featured a fresh-faced young buck called Matthew McConaughey. He is white. As he had done with Halle Berry on *Jungle Fever*, Jackson took it upon himself to share with the new talent a few of his experiences and insights. One such pearl of wisdom was that McConaughey would be earning more than Jackson within a year's time. The kid wouldn't have it. 'He laughed and said, "No I won't. Come on, you're the man," ' Jackson says. 'And I said, "Yeah, but you're the white man." Sure enough, Matthew's making more money than me now.'

While *The Great White Hype*'s domestic take of $8 million meant that paying Jackson anything like Denzel-type figures for that movie was out of the question, there were far greater box-office hopes attached to *A Time to Kill*, which kicked off shooting in September 1995 in the hothouse town of Canton, Mississippi. Assembled by Joel Schumacher, the cast for the adaptation of John Grisham's first book was a popular mix of established and new names. Whatever went on in negotiations, Jackson was glad for the role: it was another lead of sorts, with his character the keystone on whose plausibility the movie stood. As he says of the period, 'I was still making more money than I ever dreamed of.' In this instance, almost half of Washington's fee.

Top target for the lion's share of the budget was *American Beauty* star Kevin Spacey, who plays a lawyer out to convict Jackson's character Carl Lee Hailey. *Speed* screamer Sandra Bullock provided female distraction while Jackson and McConaughey vied for centre stage. The movie is essentially a courtroom drama in the Grisham tradition, but with a sickening plot at its core. Jackson's character murders two white men who have raped his ten-year-old daughter. It's a last resort act of vengeance, driven by the knowledge that the wealthy young white men would never be punished judicially in the Deep South where the movie is set. America's race problem is exposed with every scene, from the original crime to the authorities' attitudes and even the arrival of the Ku Klux Klan themselves.

After the race-heavy slapstick of *The Great White Hype*, *A Time to Kill* provided Jackson with a wake-up call about his personal beliefs and served as a reminder about the hardships of his own upbringing. Vast set pieces in the movie involved riots between fully robed and hooded KKK members and the National Guard. Jackson was not the only one who found the scenes a little too close to recent historical truth for it to be truly entertaining. In a town like Canton (population 10,000) there is still a visible black/white divide which finds the majority of each colour living in houses on either side of the railroad. There was a tangible feeling that the spectre of the real Klan could emerge at any moment. 'We were afraid something was actually going to happen in town,' Sandra Bullock admits. 'They'd say action and I would just pray that when they said cut, the riot would stop.'

Given the sheer scale of the crowd battles, Bullock's fear stood a chance of coming true. 'Imagine trying to communicate "cut" to 350 people who are all beating each other up,' the movie's cinematographer Peter Menzies Jr said to *American Cinematographer*. 'When the loudspeakers were ignored, my crew had to run into the crowd to physically stop the action.'

Bullock, of course, is white. Some black residents involved in the filming found the process cathartic. Director Schumacher recalls one woman who released decades of repression at the sight of members of the Klan hurling abuse and rocks at her father during his participation in one of the peace marches at the height of the Civil Rights Movement. 'At the time, Dr King did not want protesters to react in any way,' Schumacher says. 'But in the movie she gets to hit the Grand Dragon of the Ku Klux Klan in the face with her bag and tell him off.'

Involving the local townspeople as extras for the mass demo scenes was both an intelligent and a potentially divisive decision. But to many Canton residents, the sight of the evil Klan parading their vicious hatred on public streets held too many memories of a time only a few decades earlier for it to be glorified for the purposes of entertainment. For those who did participate, there were some bizarrely incongruous images. 'You'd be eating lunch and there would be one of these KKK guys with his hood off, laughing and talking with a black neighbour,' Menzies says. 'It was surreal.'

Joking aside, there were aspects of the shoot that turned the stomachs of its experienced team. The brutal rape scene was conducted on a closed set miles from where the majority of the film personnel were based with the ten remaining crew members hidden by a black cloth. When it was over, Schumacher and Menzies watched only one take of the 'dailies', 'because it was the kind of thing you could only watch once,' the latter says.

If building the scene had this effect on its executors, imagine the impact its real-life depiction would have had on the father of the victim. Widely considered to be Grisham's finest work, *A Time to Kill* is actually semi-autobiographical. The sickening assumption, therefore, is that this crime, or something very close to it, actually happened while he was a practising lawyer at the start of his career. By refusing to hand over film rights to the book, despite it being his first, until he was assured of huge swathes of editorial control over issues like choosing a director and casting, Grisham reveals how personal and how important the story is to him. It was certainly a pressure felt by all the actors involved.

In this situation, there really is no better man than Samuel L. Jackson. For the near four months of the *A Time to Kill* shoot in sweltering Mississippi, he resonated the anger of his character, Carl Lee Hailey. The 'biography' he wrote for Hailey was the usual thorough work – 'I walked pigeon-toed like one of my uncles, and I talked like one of my grandfather's brothers,' he explains. 'I knew who my character was, and what he embodied.' This time, though, he was able to invest the character with a large degree of his own personal experience at racists' hands. The whole ethos of biting his tongue in the face of provocation, walking away at the first sign of trouble, awoke responses in his body that he had hoped would never be triggered again.

As with the townsfolk of Canton, he shared an uncomfortable past with the movie's fictional storyline. He could also sense a familiar presence as he strolled around the town, doing things that were second nature to him, but unheard of among the residents. 'The new South is run by integrationists,' he says. 'But there is still an old South there. In Canton I used to eat in restaurants that black people didn't go to. They could, but they didn't – you know what I mean?'

It was the same story on the local golf course. 'My assistant and I were the only two black people to ever play there,' Jackson said to the *Toronto Sun*. 'It was surrounded by cotton fields so you can imagine what it used to be. I could almost hear the slaves singing.'

Given his natural affinity with the locale and the way he had his character nailed, *A Time to Kill* should have been Jackson's finest hour. It was a multi-million-dollar project from the team that had brought us *The Client* and *Batman Forever* and it featured a stellar cast – Spacey, Bullock, Donald and Keifer Sutherland, Ashley Judd, Brenda Fricker and, from Jackson's NEC days, the inspirational Charles Dutton. It provided Hollywood's first all-out attempt at capturing something of the racial maelstrom of America's not-too-distant past and a chance to open a serious debate on vigilantism. It was, on paper, everything that Jackson could wish for. And then he saw a screening. Having reached a position in his life where his colour was no longer an impediment to his success (only to his bank balance), Jackson suddenly found himself vulnerable because of his race when he least expected it. For all the good work that Schumacher and co had embarked upon with the faithful telling of *A Time to Kill*, Jackson felt they had chickened out in the final reckoning and played up the influence of the tale's white characters at the expense of his own. Somewhere, he surmised, a decision had been taken to devalue his character in the eyes of the movie-goers. This, of course, happens all the time in every movie; but in *A Time to Kill*, where the racial balance is so crucial to its success, any tempering either way could send out clear editorial signals that were never meant to be included. And this, in Jackson's opinion, whether by accident or design, is what happened.

In a nutshell, Jackson's key speech – his Ezekiel moment of the movie – was cut and the words given to new white kid on the block McConaughey. In a stroke, the sympathy for the black character was decimated. Mass audience identification with his position was thrown away.

'I was slightly upset,' Jackson says with menacing understatement. In the version he shot, his character tells Jake Brigance everything that Brigance later relates to the jury. To Jackson's mind, you needed to hear these words from the mouth of the so-called 'killer' to empathise with his position. But it didn't happen. 'Almost every reference I made to my daughter which humanises the character, was cut.' As a result, the man seen in the film now seems devious and calculating and acting out of brute revenge. 'What we shot was a man who loved his daughter so much he wanted to make the world a better place for her.'

Schumacher's response is typically conciliatory. Jackson, he says, is overreacting and there is no conspiracy theory. 'The movie was four hours and everybody had a scene that was cut out,' he said in 1996. 'But Sam did it beautifully, it was difficult to cut it out.' As a placebo, the director said he hoped the full four-hour version would eventually appear on the laser disc version. (For the record, it hasn't happened yet.)

When *A Time to Kill* in its abridged glory hit the screens in 1996 (July in the States; September in Europe), Jackson found himself asked one question more than another. A lot of Hollywood stars would have devised a tactical response after the first instance. Jackson never did. Asked what he would do if Zoe ever fell victim to such obscene violence, his reply was invariably cold, measured and honest. He would have to take action if he were in Hailey's place he told *Time Out* in 1996. While he probably wouldn't take the law into his own hands and kill the perpetrators, 'because I have the level of affluence that I have and the kind of attitude that I have, I might see to it that somebody did something more to them when they got into jail.'

It was elements of this personal investment in his character of Hailey that would be noticed by reviewers when the movie opened. After an indifferent run of Grisham adaptations – *The Firm* and *The Client* – there were low expectations of yet another trial-by-numbers outing. But surprisingly, considering that both Schumacher and screenwriter Akiva Goldsman would later bring us the execrable *Batman & Robin*, *A Time to Kill* touched a lot of people in the same way that *To Kill a Mockingbird* had done decades earlier.

'The best Grisham adaptation yet,' insisted *Empire*. 'Intelligent, sexy, and reliably gripping until the jury delivers its tantalising verdict.' Carl Lee Hailey won special mention: 'Jail-bound Jackson, as taut as a piano string, is fantastic.' The *New York Times* agreed. 'The case is that of Carl Lee Hailey, who is played by a scorchingly terrific Samuel L. Jackson and who by any reasonable measure should be the film's most important character.'

The public responded. The domestic box office for *A Time to Kill* reached $109 million – almost 10 per cent more than the throwaway fare of *Die Hard with a Vengeance*. The message as far as Jackson was concerned was clear: audiences of all colours will support intelligent film-making. Whether or not they would have flocked in their thousands to see a film in which the central white character was not artificially boosted into such a classic hero, however, would never be known.

14. I DON'T KNOW IF WE'RE GOING THAT WAY, SAM

Samuel L. Jackson is not the sort of person who can be typecast. He won't allow it. Regardless of the financial enticements available to reprise a popular role, he is not interested. Even if he were the sort to take the money and run, the chances of him following the emotional cauldron that was *A Time to Kill* with another race-challenging script were very slight indeed. No, what he needed after four months of sweat and anguish in the Mississippi sunshine was something slightly less demanding, maybe something a bit more fun. In short, what he needed was a good, old-fashioned action movie.

On paper, *The Long Kiss Goodnight* was just what the doctor ordered. Adrenalin-pumping action based around a daft plot and some wicked lines. Even its location of sub-zero Toronto offered something as diametrically opposite to *A Time to Kill*'s suffocating heat as imaginable.

Unfortunately, on paper is where Samuel Jackson's problems started, not ended. When he first picked up the $4 million Shane Black script – a record-breaking fee for one screenplay, even if the writer was responsible for *Lethal Weapon* and *The Last Boy Scout* – Jackson was immediately taken by the character of ex-con turned private eye Mitch Hennessey. It did not occur to Jackson that Hennessey was 'white'. Unfortunately, it did not occur to the writer and the movie's producers that Hennessey might be black.

It was that time again. 'I was told, "I'm sorry, I don't know if we're going that way, Sam,"' Jackson recalls. The producers, who between them were responsible for *Terminator II*, *Forrest Gump* and *True Lies*, had pictured *The Long Kiss Goodnight* as a whites-only buddy romp between a man and a woman. Think *Thelma and Louise* meets *True Romance*. It wasn't that they were anti-black, it just wasn't a consideration. Why did it matter? For one very good reason.

UK audiences, for all their faults, think nothing when the orange-skinned Kat in *EastEnders* falls into bed with the black Dr Trueman. It's a way of life in the United Kingdom that is reflected, without any comeback, on British television and in British movies. Unfortunately, for all the work of the last half a century, American television is still less likely to show anything so radical as a mixed relationship, especially one that involves a black man and a white woman. From *LA Law* to *Baywatch* to *Friends*, there is an unspoken exclusion zone around one particular type of storyline. In the country that hosted the farcical O.J. Simpson trial, the Rodney King riots and a series of racist attacks carried out by the NYPD, there were no extra viewers to be gained in the 90s and before by showing an interracial relationship. The centuries-old distrust that Shakespeare's audiences had concerning Othello's marriage to the alabaster-skinned Desdemona was still redolent in certain parts of the USA when Laurence Fishburne played the Moor in the excellent 1995 remake. Little had changed.

As Jackson is aware, it is not as straightforward or simplistic to say that the movie-producing arm of middle-class America must be racist because it chooses not to produce mixed-race pictures at the same rate at which it churns out whites-only love stories. Hollywood's problem, like that of any manufacturer of any product, is that they have to meet demand. If they don't, they go out of business. If that demand is found to be non-existent for films of a certain hue, then so shall the supply be. It's the same logic that says that viewers are more likely to watch Russell Crowe carry off wearing a skirt as *Gladiator* than Russell Grant. No hidden agenda. No social programme. Supply and demand, simple as that.

But when you happen to be that actor campaigning for the part and you are made privy to the various changes that will have to happen before you can be given it, you have to question the priorities of the major studios. There is a moral element to this process that is mostly swept under the carpet, just like the acknowledged discrepancies between black and white Oscar winners. Before Samuel Jackson could be given the part of Hennessey in *The Long Kiss Goodnight* opposite Geena Davis, one alteration in particular had to be made.

'The leads originally fell into bed together, and now they don't,' Jackson relates calmly. 'There's something threatening about a person like me having a relationship with one of their goddesses.'

Fact: most black men on the silver screen do not have sex with white women. Denzel Washington and Wesley Snipes both did in two Spike Lee films, but that was 'black cinema'. Those pictures might have earned $16 million and $32 million respectively at the US box office, but they were still not considered mainstream. They were pitched to black audiences and, in black cinema, anything goes – that appears to be the condescending logic of mainstream Hollywood studios. Look at the exploitation flicks of the 1970s.

That is not to say it never happens elsewhere; you can't miss it when examples do crop up due to the amount of column inches generated in the US press. It seems to be, however, that TV is the more likely medium in which such experiments get aired – a cynic might argue that a long-running series has a secure enough fan base to risk occasional controversy. Whatever the logic, five years after *The Long Kiss Goodnight* was being put together, *The West Wing* ran a storyline where the President's daughter dated a black man. In 1999, Ally McBeal also stepped out with a black doctor. Even *ER*'s Eriq La Salle, after almost a decade on the show, had an affair with Alex Kingston's white colleague.

More common, but still unusual, are relationships between ethnic-background women and non-black men. Strangely enough, for all their politically incorrect leanings in other areas, the James Bond films have always led the pack regarding this strand of miscegenation. Pierce Brosnan happily leapt into the sack with Halle Berry's Jinx in *Die Another Day* and Michelle Yeoh (an Asian actress) in *Tomorrow Never Dies*. By the same token, Roger Moore's 007 was rarely without a black love interest, from his first venture in *Live and Let Die* to his last in *A View to a Kill* (where he judo'd his way into bed with Grace Jones's Mayday). *High Fidelity* (John Cusack and Lisa Bonet), *Boiler Room* (Giovanni Ribisi and Nia Long) and even *The Road to Eldorado* – a cartoon – also tackled the issue. Most prominently, Tom Cruise got jiggy with Thandie Newton in *Mission: Impossible II*. And nobody batted an eyelid. When it works the other way round, however, then American producers seem to anticipate a problem.

Within a year of Jackson's experience, there would be another famous case. After decades of sterling work, one of America's greatest ever actors finally got his first solo lead role in a movie. His name was Morgan Freeman. The film, *Kiss the Girls*, was an adaptation of James Patterson's novel. Like Jackson, however, Freeman was only given the part once certain changes had been made. Despite the book building to a love affair between its black protagonist and the younger doctor, the movie balked at having Freeman enter into a physical relationship with Ashley Judd. By 1997, there had been interracial scenes in *One Night Stand* and *Bad Company*, but still there was resistance within the industry as a whole, as the *New York Post* pointed out in October 1997. 'Gays can kiss. White men can kiss black women. But a black man smooching with a white woman is still a Tinseltown taboo. What are they afraid of?'

If that was bad, there was originally talk of recasting the part of Alex Cross in *Kiss the Girls* – literally. One studio who talked about the rights, James Patterson revealed, wanted to make Alex Cross white. 'This is the first time Morgan has had a lead solo,' he said, horrified at the very idea. 'It's the first time one of the best actors in the world has had a leading role in which he's not playing a sidekick.'

For Jackson, in his 49th year, experiencing this kind problem was annoying, little else. He had faced worse insults and survived. That is not to say he was happy to see the screenplay changes, but he had long since learned to internalise his issues and vent them at the appropriate time. This was the game he had chosen to play; he would conduct himself by the rules in place in order to win. 'The sooner you know your function in Hollywood the better,' he says. 'Film-makers know that women like to look at Denzel, that's fine.' But he still regretted the missed opportunity. 'When I read the script, I loved it and all the sexual tension between the two main characters,' he says. As soon as he won the part, that was struck out. A $4 million script was suddenly rewritten. There's a compliment for Jackson in there somewhere . . .

Actually, winning the part was not so straightforward. Like a lot of things it depended on luck – Jackson's middle name – and his innate charm. It didn't hurt either that he had taken the decision those years ago to move to LA. When he happened to come across Davis and her husband Renny Harlin in a Hollywood eaterie, Jackson was quick to make known his interest in the picture. The celebrity couple, fresh from the disaster that was *Cutthroat Island*, had optioned the Black script; she would star, he would direct. The fact that Jackson was one of the few people in the world actually not to hate the pirate romp – 'hey, I liked *Cutthroat Island*,' he says – may have swung it.

Despite it being the most expensive script in history, *The Long Kiss Goodnight*'s author insists that the six rewrites it undertook were for reasons other than a fear of showing black-on-white sex. 'The problem was New Line bought a script as it was written for a $100 million movie,' Black says, 'but they only had $65 million.' As a result, a lot of work was done to streamline and economise the film. It wasn't made easier by the fact his director and star were filming in Malta at the time so communication was by fax. The most he will allude to regarding his male lead's colour change is this: 'We would try various drafts to make the plot work and the character work,' he told *Creative Screenwriting*. 'When Sam Jackson came on board we were all ecstatic.'

The way round the miscegenation problem was inventively done. At one point Davis's character comes on to Jackson's – and he actually says no. 'Not because he's not attracted to her, not because he doesn't think she's sexy or could probably use a good fuck about that time, but because he says this is bullshit,' Black reveals. He doesn't want to be used to help her erase her past – Hennessey happens to like her past. 'Scumbag' though he is, he plays a part in her redemption at this point.

Lack of sexual activity aside, there were several reasons for Jackson to maintain his composure once the part was his: six million of them, to be precise. Having lavished so much money on the script, the producers could hardly turn down Jackson's agents' demands for pay parity with other stars.

As a result he walked onto the Ontario set that first morning in January 1996, knowing he was earning the biggest pay packet of his life. It wasn't Denzel's $10 million and it certainly wasn't Travolta's twenty; but it was a sign. A sign that his brand was finally being valued.

The plot that cost so much money was, as you'd expect from Shane Black, another inversion of the buddy movie theme. This time a former government assassin, played by Davis, has amnesia and consequently spends eight years baking cookies and being a regular American Dream mom. Forced to defend herself against an intruder – nobody wields a lemon meringue like Davis – Samantha Caine begins to realise her past life might be worth investigating. Hooking up with seedy private eye Hennessey, the pair begin to hunt down her previous employers before they silence her once and for all. A stunningly slimy performance from Patrick Malahide, unforgettable as Arthur Daley's foil Inspector Chisholm in *Minder*, merely adds to the intrigue.

Getting his teeth into a physical part after the straitjacketed restrictions of Carl Lee Hailey's inner violence certainly appealed to the kid in Jackson. 'Action films are great,' he enthuses. 'Playing cops and robbers, doing all this stuff that you did as kids, except I'm shooting people and their chests are blowing up and nobody's saying, "You missed me!" '

And yet for all the running around, it was the relationship aspect of the movie – the human part – that first connected with him. 'If you accept a woman who's lost her memory and is trying to discover herself, and a guy trying to get a grip on her as well as on who he is, the stuff happening around becomes secondary,' he says.

Following the watery flop of *Cutthroat Island*, Harlin and Davis had a lot riding on the movie. With the highlights of their track records fading fast in the notoriously goldfish-memoried world of movies (Harlin had directed *Die Hard II* and *Cliffhanger*; Davis grabbed fame by the throat in *Thelma and Louise*), they needed things to go their way. Fortunately, despite an arduous and physical shoot in freezing conditions encountered during Canada's coldest winter for a decade, their luck held out. Just. But, mere hours after shooting had wrapped at a 125-year-old local landmark in Ontario, the building burned to the ground. The sight of firefighters fruitlessly trying to drill for water in a nearby frozen lake will linger long in the memories of those present.

Trying to practise his close combat skills (inspired by the years of watching all those kung fu flicks) and quick shooting prowess in near arctic conditions was a new experience for Jackson, especially when he was in costume and the whole crew was wearing Arctic Iditarod thermals. 'They got on these moon boots so their feet are all warm and toasty, and I got on Guccis with these dime-thick soles,' he moans.

The warmest day, according to the star, was minus three or four degrees. The coldest day featured a windchill factor of minus 98. The day he and Davis had to venture into the lake, he says, went as low as minus 47. If it weren't for the crew members assigned to keep butane heaters fixed on them between takes, he doubts he would be around to recount the tale today. 'As soon as Renny said, "Cut," they'd run straight to us with these heaters,' he recalls. 'We also had these warm-up huts made out of that silver spacesuit stuff.'

The important thing is, however, he looked good. Apart from *The Great White Hype* which dressed him like Sylvester Stallone's mother on a night on the tiles, he had not had occasion to dress so fine since *Pulp Fiction* – the suits part, not the beachwear. In severe contrast to Hailey's drab apparel to match his drab persona, Hennessey is all shiny black and Kangol hats, or green caps and check slacks. The difference is amazing: a full ten years seems lost between the first role and this as Jackson hurtles from one staggering set piece to another. It's as if he reshot his *Die Hard* role directed by Gianni Versace.

Another return to *Pulp Fiction* form was Harlin and Black's decision to tap into Jackson's ability to play comedy within a thriller framework. Hennessey's lines come alive with his touch: 'When we first met you were, "Oh phooey, I burned the darn muffins," ' he tells Davis's Charlie Baltimore. 'Now, you go into a bar and ten minutes later sailors come running out.' Another time sees him nonchalantly draw on a cigarette while laying prostate in a road having been flung from a speeding car. Another sees him scat a Muddy Waters-style riff detailing his day's deeds prior to busting a few heads. Later he tells Davis that he'll be waiting downstairs for her to rescue him – again. It's all great stuff, expertly delivered by a master dialogue reader opposite a bona fide action star who looks better in a white vest than even Bruce Willis. Praise indeed.

Considering the shoot started in January, every day that passed promised slightly warmer weather. With 80 per cent of the work slated for outdoors, it couldn't get there quickly enough. By the time the movie wrapped, there was still snow on the ground, but that did not stop Jackson raving about his work. This, he declared, was one superior action movie. And as for his co-star: 'Geena's going to be major again,' he insisted. Anything less for a six-foot-plus woman in a leather catsuit and peroxide hair would be rude.

In fact, Jackson's entire recollection of working with the husband and wife team is a positive one, admitting he felt like the nice brother-in-law who shared their one-bedroom apartment with them and was privy to everything in their lives. The only downside, according to Jackson, was the lovey-dovey stuff. If Davis wanted to retake a scene, hubby was more than willing to oblige:

'Oh yes, my puppy, we can do another one for you. Sam would you like another one, too?'

'Yeah, yeah. But just stop talking like that, OK?'

Jackson was even more embarrassed by the couple's talk when it actually involved him. In the closest thing the movie comes to a sex scene, Charlie pushes Mitch up against a wall in order to have her wicked way with him. No actor admits to enjoying love scenes (the liars); but you can believe them if hubby is in the room too. 'Geena's doing all this stuff to me,' Jackson says. 'And I can here this Nordic voice saying, "All right, now lick his neck. Now more tongue in his ear. Yes! Now grab his thigh." ' It was, he says, like having your girlfriend's husband in the closet with the video camera, yelling out instructions.

Amazingly for a major studio production, the turnaround on *The Long Kiss Goodnight* was so rapid that a finished version was released in time to cash in on the spend-happy pre-Christmas crowds that same year. As far as the reviewers could see, however, no corners had been cut. Those who survived viewing *Cutthroat Island* would be shocked to learn that *The Long Kiss Goodnight* was actually a superbly entertaining action movie, reckoned *Sight and Sound*, perhaps the best of the year's many shoot-'em-ups. Jackson in particular stole the show, 'injecting more aggression, sardonic wit and complexity into what is basically the black second-banana role that Danny Glover developed in *Lethal Weapon* and Jackson himself honed in *Die Hard: With a Vengeance*'. It was a view backed up by *Premiere* who said, 'It is Jackson who steals the show and provides the soul of the movie.'

Empire weighed in with four stars and the opinion that Davis has the Stallone/Schwarzenegger market sewn up. As for our man: 'much of the fun comes from the pairing of Davis and Jackson and the way Black flips their roles. Jackson is the perfect sidekick, allowing Davis to show she can be a convincing action heroine.'

Variety's main concern was whether Davis's character could prosper in a market that had already seen *Barb Wire*, *Nikita* and *The Quick and the Dead* slump. It decided she could. 'She fills the bill of a smart, tough, capable femme operative as well as anyone could. Playing a lifelong loser with a lively sense of humour, Jackson lightens the proceedings in a welcome manner.'

Released during the same season as the likes of Mel Gibson's *Ransom*, Stallone's oddly likeable *Daylight*, *Mars Attacks!* and *Star Trek: First Contact*, *The Long Kiss Goodnight* initially recouped only a measly $33 million of its $90 million budget at the US box office, although its international appeal more than doubled that return. Either way, it proved two things: that the best reviews in the world can't buy you viewers; and that nobody wants to see a female Bruce Willis. Shame.

With hindsight, Jackson feels the promotional tone was wrong. 'I think the studio made a huge mistake by not marketing it at women,' he says. 'Women like to see themselves empowered. That story had heart, and it had bullets and it had explosions and car chases.'

One of the reasons the movie did better in Europe was down to the tireless promotional efforts of our man Jackson in plugging the movie. As far as he is concerned, doing the rounds of interviews, meeting with different suits, pressing the flesh at pointless junkets is part and parcel of being a top-of-the-range actor. He is totally aware that his role on a film does not end with the wrap party.

'Talking to you is part of my job,' he told *The Times'* Martyn Palmer in 2000, 'so I don't resent not playing golf in the sun today. I've got to give the best interview I can.' If Palmer left saying, 'Man, he was cool. He was all right,' then Jackson has succeeded.

Even before the atrocities of 9/11, getting a major American star to visit such exotic and far-flung outposts as London or Paris or Madrid was never as easy as getting them to hop on a plane for a sometimes longer stretch of time between LA and NY. When the Big Names did deign to drop in, then you can be sure that local media made a fuss. Even with his seemingly never-ending cycle of films to promote, Samuel L. Jackson was a huge name in Europe in 1996. Despite his own theories, *Die Hard* and *A Time to Kill* had merely kept him in gainful employment since 1994 in most people's minds. He would forever be Jules Winnfield in the UK, and for that fact alone he would always be welcome back.

It is very rare that a star gains much from the PR stings that take place in every major city during film-opening time. Obviously they benefit from their film being seen and their salary potentially rising and, if you're so inclined, there's often the chance of a round or two on the local golf courses. Generally, though, nothing really tangible ever comes of the whole schlepping around the world thing. But, as Samuel Jackson was to learn, there is always a first time.

During a frenetic round of interviews during his brief stopover in the UK in November 1996, Jackson made himself as available and as agreeable to as many people as possible. One of the interviews he conducted for *The Long Kiss Goodnight* was on Chris Evans' *TFI Friday*, then the coolest show in town for its mix of big names, live music and comedy. After ten minutes of flattery from the host, interspersed by a few clips of Hennessey and Baltimore leaping out of tall buildings, Evans asked the question that was to change one of their lives: 'Is there anybody you would really like to work with?'

Fazed for a brief moment, Jackson thought. And then he said: 'George Lucas.' The buzz in the movie business at the time was that the first prequel to *Star Wars* was in the pipeline. Nobody had seen the script, nobody knew what on Earth – or Tatooine – it was going to be about.

Pushed by Evans, out came Jackson's love of the whole *Star Wars* saga. Turning to the camera for a moment, he said that, if you're watching George, he'd love to play a role – absolutely anything – in the next movie. And that was that. Cue applause, some daft Danny Baker joke and live music to end. As he left the Hammersmith studios in his chauffeured limo, Jackson thought nothing more of what he'd said on the show. But on a state-of-the-art ranch in a country far, far away, a certain bearded movie mogul would get to hear of the night's events.

15. WE WANT THEM TO KNOW WHO JACKIE WILSON IS

Rarely in this life does anyone get something for nothing. And rarely do things happen without there being a knock-on effect somewhere else down the line. It's the ripple effect, six degrees of separation, causality syndrome – call it what you will. Whatever the phenomenon's name, its net result was impacting on three lives in the Encino area of California during spring 1996. The more Samuel Jackson's career blossomed, the greater the demands on his time from outside his home. Many films get shot at the various studios around LA. But many don't. It just so happened, with the weeks spent freezing his butt off in Ontario coming so soon after the months in the Deep South (the Christmas period excluded), that Samuel Jackson: Family Man had taken a back seat recently.

Part of him is happy to get away. 'I love going on location,' he says. 'When I'm at home it's a lot harder than at work. I wash dishes, make beds, go to the grocery store, do all those things. I have days off when I go on location!' It's a decent claim, but the admission of such domesticity betrays the truth: Jackson enjoys his home life and has few of the airs or graces that can afflict so many movie lifestyles.

Even when he is not on location, life doesn't sound too bad. For a start there is the golf. He has been known to play 54 holes in one day. Rumour has it there is even something called the 'Jackson Clause' in his contracts which stipulates that serious golf time must be built into all location shoots. Obsessive? Him? And then there's the work. Meetings, auditions, rehearsals – they all take place in the shadow of the Hollywood sign. On top of that, it never hurts to be seen by other industry players. It's amazing the people you can bump into on a golf course or in a restaurant or at a theatre. Anywhere else it's called socialising. In Hollywood it's networking.

Away from his empire building, the Jackson take on life is very straightforward. He starts his day with a prayer thanking the Lord for getting him through the reckless years. He flicks on a TV to catch up with the news, then he has breakfast with his family if they're around. (Some of LaTanya's roles occasionally take her out of town; Zoe would eventually move out to go to Vassar College.) It's a simple life, a normal life, but then that's the kind of man he is. 'I'm a very normal kind of guy who happens to have a very extraordinary job,' he says, 'and I value my family for making sure I remember that.'

Apart from his immediate family, Jackson is also devoted to his heritage. He has lost none of the passion for the advancement of black rights and the propagation of black culture since he was a jobbing theatre trainee all those years ago. One of the worst aspects of his millionaire lifestyle in Encino is the fact that it all seems a million miles – and years – from the struggles of the recent past. The odd champagne socialist apart, most former firebrands find it tricky to maintain the anarchic fire of one's youth when the cash starts pouring in.

Supported in all things by LaTanya, his soulmate on this subject as on so many others, Jackson decided to do something about it. Watching their daughter grow up into a beautiful and intelligent young lady, they were adamant that she would not miss out on the race consciousness that had so defined their lives. With that in mind, both LaTanya and Samuel are founding members of a group called Onyx Village, an exotic kind of support group for African-Americans working in the US entertainment industry. The Village arranges events and activities designed to educate children about their heritage and open their eyes to the riches of their collective past.

'We want them to learn the tradition of being coloured,' LaTanya told *Essence* magazine. 'We're very proud of that tradition. We want them to know about the Civil Rights Movement and the ancient kingdoms of Africa.' Her husband is more direct: 'We want them to know who Jackie Wilson is. These kids go to school with mostly white kids. We decided to make them all be black together.'

Education is an important tenet in the Jackson household. Both LaTanya and Samuel worked hard for their higher education qualifications before embarking on their search for the rainbow. They would take the same approach with Zoe if she were to suddenly announce her intention of following in their footsteps. 'I hate to sound old-school about it, but I still say you've got to have an education,' LaTanya says. 'You need a degree. Why? Because you never know.'

Jackson's dedication to his family and his commitment to education showed in his next work project after *The Long Kiss Goodnight*. Picking a movie that was to be shot, starting in June 1996, in nearby Pasadena would do wonders for his relationship with his at-that-awkward-age daughter. It would also give him and LaTanya a chance to spend some time together.

As for the education aspect? Well, the project was *187*, a gritty drama set in a tough Los Angeles state school. After sharing the limelight with Geena Davis on his last project, this was his second lead role, following *The Great White Hype*. If proof were needed about Jackson's claim never to typecast himself, look no further than the route that took him from his overblown comedic turn as Fred Sultan to this role as Trevor Garfield, hassled teacher extraordinaire. Sultan never had to give up working in a Brooklyn school after being stabbed a dozen times by a kid who's just missed a pass. Sultan never relocated to San Fernando in the hope of a better life. And Sultan never faced the hideous prospect of his new life being as terrifying as his last.

'187 is the homicide code for the Los Angeles police,' Jackson explains. 'And that's what the kids in the film keep telling me – they're going to pull a 187 on me. They mark it all over my house and my car.'

Garfield is trying to regain his love of teaching and lose his fear of being in the classroom but the harassment arrives on day one and he starts, Jackson says, to unravel. 'It's a study of how this guy becomes unglued through the system.'

Garfield is a man pushed to the edge of reason and his responses to the threats are unexpected and shocking. Jackson brilliantly builds on the kind of repressed anger so starkly evident in his portrayal of Carl Lee Hailey to create a character under quite unbelievable stress. Unlike other school movies, like Michelle Pfeiffer's *Dangerous Minds* or Sidney Poitier's *Blackboard Jungle* or John Singleton's *Higher Learning*, the film does not lead inexorably towards its happy ending. 'It's a lot darker,' Jackson says. Yes, Garfield manages to pull a few tricks to interest the hard of thinking for a few lessons, and yes he strikes up a relationship with pretty blonde Kelly Rowan, but the best he can manage is to tread water and to stay alive.

Speaking of water . . . the director for *187* was Kevin Reynolds, most spectacularly remembered for the production disasters *Waterworld* and *Rapa Nui*. He and his leading man nearly worked together before *187* when Jackson won a role in the former. 'I was trying to go to Hawaii so I could play golf,' he admits. But it was not to be. When the part of Zeus in *Die Hard* came up he had to turn Reynolds and *Water World* down.

After the experience of working with such actors as Kevin Costner, it was no surprise that Reynolds was impressed by the sheer level of technical ability that his new leading man brought to *187*. For a scene where Garfield is told he is fired, Jackson was able to produce a tear from one eye on command every take. 'It kind of amazed Kevin that every time we did it I could make that tear fall on the same word. It's actor tricks, but they work for an audience.'

Given the fact that tears were never far from his character's mind, the experience of turning up for work every day and becoming Garfield was a traumatic time for Jackson. His research had told him that one in nine teachers in America has been attacked at one point and that teaching environments like the one depicted in *187* really do exist. Originally though, he thought liberties had been taken with the realism. 'I thought the writer had taken dramatic licence to make the story more exciting,' he admits. When the actors and extras playing the pupils came in and said how realistic the story was in their experiences – some said their schools were even more dangerous – Jackson soon changed his mind. 'That's when I realised this was about something a lot scarier than I had thought. It's not just drama – this is life.

'It was shocking for me to find that these kids actually leave home some days and wonder if they are going to get back home,' he adds. By comparison, Jackson's own school had been fairly sedate. The fact that it was in a proper community where everyone knew each other and their families certainly helped. 'I never had any worries about being killed going to school, that's for sure.'

As a defence mechanism, he never let himself forget he was acting. It was a job that began in the morning and ended at night. 'When somebody says, "Cut!" I let it go,' he told *Movie Maker*. 'Who knows, I may have to talk to an agent. I can't have Trevor Garfield trying to make a deal for Sam Jackson!'

Clearly Jackson is persuasive enough as a deal-broker. For the second picture running, he had picked up on a script not intended for a black actor – ironically it had fallen into his hands in Canada during the previous film that didn't want to cast him. 'Initially there was some resistance from the studio,' he explains. 'In my mind it was a much more interesting story putting an African-American in that situation, rather than putting in a Caucasian teacher.'

For all Jackson's 'devastating performance' (*Empire*), the overall feel of the film is slightly too tricksy to be taken seriously as the bleak exposé it occasionally sets out to be. But it is shocking, which is just what Reynolds intended. Who is to blame for it not being the masterpiece both men hoped for? Jackson is diplomatic. 'My job is to give them an honest portrayal of Trevor Garfield,' he says. 'It is Kevin's job to cut this thing together and make it the story I read. A lot of times that doesn't happen.' Sometimes, he says, the film that ends up at the cinema is not the movie he shot – could he be talking about *A Time to Kill*, by any chance?

By the time *187* hit the movie theatres in 1997, Jackson had chipped in with a couple of days' shooting on the directorial debut of a friend of his. Steve Buscemi's *Trees Lounge* is a semi-autobiographical flick about a failed ice-cream van driver who mopes around a lot. And that's it. It was shot in 24 days and featured Buscemi, Chloe Sevigny, Mimi Rogers and Samuel Jackson as a trucker. While its overall mood is one of charming whimsy, the movie does not bear repeated viewing. But, as *Variety* declared, 'Buscemi has come out on top by taking on people and a place he clearly knows inside out.'

Unlike his pal Buscemi, Samuel Jackson has never felt frustrated at being known only as an actor. All his life that is all he has ever wanted to do; one only has to look at the number of parts he gets through to know it is a labour of love. What's more, he is good at it. The trouble with all these Hollywood hyphenates – the actor–directors, actor–producers etc. – is that they tend to be better at one of their jobs than the other. Take that ultimate multi-hyphenate Tarantino: screenwriter – brilliant; director – impressive; actor – next please . . .

Typically forthright, even his good friend Jackson admits this: 'You can tell Quentin he's a great director and you wouldn't be lying,' he says. 'But no one is really honest with him about his acting.' Despite turning in a decent performance as George Clooney's psycho brother in *From Dusk Till Dawn*, other performances haven't been as easy on the eye and ear. The sight of Tarantino creaking around the Broadway stage in the 1998 production *Wait Until Dark* was only tolerable because (a) the play co-starred the delectable Marisa Tomei; and (b) it was Tarantino up there, in the flesh. Despite scabrous, wrist-slashing reviews, the run sold out on his name alone but then so did Madonna's season in the 2002 West End production of *Up for Grabs*.

Jackson has no desire to direct: 'Hell, no,' he says, using his something-of-a-trademark phrase. And he means it. However, in 1996, when he came across a script that was struggling to make the transition to the big screen for financial reasons, he realised that he was in a position to save the day. *Eve's Bayou* had just got itself a brand new producer.

The total budget for Kasi Lemmons's debut as writer and director was just over $3 million – virtually half of Jackson's salary for *The Long Kiss Goodnight*. But as soon as Jackson saw the script from his old New York theatre pal, he knew that although this was one of those roles that did not put gas in the Mercedes, he had to do it. No sooner had Lemmons secured her star's signature as producer and actor than independent film company Trimar greenlit the movie.

Jackson is amused by the chain of events. 'Three million? Is that all I'm worth?' he laughs. He shouldn't have worried. When the movie went on to earn $15 million at the US box office, his producer hat suddenly became rather lucrative.

Most famous to movie audiences as Agent Starling's roommate in *The Silence of the Lambs*, Kasi Lemmons had only made the switch from acting to writing when she realised she wasn't winning the kinds of parts that moved her. And she only decided to step up as director when she couldn't work out who could possibly do justice to her intricately personal tale.

'I'd written many short stories about the Batiste family,' she told *Total Film*. 'Then I started dreaming about them and they'd talk to me in my sleep. So I wrote *Eve's Bayou*.'

The film-making process is not for the faint-hearted, however, and even though everyone at Trimar loved her script, the money aspect proved insurmountable until her old friend Jackson's intervention. Even then it would be five years between first draft and premiere. By the time it came to the now-or-never crunch meeting with the studio, she was nine months pregnant and not feeling exactly hopeful. 'I was so nervous on the day I threw up,' Lemmons admits. 'I just thought, "Look at you, they're not going to give you money!" But they're crazy over there at Trimar and they did.'

The script that was causing all the commotion was, on the face of it, the straightforward tale of a black family living in 1960s Louisiana. The fact that the movie opens with its child narrator, Eve, saying 'I was ten the summer I killed my father' soon blew that theory out of the water. Jackson plays Louis, a respectable and respected middle-class doctor who is a wonderful family man in all ways bar one: he has an insatiable desire for extra-marital affairs. His long-suffering wife, played by Lynn Whitfield, in love with all the other aspects of his character, chooses to ignore the obvious when Louis says he's out late on 'house calls'.

When ten-year-old Eve witnesses Louis having sex with *Ally McBeal*'s Lisa Nicole Carson, however, the family harmony is destroyed for ever. Her various patricidal revenge ploys include tipping off Carson's cuckolded husband and seeking advice from the local voodoo practitioner, overplayed by Diahann Carroll. Anything to rid the family of her father.

It is not every movie that can reveal the main plot twist at the start and survive beyond the opening reel. We knew in *Carlito's Way*, for example, after the first five minutes, that Pacino's character would come to a painful end; the ensuing two hours were just a case of ticking off the minutes till it happened. *Eve's Bayou* runs a similar risk, but when Jackson's character meets his end it is still shocking and strangely unexpected, thanks largely to Lemmons's expert realisation of so many aspects of her characters' lives. The Creole voodoo element never borders on the far fetched; the tragic-in-love sorrow of Louis's sister never seems caricatured; Eve's own psychic visions never threaten to test our credulity in the picture; and, for all its hideous repercussions, the burgeoning incestuous relationship between Louis and his fourteen-year-old daughter Cisely is as neatly and 'naturally' played out as possible, revealed more after Louis's death than on camera. Nothing smacks of 'set piece' filming. Nothing appears by chance. Nothing is included to win audience numbers.

For all the character's moral shortcomings, thanks to Lemmons's realistic writing and yet another mesmerising performance from her leading man, Louis does not emerge as a two-dimensional panto villain. 'Most people are complicated,' Lemmons says. 'Most people have flaws they're trying to improve. Sometimes they fall victim to certain aspects of their character. Sometimes you can try and overcome it all your life.' And in her mind, at least, writing about people who are neither good nor evil is more interesting than taking sides.

For all his on-paper faults, there was enough about Louis's life to make Samuel Jackson identify with him. In particular, he empathised with the way Louis is in such demand from all the women in his life: mother, wife, daughters and lovers. Working away from home so often, Jackson admits to feeling a little shell-shocked at LaTanya and Zoe's competitive happiness to have him back. 'I understand about coming home and constantly being in that tug of war,' he told the *Guardian*. 'It's like, "OK, go to your corners, rest a minute and come out fighting."'

The entire shoot for *Eve's Bayou* lasted just thirty days, and rounded off Jackson's year nicely. After the harrowing anguish of playing Trevor Garfield in *187*, he almost ran into wardrobe for Louis Batiste's period suit and fedora. He also got into his role of producer and tried to be the cheerleader for the production. 'Sam was great,' Lemmons says. 'Very cool, very funny and very tall!' And for once, he did not even have to convince the producers that a black actor could play the role. (Co-producer Caldecot Chubb would surely not have stood in his illustrious partner's way.)

Eve's Bayou received its earliest public airings at the Telluride and Toronto Film Festivals, where Kasi Lemmons was honoured for her outstanding work. When the movie premiered in America in September 1997, critics and film-goers alike queued up to second that emotion. The National Board of Review gave her the Director's Debut Award and the NAACP Image Awards were swamped by nominations for the movie – its seven beat everything produced that year by the major studios, including DreamWorks' *Amistad*, Fox's *Soul Food* and Warner's *Rosewood*. Cash-wise, $15 million made it far and away the best-selling independent movie of the year.

For once the ladies and gentlemen of the Fourth Estate were in total agreement about the movie and its stars. Even the soundtrack seemed universally popular, especially Erykah Badu's title song, written by Curtis Mayfield. 'Cast against type, Jackson reveals a suave, romantic side to his versatile talent, which so far has been limited mostly to actioners and pulp fiction fare,' said *Variety*. 'A wonderfully absorbing tale, full of poetry and haunting imagery that's adeptly directed and superbly acted,' said *Total Film*. 'Jackson, as the womanising doctor, is convincingly charming despite his moral flaws.' 'Samuel L. Jackson's seductive but family-loving philanderer manages to be deeply likeable, in a performance played beautifully against type,' agreed *Sight and Sound*. 'Jackson brings a depth and charm to his role that makes it easy to understand both the duplicity of the man and his undeniable charm,' said *Starburst*. *Empire* went further: 'This film is that still shamefully rare pleasure, an absorbing ensemble piece in which a fine group of actors get to show their class and range, playing a black American family who are prosperous, cultured and complex.' Finally, *Neon*: 'Although the plot's bare bones imply worthiness, *Eve's Bayou* is anything but. There's far too much wit, ambiguity and visual panache at work for lumpen melodrama.'

Even its star was impressed: 'It is a powerful film that seemed to get a great reception,' he told the *Evening Standard*. 'Everyone should go see it.'

By the time the outside world had discovered the wonders of the film and foreign distribution was found to take it overseas, it was too late to squeeze it into most release schedules outside America. After the sly way it crept into theatres in the US via the festival circuit, there was a bit more money to throw at a British launch. Consequently, 6 August 1998 found Jackson at a glitzy shindig overlooking the Grand Union Canal in the newly refurbished Holloway Odeon. His movie was about to open against all the usual summer nonsense like his old mate Willis's *Armageddon*. Why would people watch *Eve's Bayou* when they could watch Liv Tyler getting tired and emotional with Ben Affleck? 'Because we have actors in our film,' Jackson told the *Evening Standard*. 'There is also a story. It has a beginning, a middle and an end.

'People like stories about people,' he added. 'There's not a lot of nonsense in this film. There are no dinosaurs or car chases' – this said, with a straight face, by a man days away from walking onto a bionic shark movie set.

The fact that the movie did so well in America caused the marketing bods at Trimar to investigate who was watching it. The result was surprising. Almost 80 per cent of the audience had been white – and this for a movie featuring no white actors. Jackson has his theory – 'Period costumes, no car chases or rap music,' he smiles – but the truth of the matter is that people will see a good movie, regardless. Although obviously a white actor would not have been considered for Louis's role, if anything, Jackson's oft-repeated point about black actors being suitable for more than 'black' parts is vanquished by these statistics.

Unfortunately, despite the fact that the movie contains little discussion of race per se – there just happen to be no white people in the town – the same cannot be said for the thousands of words that were written about it. In an article in *Cineaste* magazine, Mia L. Mask criticised one reviewer for saying 'to hail *Eve's Bayou* as the best African-American film ever would be to understate its universal accessibility to anyone on this planet.' This, on the face of it, high praise was really saying that the movie was 'too good to be stigmatised as a "black" film', according to *Mask*. In the minefield which is racism, this must go down as looking for an argument that is not there. Clearly in this instance 'black film' is just short-hand marketing speak. The original reviewer (Andrew Sarris) intends nothing more sinister than predicting *Eve's Bayou* will stand as an exceptional piece of film-making, likely to tap into the mainstream audience. For 'mainstream' read 'largely white', but since the majority of Americans are white, this is just fact.

Including *Eve's Bayou*, Samuel L. Jackson had taken part in four films in 1996. Leading man in two, co-lead in one, cameo in the fourth. He had also racked up his largest career pay cheque to date. As the year came to a close, he would have been forgiven for planning some quality time away from the 'business'. Just him, his family and his golf clubs – what could be better? Let someone else do some acting for a change . . .

16. I LIKE MY MONSTER MOVIES TO HAVE MONSTERS IN

In 2004, Samuel L. Jackson has the reputation of the hardest-working actor in town. There is a reason for that: he is.

While some stars carefully cherry-pick the next part that will cement their relationship with the Hollywood A list, others have less lofty ambitions. Samuel Jackson just wants to act, pure and simple. He doesn't mind what he has to do to his hair, what odd wigs he might have to wear, what costumes they put him in. As long as the part is an interesting one and a new challenge, he will do it. And, having just completed his role as a philandering, lying and incestuous paedophile, he doesn't worry too much about playing the good guy.

'There are certain actors who want to be liked in every film they're in,' he explains. 'I don't particularly care about that. I don't think I have to be Hollywood good-looking all the time.' For Jackson there is no greater film fault than characters waking up in the morning looking as stunning as when they went to bed – 'and you know their mouth tastes the same as when they went to sleep'.

As 1996 proved, Jackson does not even need to be playing the main character to be content. As long as he's working, he's happy. And as for those stories that he is a workaholic? He's just Elizabeth Jackson's son, that's all. Where he comes from in Tennessee, everybody in the house went to work every day bar the annual fortnight's holiday. 'I'm from a working-class family,' he says, 'that's how I know how to work. But it's not like I'm digging ditches every day. I'm grateful for the opportunities.' There is also the fact that, above everything else, acting is an art, like golf. As US legend Gary Player said, 'It's funnier how the harder I practise, the luckier I get.' It isn't through luck that Jackson has got his handicap to six. It's diligence, hard work and, most of all, practice. If he stopped playing as regularly, his tee shots would soon start drifting treewards. And it's the same with his acting. Use it or lose it. 'I work because I love my job,' he says. 'I can't sit at home and do one movie a year and continue to be as sharp.'

There are some limits, however. 'I love what I do, but I love my family more,' he insists. 'If I ever had to make a choice, the two women in my life would win every time.'

Fortunately for Jackson, no one has asked him to make that choice. And so he keeps working. And working. If outsiders thought 1996 had been an ambitious year, there was more to come. His diary for 1997 contained six films: two major studio blockbusters, one art-house project, one $12 million movie from the typewriter of a certain Mr Tarantino, one uncredited cameo – and one picture where he got to act alongside a little green guy with a speech impediment. Busy? Sure. Interesting? Absolutely.

Taking on so much work involves a lot of reading. Some scripts he likes, some he doesn't. But even if he does, there are no guarantees that even he can just walk into a part. There is a pecking order at work where casting is concerned, and Jackson is totally aware where he fits in. 'I get sent stuff they offer Mel Gibson or Harrison Ford that they don't want to do,' he says. 'And I'm sure Tom's fingerprints are probably on everything at a certain point.' Jackson even acknowledges that the star of the day at any point – like Matt Damon a few years ago – will probably get a look in before he gets a sniff. But that's just how it is.

For his first picture of 1997, Jackson found himself in exactly that position, of reading a script but not being wanted. Unlike so many other cases, however, this wasn't a question of 'we're not going that way, Sam'. The producers just happened to have somebody else in mind – in this case, Morgan Freeman, not Tom Cruise. When Freeman turned it down, Jackson was left with the choice of picking up his hero's cast-offs, or not. Ever the professional, he had no problem with it. 'I didn't have an inferiority complex just because I was the second choice,' he says, 'because I thought their first choice was right on. Following Morgan is no problem.'

The role in question was Charles Morritz in the New Line/Channel 4 production *The Red Violin*. In the movie, Morritz is a New York string specialist who dreams of discovering the perfect instrument. Hired by a Montreal auction house to assess a batch of instruments being sold by the Chinese government, he comes across a 400-year-old violin – the perfection of his dreams. Does he allow it to go to auction or snaffle it for himself?

As a schoolboy trumpet player, Jackson empathises with Morritz's musical passion. As LA's resident obsessive, he also knows a compulsion when he sees it. 'I totally understand his obsession with perfection,' he admits. 'Morritz has spent most of his career searching for this perfect acoustic instrument. Now he has it in his grasp.'

The idea of playing a basically decent guy having his morals so severely tested is what attracted Jackson to the role. 'Morritz is morally ambiguous,' Jackson says, which to his mind makes him far more interesting than a straight good or evil character who might have an obvious agenda – the same view as Jackson's friend Lemmons gave on his character in *Eve's Bayou*. It also helped that he had never played a character like this before. 'I've proven I can play bad, mean, ugly and cruel. Now, I want to prove I can play the guy next door.'

He even hoped he could learn something from Morritz. 'What he does is something very foreign to me and I like to do roles that allow me to discover hidden things about myself and to watch other characters and what they do.'

The biggest name among a cast of thousands (mainly Chinese), Jackson's scenes were filmed on location in Montreal, hometown of the movie's writer and director Francois Girard. Italy, China and Oxford provided the remainder of the film's backgrounds. With shooting beginning on 19 February, he once again had to endure another bracing Canadian winter. At least he had the thought of spending March and April in sunnier climes to get him through.

It didn't help Jackson's temperature that Morritz was written to be old – Morgan Freeman-old. One visit to the barber's later, and Jackson was sporting a William Hague cut. Not exactly flattering, and not exactly warm, either.

A lot of the pleasure of *The Red Violin* comes from Girard's use of music as a character, and from his portrayal of the violin's life through all its 400 years. As you would expect from the man who brought us *Thirty-Two Short Films About Glenn Gould*, it is not exactly linear. It's also not exactly what springs to mind when one thinks of a small Canadian film.

'It's a big film in my mind,' Jackson says. 'I thought the story was fantastic and I wanted to be part of an epic in the great Hollywood sense of what an epic is. It is also very independent.' The fact that there was not a big studio machine behind the film meant it had to be driven by the passion of the writers, director and producers. In Jackson's opinion, that effort transfers to an audience 'in a very palpable way'.

Critics largely agreed. 'A pleasingly sour little yarn,' said *Sight and Sound*. 'There's enough emotionally involving content to offset the occasional lack of plot clarity,' said *Empire*, adding, 'Jackson is oh-so-cool as usual, if not entirely convincing as an antiques expert.' *Entertainment Weekly* came up with header of the month for its 'Take a Bow' to support its claim that the complex structure of the work deserved to be marvelled.

Final thought comes from the latter publication: 'As for what big-time badass Jackson is doing fondling a fiddle and talking about wood varnish in an artsy Canadian project, I think the answer is, anything he wants!'

While *A Time to Kill* writer John Grisham appears to have the lawyer-turned-author market pretty sewn up – *The Pelican Brief*, *The Juror*, *The Chamber* can all be added to his earlier list of novels – there is another man who has done OK transposing his science background into similar fiction gold.

A former trainee doctor in the emergency room at Massachusetts General Hospital, Michael Crichton saw the potential early on for writing about his work. In 1970 he published *Five Patients*, a factual book based on his experiences on the wards. A quarter of a century later, this would become the backbone for a certain little TV series called *ER*. But Crichton was also interested in science fiction, especially in the 'what if?' variety set in the very near future. While still juggling a medical career, Crichton published a series of novels under the pseudonym 'Jeffrey Hudson' – hardly a name to have anyone rushing to the bookstores – that would eventually be turned into the successful movies *The Andromeda Strain*, *Westworld* and *Coma*.

In 1993, Crichton had his biggest success when his story of *Jurassic Park* was transformed for the silver screen by Steven Spielberg. In what has become a theme in his work, that movie featured a small group of disparate scientific backgrounds faced with a futuristic fantasy turned killer. It also featured an actor called Samuel L. Jackson. Four years later, author and actor found themselves working together again. This time the film was *Sphere*, adapted from Crichton's 1987 novel about a small group of disparate scientific backgrounds faced with a futuristic fantasy turned killer. It only needed Wayne Knight to ham off into the sunset with a bunch of eggs to complete the similarities.

While the monsters in *Jurassic Park*, as Jackson admits, stole the show, the creature with murder on its mind in *Sphere* is not even seen. In fact, even where it has come from – yet another galaxy far, far away – is not shown. *Sphere*, in fact, is a space monster movie shot not in space at all, but totally under water.

The fact that *Sphere* is more of a psychological action flick along the lines of *Solaris* or *Forbidden Planet* suited director Barry Levinson down to the ground. Having built his reputation in comedies like *Good Morning Vietnam* and drama such as *Bugsy* and *Rain Man*, he had actually been looking for a sci-fi movie that didn't rely on computer-generated aliens. 'My problem with doing science fiction is I don't know how to deal with the monster,' he admitted to *Starburst*. 'I saw *Sphere* as the *Who's Afraid of Virginia Woolf* of science fiction' For the director, it was more a psychological drama where, ultimately, it's the human characters who are the closest thing to monsters.

Three science bods – Professor Norman Goodman (Dustin Hoffman), bio-chemist Beth Halperin (Sharon Stone – really) and sceptical mathematician Harry Adams (Samuel L. Jackson) – are rounded up by shifty government type Harold Barnes (Peter Coyote) to investigate a vessel that appears to have been submerged at the bottom of the South Pacific for three hundred years. (Or in *Jurassic Park* shorthand, Jackson plays the Jeff

Goldblum character, Hoffman is Sam Neil and Stone does her impression of Helen Hunt.)

Two things had to happen before Jackson, fresh from Montreal and his stint as a sexagenarian antiques dealer, shot one scene in front of a camera. He needed to learn to dive and he needed to sort out his hair.

According to producer Andrew Wald, all the cast spent two weeks training with diving instructor Kris Newman. 'They all elected to go on and become fully certified,' he says. 'Dustin Hoffman was not a big diver, but Sharon Stone and Queen Latifah had previous diving experience.'

Despite her experience, it was Stone who, according to the *National Enquirer*, got into deep water difficulties and had to be rescued by co-star Jackson. In an act of miscegenation that would never have made it onto the screen in many movies, Stone was allegedly only saved by Jackson administering repeated mouth-to-mouth resuscitation. In reality, according to Stone, the only gossip was that all the cast had urinated at some point in the set's large water tanks.

More prosaically, 'They all had to become comfortable with their hand-eye co-ordination underwater,' Wald explains, 'so they could do practically anything.' Training involved excercises ranging from underwater egg and spoon races and rolling bowling balls with a stick to swimming through a proper airlock. (For the record, Hoffman seemed to have his co-stars licked on the egg and spoon races.)

He may not have as much as dipped his toe into the scuba world before, but Samuel Jackson was hooked in no time. What did anyone expect of the former oceanography major? This was the chance his teenage equivalent had always dreamed of; his adult self didn't need to be asked twice. On the face of it, diving is a solitary pastime, much like golf, which appeals to his personality. But in this instance Jackson couldn't wait to share his new-found passion with his family. While LaTanya stayed on terra firma, Zoe and her dad were soon diving regularly together. 'I've got a little leisure life going,' he admitted to the *South China Morning Post*.

While the diving requirements of the film were soon met, Jackson's artificially aged hairstyle from his portrayal of Charles Morritz proved sterner opposition. There were wig options, of course – he was no stranger to this. But then there were the extra problems of keeping it natural-looking for the underwater scenes (anyone who remembers Sean Connery's syrup clinging on for dear life during *Never Say Never Again* will appreciate the predicament). Jackson had the answer.

'The day after I finished *The Red Violin* I had to go to *Sphere*,' he recalls. Turning up with the front part of his hair cut out and the rest dyed white gave him only one choice. 'Barry said, "Go ahead, cut it off. Let's see what it looks like." I shaved my head and he liked it so I ended up keeping it.'

Because of a part in a fairly obscure Canadian movie, Jackson was forced to change his hairstyle. It may have been coincidence, but in so doing, he only added to the growing belief that he was the coolest man alive. Remarkable as it sounds, he would win major parts because of it. Even more remarkable, he nearly didn't get to benefit from his follicular sacrifice in *Sphere*.

It's an unwritten law in Hollywood that water + cameras = a movie that goes way over time and budget. Think *Jaws*, think *Titanic*, think *Waterworld*. Despite a lengthy pre-production phase, Warner Brothers got wet feet at the prospect of their $100 million investment becoming, quite literally, just a drop in the ocean of the film's final cost. The result was a one-month shut-down to reassess costs. 'Any movie dealing with water is going to be a cause for concern because a lot of big movies start out with one figure and balloon to another after production starts,' executive producer Peter Giuliano says. Levinson's reputation for always meeting his budgets was tested further when Warners decided to trim the budget to $85 million and knock the shooting schedule down to seventy days from ninety. In the end, they used only 65.

Part of the reason Levinson was able to please the bean-counters back at Burbank was his take on 'deep sea' filming. James Cameron's *The Abyss*, which has striking similarities to *Sphere*'s plot (Crichton's novel predates the 1989 film) went to enormous lengths to recreate the realism of thousands of leagues under the ocean – much to the detriment of his cast and crew. 'You learn from others' mistakes,' laughs Levinson tactfully. Cameron's decision to use deep water for autheticity's sake meant actors and crew had to decompress when they came up, costing the production days in wasted time. '*Water World* was out on the ocean,' Levinson continues, 'and whenever you do that it's going to multiply your problems, because you have very little control over Mother Nature.'

Not only did the *Sphere* actors not need to decompress after a morning's shoot, they barely got their helmets wet. As soon as tests showed that seven feet deep could be made comfortably to look like 2,000, it was just a case of sourcing a location for building five tanks forty-feet wide and up to 26-feet deep. Mare Island naval station, a decommissioned military base in Vallejo, near San Francisco, provided the solution. After another chilly Canadian winter, it meant Samuel Jackson could still play family man and turn up for work.

For a guy not normally given to being starstruck, it actually took Jackson longer to acclimatise to his co-stars than it did to the idea of spending half his time in a tank, listening to Levinson barking orders through an in-helmet microphone. 'My first day on the set, I had to do a major dramatic scene with Dustin,' he recalls. 'It took me half the day to actually accept that I was acting with one of the most respected actors in the business.'

Part of his awe was because of his pre-determined opinion of Hoffman's reputation. This was the man who, famously, was told by *Marathon Man* co-star Lord Olivier after hours of trying to 'get into character' by improvising a shouting session between the two men, 'Why don't you try acting, dear boy? It's much easier.' Brando aside, Hoffman gave new meaning to Method Acting, according to reports.

Jackson discovered otherwise. 'He's just a funny man to be around,' he says. 'He's stopped being that obsessive person who calls people up to talk about his role or throw stuff at you.' And, Jackson suggests, he probably didn't fancy spending five days in a submarine just to see what it was like. The set, in fact, was a pleasurable place to be. Levinson has a reputation for working well with actors – this was his fourth film with Hoffman, a notoriously intense star – and this was no exception. Whether the script, the result of four screenwriters' efforts, justified his work is another thing, but as far as the camaraderie on set went, everyone got on just fine. 'It was great,' says the wily Peter Coyote. 'Everyone except Sharon was in the same make-up trailer so before the day even started, we had goofed around, told jokes, teased each other and gossiped.'

The plot twist in *Sphere* comes from the fact that there is no visible monster. The 'sphere' in question has the ability to distort human minds, bringing to life their fears. It is Harry, Jackson's character, who proves most susceptible to the mind-tampering and needs to be rescued from the clutches of alien 'Jerry' before his own deep-sea phobias – giant squid, shoals of killer jellyfish and, best of all, a tumultuous influx of copies of *20,000 Leagues Under the Sea* – kill them all.

Unfortunately, while the atmosphere on set and under water was light, the tension and claustrophobia of the scenario rarely got above the same level. The end result was, unfortunately, $85 million of anti-climax. Even Jackson, normally a nailed-on cert to steal any show, seems oddly withdrawn in the finished product. In-jokes at his compulsive behaviour aside (his character's obsession with the aforementioned Jules Verne title), it was a fairly innocuous performance. Reviewers agreed on the film's global release in February/March 1998.

'Think *The Abyss* meets *Event Horizon* but nowhere near as interesting or terrifying,' said *Total Film*, directing viewers towards the Laurence Fishburne film. The *New York Times* said: 'Hoffman's cool authority is well used here, as is Mr Jackson's muscular intensity and discreetly mocking air. But ultimately *Sphere* is much too occupied with its scientific mystery to come up for air.' *Variety* pulled no punches: '*Sphere* is an empty shell. Derivative of any number of famous sci-fi movies and as full of promises as the Wizard of Oz.' *Premiere*, its tongue firmly in its cheek, was dismissive of the actors' ability to represent the science set. 'Now, while Hoffman, Stone and Jackson are all terrific stars, the only mission they could credibly undertake together would involve a limo trip to the People's Choice Awards.'

As for its stars, well Samuel Jackson as ever dutifully trod the chat-show circuit plugging the movie. For a while, though, the biggest mystery concerning the movie was when it would be released. 'Everybody keeps saying Christmas,' Jackson told *Neon* in autumn 1997, 'but I keep thinking everybody's running from *Titanic*, and nobody's gonna release a movie over Christmas until they figure out what that thing is doing.' In the event, *Sphere* was held over till spring 1998 – not that it helped.

Looking back, Jackson is slightly miffed at the missed opportunities of his $85 million foray into the deep. 'I prefer my monster movies to have monsters in,' he says. 'But, hey, that's just me.'

17. ACCEPT NO SUBSTITUTE

Towards the end of the *Sphere* shoot, Samuel Jackson started disappearing at weekends. It wasn't for golf or even to practise his new hobby of scuba diving. It was, of course, for yet another film. And, once again, the influence of *The Red Violin* was still strong.

'While I was doing *Sphere* I had to get fitted for the wig I wear in *Jackie Brown*,' Jackson says. 'They fitted it onto my bald head, so I couldn't grow my hair while I was wearing that wig.'

Jackie Brown was the new movie by Quentin Tarantino. After the brilliant self-penned mastery of *Reservoir Dogs* and *Pulp Fiction*, and even *From Dusk Till Dawn*, *True Romance* and *Natural Born Killers* to some extent, it surprised everyone in the movie business and beyond that this new work was an adaptation of an Elmore Leonard novel called *Rum Punch*. But, lest anyone labour under the misapprehension that Tarantino had dried up, he still had something to say and the finished screenplay was wildly different in tone to the source material. For a start, the female protagonist was switched from a white woman to a black woman, immediately shifting the cultural emphasis and audience of the movie. Even the movie's villain fluctuated vis-à-vis his race.

'I was that character when I was writing it,' Tarantino admits of Ordell Robbie, eventual supa-nigga extraordinaire. Ordell, he says, exists in the same world the writer inhabited as a child. 'To tell you the truth, if I was an older man and I was black, I would've played it.'

Considering Jackson has said that Tarantino is black – he just doesn't know it – it was always a possibility that the actor and character would combine. 'That's the truth,' the writer says. 'That's the product of the environment and upbringing and that's just a side of me that got exorcised in this movie.'

In the end the auteur and frustrated thesp didn't take a role, despite recently starring – not too jarringly – alongside George Clooney in *From Dusk Till Dawn*. 'People have taken me for granted a little bit,' he told *Empire*, 'so I wasn't going to put myself in the movie or put in a fun cameo for the heck of it.'

As soon as he'd come to his senses about not casting himself, there was only one alternative. 'It was a no-brainer to cast Sam as Ordell,' Tarantino says. 'I could hear him saying the words as I wrote them. Sam gets the music out of my dialogue like no other actor does.'

For his part, Jackson was in as soon as Quentin showed up with a script. The idea of Tarantino taking the role instead, however, prompted a typical response from the actor: 'Yeah, right.' Comparisons between Jules and Ordell were inevitable, of course. On the face of it, both were cold-blooded killers, but that's where the similarities end, according to the man who brought both to life. 'Whereas Jules is a moralistic kind of guy, Ordell has no morals,' Jackson explains. 'He has just one steadfast rule. Nothing and no one is going to get in his way.' In other words, if you're part of his solution, you're a great person. If you're part of his problem, you're history. But the fact that the character was also 'personable, opinionated and funny', meant there was something for Jackson to get his teeth into.

The last words could describe the director, and for that reason Jackson could never turn down the chance to work with him again. It's almost a bonus that Tarantino writes such three-dimensional characters and gives Jackson a real opportunity to work on the 'biography' for his parts. Killers are no different to any other career-minded people, he says.

'I don't believe assassins sit at home sharpening their knives and polishing their bullets,' he says. 'They go to the store and drive their kids to school. They're normal people who just happen to have interesting jobs.'

Jules maybe. But Ordell – 'normal'? 'Ordell is the first purely evil character I've played,' Jackson admits. 'He'd kill you without thinking twice. But I knew Quentin was going to write him some incredible dialogue. I'm a stage-trained actor so words are the most important thing to me. But at the end of the day, Ordell is the ultimate super-cool nigga.'

Based on the 'Dutch' Leonard book, *Jackie Brown* was essentially a complex money-stealing plot involving a gun runner (Ordell), a flight stewardess down on her luck (Pam Grier as the title character), a just-out-of-jail hoodlum (Robert De Niro), a pothead surfer girl (Bridget Fonda), a bail bondsman (Robert Forster) and a cop (Michael Keaton). The interplay between the characters, as you'd expect, is superb. Grier, plucked from Tarantino's childhood memory of watching all those Blaxploitation movies in which her characters, Coffy or Foxy Brown etc., were forever killing and getting their breasts out, holds everything together as the titular star. Forster, also rescued from a dead career thanks to the director's love for his work in early 70s pictures and TV series *Banyon*, thoroughly deserved his Oscar nomination for Max Cherry. (Ironically, both had auditioned for Tarantino before: Forster for the part in *Reservoir Dogs* which eventually went to Laurence Tierney and Grier for the part of Jody in *Pulp Fiction*.) Jackson, however, provides the star turn, prowling around the set with a menace not even seen in Jules Winnfield. The venomous look he manages to produce for Fonda's character when she refuses to answer his phone early on gives every indication that this is a character capable of killing several people before the film's end. And when, showing henchman

Louis a bullet-wounded corpse in his Oldsmobile trunk, he says, 'It's an employee I had to let go,' the audience is left in no doubt.

Ordell reaps his power and money from gunrunning. Showing De Niro's Louis a sales video of the latest rapid action hardware, fantastically called *Chicks With Guns*, he salivates at every weapon that comes on screen – the bikini-clad women don't get a look-in. 'The AK47,' he drools. 'When you absolutely, positively got to kill every motherfucker in the room, accept no substitute.'

Garbed in a variety of stunningly ostentatious costumes – often colour-co-ordinated track suits and Kangol caps – Ordell is a villain of the old school. In fact, Jackson had a very specific inspirational source when fine-tuning his character, although Tarantino required some convincing that it would work. But with the actor's head still shaved from *Sphere*, at least there was virtually a blank canvas to work with.

'I had the wig made and a little braid for my chin and suddenly everybody realised it would work,' he says. 'It comes from my affection for Hong Kong films, where the villains tend to be very distinctive.'

For the weekends where he shuttled between San Francisco's *Sphere* set and LA's *Jackie Brown* shoot, slipping between characters was actually a lot easier thanks to the hairpieces. 'I would put the hair and the braid on and I would immediately be back as Ordell,' he explains.

More distinctive than playing two diverse characters was working with two equally talented but wildly different directors. 'The atmosphere on the set was very different,' Jackson explains. 'Barry's very quiet, whereas Quentin fills the room, you know he's there. He'll laugh out loud during a take.'

Just like on *Pulp Fiction*, the key to Tarantino's films being happy places is the work he puts in before the camera starts. 'We'll have dinner gatherings or he'll have a big dancing night where everybody goes dancing together,' Jackson says. 'And every week he has a screening of some B movie he's chosen.'

Another way that Tarantino gives life to his extreme characters is through their drives and ambitions. As written in Leonard's novel, Ordell, the vicious, stop-at-nothing criminal, has a dream: to earn a million dollars and retire. To date he has half that – and Jackie Brown is his means of transporting it from a Mexican bank to LA. Before getting his head round the violent aspects of the character, millionaire actor Jackson had to appreciate his motivation in order to construct a 'biography'. Most taxing of all, was sharing Ordell's obsession with earning a million dollars. 'Because I've done the things I've done, I know a million dollars is not a lot of money,' he told *Empire*.

Having worked with one icon of the silver screen on *Sphere* – Hoffman, not Stone – Jackson was even more awestruck to be thrown together with another legendary character in *Jackie Brown*. 'On the first day I was doing a scene,' he says, 'and you want to do your job, but in the back of your mind you're thinking, "I'm doing a scene with Robert De Niro." ' As is often the case, the pre-publicity – the violence, the attitude, the sneer – didn't live up to billing. In fact, given half a chance you'd hardly know the great actor was there. 'On the set I'd hear this quiet little voice,' says Jackson laughing, 'and I realised it was Bobby talking to me. He's so unassuming and shy it's incredible.'

His character, Louis, is one of the great understated roles in movie history. Almost wordlessly, De Niro builds a three-dimensional picture of the slow-witted ex-con that relies less on Tarantino's inspiration than any other character in the writer's career. And that's why De Niro was worth a relatively vast chunk of the movie's tiny budget – a whole million dollars. Jackson, in comparison, was happy to pocket a quarter of that just to work with Team Tarantino again. In principle, unlike the likes of McConaughey or Damon or Affleck, De Niro was the calibre of star that Jackson didn't mind coming off worse than. 'I don't begrudge Bob getting what Bob gets,' he insists. 'He gets that because he's De Niro and his agents can negotiate better deals than my agents.' At least with De Niro there was no resentment that the lesser-talented white guy was earning more because of his skin colour.

Other stars of the movie were as overwhelmed about their leading man as Jackson was with De Niro. Robert Forster picked up immediately on Jackson's training: 'I've never worked with anyone as good,' he admits. 'This guy is from the theatre so he prepares in a way that I try to.' Lawrence Bender confirms his director's feeling when he says, 'Sam Jackson says Quentin's lines better than anyone else alive.' Michael Keaton, who plays the unnervingly twitchy cop, Ray Nicolet, opines: 'I'd say that Samuel Jackson is the most graceful actor I've ever seen. It's really impressive the way he works.'

'Sam has a lot of power in his work,' says Pam Grier, his young adulthood hero. 'He has such intensity and presence that I wondered, having seen his *Pulp Fiction* character, where he was going to go with this part. And he did a phenomenal job.'

For his part, Jackson was just as thrilled to be working with Grier. 'I looked up one day in the script and I'm standing there and I've got my hands round Pam Grier's throat,' he gloated to *Neon*. 'I'm going, "Oh man, I'm choking Coffy." '

His acting aside, Bridget Fonda actually found Jackson a human voice on the busy set. 'Sam is just a riot,' she says. 'He cracks me up and we had a great relationship in Melanie and Ordell. You sort of like his character in spite of hating him because of Sam.'

Even the character's creator was impressed with the guy who played him. 'Samuel L. Jackson added to the part, I felt,' says Elmore Leonard. 'There was one scene which starts on a balcony then comes down to where he wants Beaumont in the trunk. They expanded on that scene from the book because they liked what Sam did with it.' Even Tarantino joins in the hagiography. 'Sam is just perfect, almost too perfect. He was terrific. There's a little part of Sam that is Ordell.'

On the face of it, Tarantino is correct – apart from the wig and braid, Jackson's character is identifiable by the fact he wears a selection of Black Panther-style berets throughout the picture; black, white, orange – always matching his outfit. In real life, Jackson too had been sporting the Kangol headwear for some time. For some reason, Tarantino was suddenly besieged in interviews – after the regulation 'do you think your films are too violent?' question – by the 'why are Sam and Pam wearing those daft hats?' line of enquiry. 'Sam wears those Kangol hats a lot in real life,' the director says. 'They're really big in the black community. Go to a black mall, you'll see a sea of Kangol hats.'

Fifty per cent more expensive than *Pulp Fiction*, weighing in at a ridiculously paltrey $12 million, *Jackie Brown* took a relatively disappointing $40 million in America despite its heavy reliance on the LA South Bay area's indigenous black culture. (Leonard's *Rum Punch* was originally set in Florida; Tarantino transposed the action to the area where he grew up, giving such unfashionable boroughs as Carson, Hawthorne, Compton, Hermosa Beach and Torrance's Del Amo Fashion Centre their day in the movie sun.) Interestingly, the movie was better received financially in Europe. In its defence, it came out at a time when audiences were still flocking to see *Good Will Hunting, Titanic, LA Confidential, As Good as it Gets* and Scorsese's *Kundun*.

It was not only at the box office that *Jackie Brown* failed to live up to the phenomenal standards set by *Pulp Fiction*. With hindsight, there was more than a hint of *Schadenfreude* as a noticeable Tarantino backlash kicked in from a media industry sometimes desperate for its stars to fail. Reviews were mixed as a result, but largely as a result of Tarantino being compared to his own phenomenal standards; if *Jackie Brown* had been made by any other director, the reviews would have been considerably more favourable.

The *LA Times* led the cheerleading: 'It's a movie as wise as it is funny and Tarantino has surrounded Grier and Forster with Jackson's often hilarious but also icy thug whose swagger suggests that he may fear he's not as smart as he insists he is.' 'Jackson is perfection,' said *Rolling Stone*, 'combining charm and menace with uncanny brilliance . . . Sorry to disappoint those who long to see Quentin Tarantino fall on his famously flashy ass, but the overlong, over-indulgent *Jackie Brown* scores a knockout just the same.' The *Evening Standard*: '*Jackie Brown* hasn't the bravura sequences, the flash acting, the swallow-its-own-tail plot dazzlement of *Pulp Fiction*, but it is a distinctive piece of work. No mistake, Tarantino is here to stay.' Among the naysayers were the *Boston Globe* who reckoned that 'at more than two hours it's simply too long. It just isn't as boppy to watch as Leonard is to read.' *Empire* combined a generally positive review with the opinion that 'the movie teeters on the edge of tedium occasionally, a flaw not helped by its running time'. The *New York Times* confirmed the overlong consensus: 'The film lacks the ingenious structure and taut pacing of *Pulp Fiction* and one scene is shot from four different perspectives.' *Total Film* stands alone at criticising the dialogue: 'Lines like "Look, I hate to be the kinda nigga does a nigga a favour then, bam! – hits a nigga up for a favour in return . . ." smack of laziness.'

Recognising that a lot of the criticism was aimed less at the movie than at the personality of the man behind it, Samuel Jackson was quick to speak out in Tarantino's defence. Unfortunately, before 1998 – the year of *Jackie Brown*'s release – was out, Jackson would be defending his friend from charges a lot more damaging than simply making a boring movie.

Given Tarantino's near worship of black culture and his obvious respect for his black actors – he has said, 'We all have a lot of people inside us, and one of the ones inside me is black' – it seems hard to believe that one of the film's strongest and most outspoken critics was himself a black film-maker. It was, of course, Spike Lee.

No sooner had *Jackie Brown* been released, no sooner had the Kangol-wearing Tarantino started on his relentless (self-) promotion circuit, no sooner had the plaudits for this innovative piece of black cinema started to trickle in, than Lee announced to the press the one criticism guaranteed to get him an audience.

Jackie Brown is racist.

His reasoning? The movie's characters overuse the word 'nigga'. Lee had counted – there were 38 instances. Watching the movie, he said, his wife was offended by it. It did not matter to him that the words came predominantly from Ordell's mouth – a black mouth. What mattered was they had been written, scripted and directed by Tarantino – a white man. If, Lee said, he had used a word like 'kike' so many times in one movie, he would expect to be hounded out of business by an outraged public.

Tarantino, as might be expected, ignored the obvious logical ripostes and went for something a little more brazen. 'I'm a white guy who is not afraid of that word,' he told *Black Film Makers*. 'I just don't feel the whole white guilt and pussy-footing around the whole racial issue.'

Conjuring images of Steve Martin's character in *The Jerk*, his background is interesting and varied enough to explain his views. Like Jackson, Tarantino's father wasn't around too much during his youth, so his mother had to work. Left to his own devices, he found himself naturally gravitating towards the black kids in his area and he started hanging out with those. Ask him to name his favourite movies and the Blaxploitation staples of *Coffy*, *Foxy Brown* and *Shaft* will top his list.

Stung by the criticisms all the same, Tarantino refused to enter into the debate, realising that nobody ever comes out well in an argument about racism. It's like trying to answer the question: 'When did you stop beating your wife?' There was nothing to be gained, he reasoned, by defending himself publicly. The media, of course, will never accept silence for an answer so, seeing his friend being hung out to dry by a rabid press eager to see this enfant terrible of cinema dethroned, Jackson stepped into the fight.

Immediately the dynamic of the argument changed. There was nothing that Lee or those who jumped on his bandwagon could say that Jackson could not counter – with knobs on. The fact that Jackson and Lee had some history as well just made spectators salivate all the more at the encounter. Whatever the motive, for a while it seemed like Jackson would talk about little else during interviews.

Tactic number one in verbal combat: belittle your opponent. 'I haven't been witness to any special elections that made Spike Lee the official spokesman for black people the way he thinks he is,' Jackson said in *Neon*, warming to the fight. 'Spike's just angry at society because he doesn't feel the playing field is level,' he told the *Guardian*, suggesting Lee was angry at being too short and not classically handsome enough to get the girls when he was younger.

Tactic number two: expose the hypocrisy of a man who has built a whole career out of making racially divisive movies taking issue with another film-maker who has been less confrontational.

'Black artists think they are the only ones allowed to use the word,' Jackson told the *Sunday Telegraph*. 'Well, if that's his argument then Spike has no right to write "white boy", "cracker", "honky" or whatever else he does in his scripts.'

To the *Voice* he added, 'I heard the same argument against using the word nigga from the Hughes brothers, who used the word about a hundred times in their film *Menace II Society*.' Pointing out that Tarantino and the Hughes brothers shared a similar upbringing emphasised the point.

Not only do Lee's pictures contain words like 'honky', but they are also used in a pejorative context – something Tarantino does not do in *Jackie Brown*. The hypocrisy is stunning. Jackson, again, devises a sensible path not based on knee-jerk reaction. 'I am not offended by what people say,' he says. 'I am offended by what they mean when they say it.' By way of example, he cited in the *Observer* the way the word is used by white guys to cause offence in *Reservoir Dogs*. 'As a sophisticated audience you're supposed to understand that difference.'

Tactic number three: throw in a few facts. 'I know Quentin isn't racist,' Jackson says, 'and so does Spike.' Proof, he said, was in the fact Lee cast Tarantino in *Girl 6* – in a scene with a bare-breasted Theresa Randle (a black actress). 'I said to him, "Was he a racist before or after that?" ' Jackson asked in the *Guardian*. 'Spike said, "That's different." I was like, "No, Spike, it's the same thing." '

Tactic number four: take the higher cultural ground. 'It's art,' Jackson says. 'You can leave the film or tell people not to go and see it or not to read the book, but you don't censor somebody else's art because you are offended by it.

'In my opinion, Spike's the last person who should try and censor somebody's artistic endeavour,' he says. 'People have tried to do that to him for years and for him to do the same is ridiculous.'

Tactic number five: goad the opposition. In particular, Jackson picked on interviews where Lee had said if he made a movie overusing the word 'kike', he would never work in Hollywood again. 'Well, if you ain't got the balls to say it, how do you know?' he suggested. 'Try it and see.'

Considering Lee had managed to enrage the Jewish community quite enough without it in *Mo' Better Blues*, this argument must have hurt. 'Spike has offended a lot of people in his life,' Jackson says. 'He markets his movies through controversy.'

Tactic number six – the killer blow: A few home truths. 'Personally my feeling is that Spike's anger stems from the fact that he sat down and watched a good black movie and he hasn't made one himself in a while,' he told the *Sunday Telegraph*.

The Jackson/Lee farrago raged in the media for several months during 1998. Jackson came out of it looking like an eloquent, rational human being while his former mentor came to resemble an embittered, jealous has-been. At the heart of their dust-up was the original problem of almost ten years earlier when Jackson had refused to work on *Malcolm X* for scale. They later patched up their differences ('I guess Spike got over it, anyway, because I noticed in *Bamboozled* he out-nigga'd Quentin by about thirty times in the first fifteen minutes') but it was fun while it lasted.

Almost a sideshow to the main event, however, was a real discussion on the use of the N-word. Away from hostilities, Jackson admits that during his childhood, during Segregation, 'nigger' was definitely 'a rock-throwing word. But at some point, as we got older, a "nigga" was something you wanted to be, because you didn't want to be a negro or a coloured.'

Like all aspects of language, the word has evolved. Central to its early rehabilitation were the Blaxploitation films of the 1970s. Suddenly the word was being used in a 'cool' context. Comedians also had a role to play. There is no topic that cannot be touched upon with the right humour (as Tarantino had shown with the accidental head shooting) and people like Richard Pryor in the early 1980s openly introduced themselves as 'niggers' – and proud of it – during their sets. Lenny Bruce went further, accentuating the word's devalued currency by using it to death. Everyone has heard conversations where the word 'fuck' is used as noun, verb and adjective, almost to the exclusion of other vocabulary. It is the same principle: 'That's kind of like where Lenny Bruce was hoping to get,' Jackson says. 'You take the power from a word by overusing it.'

Part of the reason for the word's acceptance back in popular culture has been its altered spelling, pronunciation and usage. In 1989 an annoyingly brash rap group announced themselves on the music scene. They were NWA – Niggaz Wit' Attitude. At a stroke, the word had been reclaimed by big-budget entertainers; newspapers printed it, television journalists said it: 'nigga' was back in vogue and it was nothing to be ashamed of.

And yet, as Pascoe Sawyer writes in *Black Film Makers*, 'Studies in America show that "nigger" is still the most commonly used insult in racially motivated attacks on black people. For most people, black and white, "nigger" still means: the lowest of the low.'

(There is an excellent scene in *True Romance* where Dennis Hopper is killed by Sicilian gangsters for suggesting that the bloodstock of all Sicilians originally came from black settlers: 'That's how blonde hair and blue eyes became black hair and dark skin ... you Sicilians still carry that nigger gene.')

As he says, Samuel Jackson is of the view that the word is only a vehicle for the sentiment. He prefers it to be pronounced and spelled in its newer form, but that doesn't matter as much as what you think of when you say or hear it. Context is all, which is why it was fine for Jules to contribute most of the 28 occurrences in *Pulp Fiction* and for Ordell to get the lion's share in *Jackie Brown*. 'It's how Ordell speaks, it's not negative,' Jackson says. 'To him, it's like saying, guy, fella, whatever. No big deal.'

It's also the way Jackson himself speaks. 'Sam Jackson uses nigga in his speech, that's just who he is and where he comes from,' Tarantino says.

Admitting this, Jackson says it's precisely Tarantino's remarkable affinity for black dialect – not just his – that allows Ordell to pull off such controversial dialogue. 'Quentin has a 95 per cent ear for African-American language,' he says. To date there has only been one instance where he felt the auteur was straying into the realms of being offensive and that, strangely enough, came more down to his pronunciation. It was the 'dead nigga storage' scene in *Pulp Fiction* and Tarantino was either going to take advice from Jackson or run into trouble. 'I kept saying, "Quentin, as long as you say 'nigger', it's going to be like fingernails on a chalkboard," ' he recalls. ' "You've got to say 'n-i-g-g-a-h', nigga." ' In other words, show that he is familiar with the word and its cultural import and has used it in mixed company and 'not just with some white guys'.

For a final thought on the subject, Jackson is intrigued by the fact that the N-word carries more negative weight in Europe than in America. This is, he surmises, because that gang culture and rap language had US origins and its impact is still being felt overseas. The UK has only just stopped laughing at Ali G's use of the phrase 'Is it coz I is black?' The idea of him saying, 'Is it coz I is a nigga?' would probably make even Channel 4 blanch. 'It's because the evolution of your society is a little different from ours in terms of the use of the word,' he told the *Voice*. 'I don't even think you guys use it amongst each other and we always have.' It was more likely to be kids who have adopted the hip-hop culture and attitude who felt comfortable using it, and probably that same group, therefore, who were least offended by it. 'The less power you give a word, the less power it has over you.'

While Quentin Tarantino had no problem hearing or utilising Jackson's street dialect in his work – 'there is no word that should stay in jail – it's all language' – no sooner had the actor wrapped on *Jackie Brown* in June 1997 than he was confronted by a director with a completely different view. This new director, in fact, found the word 'nigga' so distasteful that he banned Jackson from saying it while on set. 'That made me mad,' the star admits. But he agreed to the terms, which in itself was a surprise. It is not every day that Samuel Jackson will let anyone – employer or not – dictate how he conducts his life. But then, in all honesty, it was not every day that he got to work with George Lucas.

Part 3

THE 'L' STANDS FOR LUCKY

18, WELL, HE'S BLACK

In 1997, Samuel L. Jackson was asked by the now-defunct *Neon* magazine what his opinion would be if Zoe announced she wanted to become an actress. As ever, he was candour itself in his reply. 'I'd say, "Great, I'll give you the names of some people and tell them you're my daughter," ' he says. 'This business is built on nepotism.' Even if Zoe couldn't act, it would probably take three or four films before anyone noticed – but somebody would sign her up just because of whose daughter she was.

'I say let her do it. Or at least give her a chance to fail. My wife's a good actor. I think I'm OK, so she might have some good genes.'

If Zoe did opt for the acting life, it would be interesting to see how her parents reacted to her constantly travelling and being away from home. They would find out soon enough when she left for Vassar, but if LaTanya's loathing of Samuel being away was anything to go by, she would not cope well with her daughter's absence.

'LaTanya thinks she owns me,' Jackson explains. 'She has this thing about putting me in a box and being with me 24 hours a day. She thinks of me as her personal property.' Guilty as charged, LaTanya says. 'When he goes away to shoot, it's very hard for me, because when I come home I expect that he is going to be there then or later on.'

After what must have been a difficult 1996 for LaTanya, her husband had mostly managed to find films in West Coast California, keeping the family together throughout the first half of the year. All that was to change in June, however, when a new movie to be shot in New York, Chicago and Tennessee started shooting. This time, however, it was LaTanya packing her bags for a month or so of hotel living. She had won the role of Deputy Marshal Cooper in the Tommy Lee Jones and Wesley Snipes movie *US Marshals*. A follow-up to Harrison Ford's *The Fugitive*, the flick saw Jones recreating his role as Marshal Sam Gerard – but there was a huge Harrison Ford-sized hole where the original film's star had refused to participate in the seemingly redundant sequel. Little matter, it was still a big budget picture and LaTanya had a piece of it. As long as she didn't rub up the notoriously grouchy Jones the wrong way, this could put her big screen career back on track.

Anything LaTanya could do, of course, Samuel could do better. She was off to the other side of the country? He would go to England. She was in a big budget action film? He would sign up for the most anticipated action flick of the decade. As for LaTanya's hopes of being in a hit movie – Samuel knew even before he'd turned up that he was stepping into a possible billion-dollar success.

A year earlier, Jackson had appeared on Chris Evans's *TFI Friday* and announced to the world his love of the *Star Wars* films and his desire to work in any new ones. Word got back to Skywalker Ranch and its proprietor was interested.

'I was able to use my celebrity to worm my way into the *Star Wars* prequels,' Jackson grins. Sadly Evans's celebrity didn't make quite the same impact on the actor. 'This guy who'd just married some nineteen-year-old – I can't remember his name – asked me who I'd like to work with. I knew about the *Star Wars* films so I said George Lucas.'

Lucas heard about it and they met at his ranch. Was Jackson serious about wanting a part? 'I told George I would be a storm trooper with a helmet on,' he says. 'It didn't matter if nobody else knew I was in it, as long as I did.' Lucas said he had something a little bigger in mind – maybe even a Jedi.

In the end it was not only a Jedi Knight but Mace Windu, a member of the Jedi Council. And we all know who leads that Council. For Jackson, it was the cherry on top of a pretty amazing year. 'One day I'm standing across from Dustin Hoffman,' he says. 'And the next week I'm working with Robert De Niro. And now I'm doing scenes with Yoda. I can retire now.'

For as long as Jackson had been on the celebrity circuit he had never witnessed a media scrum like the one surrounding everything to do with *The Phantom Menace*. In truth, he wasn't alone; no movie in history had been so highly anticipated. As soon as Jackson's name was linked with the project he started being plagued by demands for insider information. It didn't matter that he was often plugging other movies like *Eve's Bayou* or *187* at the time. Like everyone associated with the project, Jackson was sworn to secrecy. The movie did not even have an official name until shortly before its release. For a while, he was even kept in the dark about his role. It was the day before shooting when they let him see a script, or at least a section of one. 'I don't have a clue what the movie's about,' he said after chipping in with his part in 1997. 'I saw the six pages of the script I'm in, but I don't know what happens before or after that.'

For months, interviews went something like this:

Q: What's the movie about?

A: I'll tell you, but then I'll have to kill you.

Q: Are you a good guy or bad guy?

A: I can't tell you, but I do all of my thing with Yoda. And I can tell you he looks the same.

Q: Tell us something about your character.

A: Well, he's black.

Jackson, of course, had been hooked on the exploits of the Jedis since that hazy screening back in 1977. 'I remember seeing the first screening on 44th Street. Nobody knew anything about it,' he says. 'The only people there were drug addicts.' Jackson liked it because it seemed like one of his favourite old-fashioned Errol Flynn movies but set in outer space. For a while he thought he was in the minority – there were no queues around the block when it opened. Then people like him started talking about it. 'Then the word went out. I just thought, "I wish I could be in it." '

Shooting took place in Leavesden, England in June. Jackson was required for four days. On day one he was given his pages; day two he shot his first scene. Any possible problems raised by not knowing his contribution's context within the whole piece were negated by Lucas's trademark thoroughness. 'Each little scene had a goal and the goals were pretty simple,' he says. One scene involved assessing Anakin, the mop-topped boy who would become Darth Vader; another saw him reprimand Liam Neeson's Qui-Gon, all the while conveying just how serious things were becoming for the Empire. 'I also had to maintain some sense of calm in that and not look panicked. Jedis don't panic.'

Even with minimal guidance, Jackson's theatre habit of building a biography for his characters enabled him quickly to nail down the essence of Windu. 'I wanted to look like a person who was in control of his emotions,' he told *Starburst*, 'who could understand and assess the situation, who had some sense of seeing into people and who was a leader.'

It was slightly daunting for Jackson with Lucas watching rehearsals, but the actor knew he was on the right lines when the director made no comment. 'I'm not a needy kind of actor who says, "Is there anything else you want?" ' he says. 'I don't need that kind of attention. They don't say anything? Then I'm cool.'

Apart from fulfilling his dream to work with Lucas, Jackson was also delighted to learn that the director worked in a very actor-friendly way. 'You don't have to worry about too many takes, because George doesn't care,' he laughs. 'George is like, "Yeah, do that." There can be an airplane crashing behind you, and George will print it. He's the guy who's there.'

Once Jackson had got over the joy of discovering he was going to be a Jedi, he had to get over another hurdle. He didn't have many lines, but one of them was 'May the force be with you'. Could he say it without his boyhood enthusiasm creeping out? 'The hardest thing was to keep from grinning,' he admits. It being the first film, he was aware that Mace's utterance could mark the first appearance, chronologically, of the magical phrase – if he could get hold of a copy of the full script he could find out. Sadly it wasn't to be. 'Seeing the film, Liam beat me to it.'

Even better than the rehearsals was to come. First there was the thrill of finding a full Jedi outfit in his dressing room. 'I put it on and stood in front of a mirror posing for a while, thinking, "Yeah, I'm a real Jedi."' When he went back onto the set, a crew member came over carrying a case. He flipped it open and said to the awestruck actor, 'Pick a lightsaber.' Suddenly Jackson felt like a ten-year-old boy again, tearing around his grandparents' house – it took all of his concentration not to let it show. 'It was the hardest thing for me to stop going [makes fighting gestures] swoosh, swoosh!' Another career goal ticked off, even before he had filmed a minute.

After four days of bliss – 'I felt like a big kid' – Jackson was as eager as everyone else to see the finished film. A lot of his scenes had been done against blue screens – the backgrounds would be drawn in later at the Skywalker Ranch. Watching the film would be the first time he got to see the views outside the windows at the Jedi Council meeting. What's more, despite telling the press that Yoda looked the same, the little Jedi Master that Jackson acted opposite didn't exist: the character was entirely created by CGI technology later, like *The Lord of the Rings*' Gollum or Ang Lee's *Hulk*. Jackson had to walk along while Frank Oz or a stand-in voiced the lines from off camera.

If the hubbub before the movie's launch was intense, the frenzy that surrounded its actual opening was off the scale. Merchandise, tie-ins, fast-food promotions – you name it, it happened. Non disciples were thoroughly sick of the words Phantom and Menace long before it opened. Many genuine aficionados felt the same. '*The Phantom Menace*,' said the *Hollywood Reporter*, 'is the first film that will make money even if nobody buys a ticket to see it.' On the plus side, Jackson was captured in plastic for the first time: 'I got to be an action figure and it actually looks like me,' he enthuses. 'I was one of the few people in *Jurassic Park* that didn't get an action figure, so this was a great vindication.'

For a while, the Windu doll was outselling Obi-Wan Kenobi's. 'It's probably because more black people are buying them,' he laughed to one interviewer. Speaking of which: he was pleased to notice there were more 'brothers' in *The Phantom Menace* than there were in the first trilogy, and not just making up numbers, either. 'We even got a brother who is Captain of the Queen's guard,' he says before pausing for a moment. 'OK, she does get captured a lot. You've got to figure that brother's not going to have that job for very long.'

The first *Star Wars* film, *A New Hope*, was not well received by critics. C-3PO was named as the most annoying film character of all time. Fast forward three decades and *The Phantom Menace* was pulled apart by reviewers who named newcomer Jar Jar Binks as 'the most annoying film character of all time'. Lucas took the criticisms in his stride, pointing out how bad dialogue, wooden acting, over-reliance on special effects and weak, written-for-children storylines had all been said of the first three films in turn. Some critics seemed even to lift their review of one movie and recycle it for the next in the series. 'You'd think that after a while they'd figure out that that's what these things are,' Lucas says. 'It's always going to be like that because I see it as one movie, not six.'

Jackson, as might be expected, was more outspoken, upset that people viewed the film with cynical grown-up eyes rather than the sense of wonder they would have felt as a kid. 'All these adults who really loved *Star Wars* forgot that when they saw it they were teenagers,' he said, 'and they don't know how to look at a movie like a teenager again.'

He also took public umbrage with the various barbs of 'racism' aimed at Lucas – hadn't he been here before, defending another director a year or two earlier? This time it was said in some quarters that the two viceroys were Chinese, Watto was a Jew and Jar Jar was a *Gone With the Wind*-style manservant. 'If you can't watch a movie without putting racial connotations on the people, then you've got a problem,' he complained. Spoken like a man who has never had a problem with the lack of black characters in movies nor, of course, ever felt aggrieved that even his beloved *Star Wars* was basically a white man's movie.

Off this well-beaten track, the *New York Times* was surprisingly upbeat, delivering the most positive spin on the new film. It hated the media overkill, of course, but said, 'Stripped of hype and breathless expectations, Mr Lucas's first instalment offers a happy surprise: it's up to snuff.' *Entertainment Weekly* disagreed. 'Skittery and overstuffed. Some of it is fun, but the main struggle you see played out is that of George Lucas nervously fighting to give everyone in the galaxy their money's worth.' The majority of critics were closer to the latter view than the former. As with the first three movies, of course, the reviews were irrelevant. *The Phantom Menace* earned $430 million in the US alone. And Samuel Jackson had been part of it. Eat your heart out *US Marshals*.

With LaTanya away, it was just as well that *Phantom* only took up a couple of Jackson's days in June because he had sole charge of Zoe for the next few weeks. Coinciding with her summer break, it meant there was plenty of time for the pair of them to go scuba diving. There were also opportunities to catch up on their shared love of kung fu films and he even attempted to get her on the golf course.

It's a truism, but like a lot of parents who have come from broken homes, Jackson takes his family responsibilities very seriously. Zoe, he says, is the reason that he and LaTanya are still together. If ever they have reached a point where either of them considers opting out of the marriage, one look at their daughter puts them straight. 'I firmly believe kids deserve and need two parents,' Jackson says. 'It's to do with how I was raised.' It's too easy, he says, to let an argument escalate out of control and to call time on a relationship. Luckily, neither he nor LaTanya has ever allowed things to get that far. 'I'm sure LaTanya and I have both been there,' he told *Essence*. 'But what brings us back is Zoe.'

Another truism is that absent parents often seem to get on better with their children than the permanent fixture. Growing up, Zoe and her dad had a perfect relationship in many ways. He wasn't always around, but it was for work reasons, not a relationship problem. When he was there, they were fun times because father and daughter would hang out more like buddies than anything else. As with any parent doing most of the raising on her own, there was a tendency for LaTanya to be seen by her daughter as the harsher one. More than once, Dad has come home and had to step between the warring tongues of Mother and Child. 'We're both laid-back and cool,' Zoe says of her and her father. 'My mom is more high-strung.' LaTanya admits that she can be 'the heavy' at times, but when she's the only one around, someone has to be. Samuel, on the other hand, swans into town after a month or two away and acts more like best friend than a strict disciplinarian. 'I'm her protector,' he says.

The bond between husband and wife, though different, is just as strong as between father and daughter. One incident proved the point, although LaTanya rather wishes it hadn't. Asked by a photographer at a big showbiz event who he considered the most beautiful woman in the room, Jackson had no hesitation in naming his wife. 'They were like, "Who, her?" ' LaTanya says. 'I was undone, like, Oh God, just swallow me up in the floor.'

It was while squiring his wife to another showbiz bash earlier in the year that Jackson had a chance encounter that was to influence how he spent the remainder of 1997 once his wife had returned from Chicago. It was at the 69th Academy Awards that he happened to bump into old friend Kevin Spacey whom he'd met when they had both been in *A Time to Kill*. Spacey had just picked up his Best Actor Oscar for *American Beauty*. Conversation revealed that they were both considering the same script. A deal was done.

'I met Kevin at an Awards party and it turned out we were both reading the same script,' Jackson explains. 'I told him I'd do the film if he did it, and he said the same thing. And that was it.'

For Spacey, the choice was slightly harder. No one wants to come off looking second best, especially when you have his Oscar-winning credentials. Having seen at close hand Carl Lee Hailey's character destroy the rest of the field in the Grisham picture, he had to be sure that the movie offered equal opportunities. 'Jackson tends to blow his co-stars out of the water,' he says. 'Well, most co-stars,' he adds slyly.

The movie under discussion was *The Negotiator*. The project had actually been floating around Hollywood for a couple of years, originally developed as a Warner Bros vehicle for Sylvester Stallone, who owed the studio a picture. Following on from his impressive turn in *Cop Land*, Stallone passed on the chance to play another policeman. As befalls the majority of scripts, it sat in Hollywood limbo for months before *Friday* and *Set it Off* director F. Gary Gray was offered the opportunity to direct it. Since the movie boils down to a taut two-header, he knew he needed actors above the usual superficial standard. In the end he went for two men who had earned their stripes doing stage work; one of them famously in independent theatres in London. 'I was asked for my first choice,' Gray says, 'and I said I'd love to have Sam and Kevin.' And he got them.

The Negotiator is actually based on real-life events. A St Louis hostage negotiator alleged that he had been framed, as they say in *The A-Team*, for a crime he didn't commit and so staged his own siege in the hope of flushing out the real culprits from among his colleagues. In the movie version, relocated to Chicago, Danny Roman is the top man with the plausible nature; Chris Sabian is the guy from another precinct enlisted to try to talk him down. The stage is immediately set up for a potentially explosive face-off between two of the strongest actors working in mainstream pictures today.

Shooting started in Chicago on 12 September 1997 – no sooner had LaTanya left the windy city than her husband was jetting in. Typical. Before then, however, Spacey for one was confident the script was something different. 'I often go to movies of this type and they're just dumb,' he says. 'I had worries that were addressed during the script and rehearsal process – just to make sure it was not going to be silly.' His main gripe was the clichéd ending that big budget cop thrillers always feel obliged to stage: in the first draft, *The Negotiator* was going to be no different. 'The original script ended in a train station with the evidence in a locker and 150 cops all pointing guns at each other. And I said, "Guys, I don't want to do the *OK Corral*." ' Been there, done that. The finished picture climaxes with just three people in a room.

After the tease of *A Time to Kill* putting them in the same picture but with hardly any scenes together, Jackson thought *The Negotiator* would be the perfect tonic to pit the two actors against each other. 'This seemed like the ideal project,' he says. 'Both of us doing something where we are actually talking to each other.'

They may have been talking to each other, but that was all. Like all good hostage situations, the majority of the action sees the men communicate largely by phone rather than being in the same room together. True to normal Hollywood convention, each man's part was shot separately. Out of line with convention, each actor played a full scene even when it was not his turn in front of the camera. Most actors would have skulked in their trailers while stand-ins delivered the unrecorded lines for the star to act against. (Many of Jackson's lines with Yoda had been said to a stand-in rather than Fozzy Bear and Jedi Master 'voice' Frank Oz.) Not here. 'I was there all the time,' Jackson says. 'There's no way another actor could read the lines to him the way I would do it so he could react dramatically the way he needs to.' A lot of actors, he reveals, wouldn't have put that effort in, preferring to disappear to their trailers until their face can actually get on camera. As a consequence, in Jackson's opinion, if a star does help out it's so half-hearted he often wishes the stand-in could do it instead – 'at least you know the stand-in is going to act'.

Jackson has a high regard for his own talent; not just his ability, but the hours he has put in and the effort he makes on a daily basis, whatever the role. Going up against Spacey was a real eye-opener for him because it was as close as he'd come to meeting a worthy co-star. 'It's a joy to step into an acting situation with an actor you respect and admire and who understands the process as well as you think you do,' he says. The result is he leaves the set fired up by the experience, not drained from having spent the day watching a less talented co-star play catch-up.

Unfortunately, Jackson's opinion of the man at the movie's helm was less glowing. To be fair, his opinion of directors as a breed is low to start with. 'I never think about directors,' he says. 'They just kind of come with the project, so nah, I'm not interested in seeing them in action.'

As far as he is concerned, directors have virtually nothing to do with getting a good performance out of him; all they can do, therefore, is get in the way. Because of the nature of the job, the majority of directors that he has worked with, he explained in 2000, have probably only worked on between five and eight pictures. Our man Jackson, on the other hand, had experienced almost ten times as many. And that, he reckons, gives him the right to speak up if he thinks a director is going about things the wrong way. 'I'm the one that's ultimately up there on screen getting criticised for doing what some stupid ass wanted me to do,' he told the *Sunday Herald*. 'So I don't do anything I don't agree with.'

And what was F. Gary Gray's problem? 'He's kind of like a fly sometimes,' Jackson explains. 'He buzzes around and creates another kind of tension on top of the tension that's already in the scene.' Gray bullishly takes the comment on the chin. 'I have to do what it takes to get the film in the best possible shape,' he countered in *Premiere*, 'and if that requires me to buzz around and instigate, that's fine. I would prefer they hate me now and love me later.'

One of Jackson's reasons for 'hating' his director possibly arose when he had to step out onto a ledge on the twentieth floor of the R.R. Donelly Building in downtown Chicago. Scuba diving he can learn. High-wire gymnastics, on the other hand, are beyond the pale. 'Am I supposed to stand there?' he asked Gray when directed to the ledge. 'I'm not standing there.' He was not joking. Only a fully supported harness linking him to the inside of the building swayed him. As he stepped out to face a helicopter hovering fifteen feet away, with actors training laser-sight weapons on him, he must have cast a nostalgic thought towards the benefits of the blue screen magic on his last film.

'I was bolted to the floor on the twentieth floor, the windows were out, there were helicopters right in my face, and the wind was blowing,' he recalls. All this for two days as they tried to nail down the shot. 'Lucky I'm a real rollercoaster fan,' he says.

In his usual thoroughness, Jackson did a little investigating into how real-life negotiators think. How did he do it? Around eighteen holes, of course. 'I played golf with a few of them,' he admits. 'You spend four hours on a golf course with a bunch of guys, and you'll find out what they're about.'

Gray had a less casual approach to research and went riding with the Chicago bomb and arson squad. 'I acquired a new-found respect for police,' he admits. 'All day long on the radio, we'd hear, "Shots fired! Shots fired! Shots fired!" '

As a result, scenes involving the occasional closure of thirty downtown blocks during the seventy-day shoot, much of it at night, were reorganised into a tighter, more 'police-like' manoeuvre.

At early screenings of *The Negotiator*, it became obvious that most audiences reacted positively to one particular line that hisses from Roman's clenched teeth: 'I'm not going to jail today.' In mock disappointment, Jackson could see himself being stopped in the street already. 'Oh no,' he said in 1998. 'I can see that's going to become my next airport catch-phrase.' Ever since *Pulp Fiction* he had been accosted by people yelling, 'Hey Sam! Know what they call a quarter-pounder with cheese in France?' Or worse, he adds, 'They'll say, "Sign my wallet, you bad motherfucker!" '

As with so many of Jackson's films, there was little to fault his performance within *The Negotiator* (although *Entertainment Weekly* suggested it). Unusually, he palpably met his equal with Spacey. Any faults with the finished movie, therefore, lay with the director or the script. A $45 million domestic return – which recouped the movie's cost – set the tone of not-too-bad, not-too-amazing that seemed to be backed up by the majority of reviewers.

'The film drifts from examining dualism and Otherness into becoming disappointingly routine cop melodrama,' said *Sight and Sound*. It doesn't even maximise the use of its actors' talent: 'for much of their time together on screen they have little to do but showboat at each other.' The *New York Times* was struck by how mundane the characters' language was given each actor's experience with exceptionally verbal parts. 'Mr Jackson is far too commanding and clever an actor to make his character seem that uncomplicated, but the script doesn't leave much to the imagination.' While the *Washington Post* declared the plot to be 'about five rewrites shy of intelligibility', *Total Film* hit the nail on the head: 'There's absolutely nothing wrong with what either Spacey or Jackson do in this film. It's just that taking a Stallone movie and treating it like *Macbeth* doesn't make it *Macbeth*.'

In its defence, *Empire* applauded the picture for 'bringing conversation (and an almost theatrical claustrophobia) to the action flick', as part of a four-star review. The *Dallas Morning News* found Jackson 'one for the ages, so enjoy him in his prime. Both performers are brilliantly unpredictable, capable of making you nervous with their presence alone; as a pair, they're a fuse waiting for a match.' Like *Total Film*, the *Los Angeles Times* had a nice enough time at the pictures without really believing a word of it. 'This film is intensely watchable,' it stated, 'even though a lot of what's happening doesn't stand up to a moment's scrutiny.'

Even before the movie was released, Jackson was prepared for the flak. Maybe the pressures of leading a film were getting to him or maybe he had finally met his match alongside the mesmerising Spacey. Whatever the reason (and let's hope it wasn't jealousy) his self-defence caveat in case the film bombed seemed oddly negative: 'I know I'll be the one punished if the movie flops,' he said, 'and not Kevin. He's got his Oscar.'

Winding up on *The Negotiator* – or the Chicago play as perhaps it should be called – in November, Samuel Jackson could look back on his most productive year as an actor. *The Red Violin* had taken him to Montreal, *Sphere* had taken him diving for another big pay-cheque, *Jackie Brown* had reunited him with Tarantino and, surely, another stab at major honours; *The Phantom Menace* fulfilled a thirty-year dream while *The Negotiator* saw him headline a major action thriller in his own right. Spacey brought the art-house audience, following his chilling John Doe in *Se7en* and his thespian image; it was Jackson who, as alumnus of *Die Hard* and *Long Kiss Goodnight*, had the gun-wielding résumé.

On top of the sheer volume of movies he had worked on, Jackson had also seen his personal stock rise thanks to his association with some major names. As he says, Hoffman one week, De Niro another, Yoda the next meant that his face, his name and his talent were being seen alongside the greatest box office draws of the century. It could only help his financial bargaining power to be implicitly allied to commercial hits in producers' minds.

Obviously, then, the very last thing Jackson should have done to capitalise on his mushrooming reputation, was to contribute a completely uncredited scene to a film for minimal payment. But that is exactly what he did.

On 1 October filming began of yet another Elmore Leonard adaptation. *Out of Sight*, helmed and reworked by Steven Soderbergh, was also another Jersey Films project – Danny DeVito's company, of course, produced *Pulp Fiction*, so the lines of communication were there. It starred so-far-so-bad movie wannabe George Clooney opposite new mouth on the block, Jennifer Lopez. Completely against the run of both actors' form, Soderbergh teased superb performances from each and matched it with a visually innovative and well-paced thriller.

Clooney plays Jack Foley, a multiple bank robber recently escaped from prison. Lopez is cop Karen Sisco charged with bringing him in. Thrown together by a series of interesting circumstances, the couple fall in love – but that doesn't help the fact that she has to bring him to justice. The movie climaxes with J.Fo begging J.Lo to kill him so he does not have to spend the rest of his life in jail. She shoots him in the leg. The film's final scene sees the patched-up con joined in the police van that will take him back to Glades by a certain laconic multiple escapee. Out of nowhere, completely unannounced in the publicity and in the credits, that escapee is Samuel L. Jackson.

It is a virtuoso turn that dictates the entire ending. Sisco has paired the two villains for the nine-hour journey in the hope that her lover will pick up a few tips. 'It's a short scene,' Soderbergh says, 'so we needed someone that, when they implied that they were the pre-eminent escape artist in the country, you believed them right away.' As it dawns on Foley that Sisco is trying to help him, the small van becomes alive with the sexual energy that had crackled in the trunk earlier. The smouldering smile that creeps from Lopez's lips as the camera pans to her from Clooney conveys more sensuality in two seconds than most films manage in ninety minutes. It also announced her as a major acting talent. If she ever gets bored of getting married every year and making music, there's definitely a career for her here in serious movie making.

If getting Jackson involved proved an unexpected coup, *Out of Sight*'s second *Jackie Brown* cameo star was even more diverting. Although the Tarantino picture had yet to be released, Soderbergh, through Jersey, had been following its progress and seen early work. He was particularly taken by Michael Keaton's gum-chewing, head-flicking cop and thought it would be good to get him in *Out of Sight* to play Sisco's pathetic, adulterous FBI boyfriend. Not the actor, you understand – the character, Ray Nicolet. 'As far as Tarantino and I could determine, that's a first,' the smiling Soderbergh says. 'I don't think that's ever been done before where two unrelated movies share a character that is played by the same actor in both. We giggled at that.'

With Keaton supplying the movie in-joke and Jackson weighing in with the climax-saving gravitas, *Out of Sight*'s marriage to *Jackie Brown* proved an irresistible mix. As Soderbergh says, blink and you'll miss him, but name one other actor who could be trusted to act as the glue for a series of plot strands within one brief monologue in the back of a police van?

19. JURASSIC SHARK

By 1998, Samuel L. Jackson's position in Hollywood was secure. Secure and pretty defined. There was no character he could not play, no part he could not do justice to, no role too small for him to consider or too large for him to pull off. For sheer breadth of work and experiences, there was no one to touch him.

That was not to say that he was happy. He was – to a point. But it did not matter how well known he became, how much personal acclaim he reaped from his various movies, the pay disparity thing still bothered him. 'I don't know if I can be any more famous than I am now,' he told the *Guardian* in August that year. 'I can make more money, but I don't know if I can be more famous.'

To the outsider, it might seem that after working on movies like *The Negotiator*, *Sphere* and *The Long Kiss Goodnight* and picking up five, six or seven million dollars for a month or two's work on each, Jackson could hardly have been close to sitting, Kangol cap in hand, begging in a tube station. But it's relative. Jackson wasn't earning, despite some amazing performances, anything like the big white stars. 'In order for me to live like Tom Hanks, Mel Gibson and all those other $20 million players, I have to do five or six movies a year,' he explains. 'I earn the same as someone like Bill Pullman.' If you're tempted to say 'who?' at this name, Jackson has the ready riposte: 'Exactly!'

There is another reason he works so hard, and it is not a positive one. 'Everyone's phone stops ringing at some point,' he says. 'Gregory Peck, Burt Reynolds, Laurence Olivier. It happened to them all. So I work while I can.'

Fortunately, with his team of agents and managers on the case at all times, finding those five or six pictures a year isn't the problem it might be. As long as the character is interesting and new – those are the rules. 'When I don't know what I'm doing two pictures down the line I'm not a pleasant person,' Jackson admits. 'I'll call up my agent and ask, "Do I need to get a new agent?"'

It doesn't help Jackson's almost paranoid obsession with tying down the next role that he cannot even be sure where his competition is coming from. 'The whole game has changed now,' he says, noting how athletes, pop stars, rappers or comedians have all been in vogue in Hollywood at some point over the last five years. 'It seems like the rule of the day is, "Do anything but go to acting school to become an actor." And that pisses me off, make no mistake.

'Acting is one of those things I've always been able to do,' he states. 'It's not for everybody, yet everybody thinks they can do it. They can't.

'You can get people into theatres the first weekend because you have Ice Box, Ice Tray and Ice Pick in your movie,' he told *The Times*, 'but by the second week, word is going to be out.'

Rappers would become a *bête noire* for Jackson over the next year or two, drawing him into a public debate with Ice Cube. For now, though, he would bite his tongue, especially with a film coming up that featured another hyphenate of dubious extraction, L.L. Cool J.

At least 'real' actors, as he viewed himself, were still the demesne of the awards circuit. With so much good work behind him in 1997, he was pretty confident of a sniff come trophy time. Unfortunately, his biggest chance was with *Jackie Brown* and that particular movie, perhaps as a backlash to the Tarantino effect, was rumoured to miss out. The rumours weren't wrong. Come Academy Award time, only Robert Forster's Max Cherry picked up a (deserved) nomination; the masterly menacing performance of Jackson as Ordell Robbie was amazingly overlooked. Could this have been the Academy's revenge for the harsh words they'd been on the receiving end of since 1995?

Jackie Brown didn't even get a nod for Best Picture which baffled its star. 'All I know is, I voted for it,' he says. That's right – Jackson was now a fully paid up card carrying Academy member and he got to have a say. Not that it did him any good.

There was more luck going with the Golden Globes. Jackson picked up a nomination for Best Actor and Grier for Best Actress, although neither of them won. On a wider note, a not so staggering nine 'people of colour' were nominated for Globes that year, a record according to the *Hollywood Reporter*. Apart from Jackson and Grier, these nominees included Ving Rhames for his post-Fred Sultan portrayal of Don King and Jennifer Lopez, surely the lightest woman of colour in town.

While the Golden Globes kicked into disappointing gear in January, across the way from the Beverly Hilton a new film festival was in swing. Honoured with the Director's Achievement Award from the Nortel Palm Springs International Film Festival was Kasi Lemmons for the Jackson-produced *Eve's Bayou*. As producer, Jackson shared the Independent Spirit Awards' Best First Feature honour; as an actor, he was nominated for Outstanding Lead Actor at the Image Awards and Best Supporting Actor at the Golden Satellite Awards. At the Black Film Awards he went a step further, picking up Best Actor. It was a thrilling time for the surprise hit and the surprise producer. At least one of his projects was getting lucky in LA that season.

As usual with Tarantino's movies, the greater acclaim for *Jackie Brown* still seemed to be coming from a Europe more inclined to drink in his words than choke on them. The third week of February 1998 found Samuel Jackson and friends partying in Berlin on the back of the city's Film Festival. Picking up the event's prestigious 'Silver Bear' award for Best Actor was none other than Mr Jackson himself. An 'outstanding single achievement' Bear went to Matt Damon for his writing/starring double-header in *Good Will Hunting.*

When he wasn't collecting awards, Jackson was certainly in demand to present them. With a large chunk of the early part of the year devoted to hawking round his latest releases, he started to pop up behind the lectern at a number of 'and the winner is . . .' events. First up was the Brits, the UK's answer to the Grammys, held at the vast air hangar that is Earls Court. In town with co-promotee Pam Grier to attend the London launch of *Jackie Brown* and the obligatory celebrity party afterwards (this one held in the lugubrious surroundings of Ladbroke Grove), Jackson strode onto the glitzy stage in front of an arena full of screaming pop fans to present the award for Best British Single to about-to-self-combust girl combo All Saints for their song 'Never Ever'. 'That was cool,' he says. 'Oh man, all the kids down in the front in their own little mosh pit. I always wanted to be a rock star and have forty thousand people in the palm of your hand.'

Never a man to settle for having a favourable experience only once, no sooner had he said this than Jackson was signed up for another screaming teen-fest. This was a bigger deal. On 30 May he had to walk out and host the MTV Movie Awards. All of them. Cool or what? Unfortunately, when it came to his nomination for Best Actor, the *Jackie Brown* star was once again left empty-handed.

Somewhere in the middle, he even found time to get all tux'd and Kangoled up for the big ones – the Oscars. In a way, it was easier to enjoy the whole event when just handing over an award than being in the running for receiving one. Sort of. 'Yeah, you get dressed up, hang out with a lot of people, present some awards, bounce from party to party for a couple of hours and roll on in. I just take it for granted.'

While the start of the year traditionally focuses eyes on LA's acting hub, it seemed a good time to release a reality-style movie diary about one of the area's most historic (as anything in such a new town can be) attractions. Called *Off the Menu: The Last Days of Chasens*, the film was a documentary charting the closing weeks of the restaurant which had first opened its doors in 1936. No sooner had news of its end got round than bookings went through the roof. Captured on celluloid by directors Shari Springer

Berman and Robert Pulcini, Chasens' dying days sees the likes of Samuel Jackson, Jackie Collins, Jessica Lange, Quentin Tarantino, Johnny Mathis and Jay Leno all pile through its doors.

While being seen in Chasens seemed to be important for a lot of celebrities, it is not the kind of thing that drives Jackson on; it's not what he signed up for when he ticked the box marked 'star' all those years ago. Perceived status through pay equality he cares about; status through certain exclusive club memberships he doesn't. He laughs, for example, when asked if he belongs to the same golf club as fellow swinger Will Smith. 'Will belongs to the most elitist golf course in California,' he says. 'I wouldn't pay the kind of yearly fees Will pays for his club in a lifetime of golf.' That's not to say Jackson doesn't reap the odd benefit from his international fame. 'I do OK, I get invitations to play at some great courses.'

While he wouldn't take too kindly if you yelled out to him as he was lining up a fairway shot, Jackson remains that most remarkable Hollywood star: an approachable one, and one who knew what he was getting into when he entered the business. 'I don't stop people from taking my picture when I'm walking down the street,' he says. 'I make people say "please" when asking me for an autograph, but I don't say no. I don't walk around with bodyguards.' Why not? Because, he says, it's not the Oscars Academy or the Golden Globes judges who decide who is a star; it's the guy on the street who pays his eight dollars for a movie ticket.

Speaking of spending, it was round about Oscar time that year that Jackson revealed a little of the family's purchasing habits. He owns, he admitted, about forty pairs of glasses at around $400 a pop. LaTanya, however, works to larger scale. 'She won't stop shopping,' he said. 'She doesn't buy normal things. She buys cars and houses and stuff.'

For all his gripes about being the poor relation to obscure white actors, Jackson admits that he does all right. At the same time as he was confessing all about his joy of specs, he also acknowledged a perceptible shift in emphasis regarding parts offered to him. 'Even on this short "A list" of black actors, a lot of the scripts that I get don't have the fingerprints of other people on them any more,' he said proudly. 'I don't have those kinds of problems.'

Having said that, the start of the year presented Jackson with a phenomenon he had not experienced for some years. 'I have no idea what my next job is,' he told *Empire* in February, 'and that's the first time that's happened in three years. Everybody else seems to think I need a break, and I'm like, "Get me a job!" '

· Clearly the message got through. However, his big role for 1998 – his only one, in fact – was not one of those parts that necessarily required a member of the 'A list black actors' set. But he won it all the same.

After the disappointingly low body count in underwater monster movie *Sphere*, Jackson had been looking to find a more traditional blood-thirsty vehicle to exorcise another of his schoolboy ambitions. 'I used to love good, old-fashioned monster movies as a kid,' he says. 'We'd watch them then go home and somebody would pretend to be Dracula or Frankenstein and chase us and we'd run from them.'

On the monster front, *Sphere* proved something of a damp squib. On the face of it, at least, this new picture would not fall into that trap. '*Deep Blue Sea* was an opportunity to finally be in a movie like that,' Jackson says, 'and have to run away from something that was bigger and stronger with sharp teeth.' Obviously the velociraptors of *Jurassic Park* weren't scary enough for him. 'It was great to find something you could go, "Oh! Oh! Look out! Go this way – aaaaaaarghhh!" Even though I didn't get to be that panicky, it was cool.'

In case you hadn't worked it out, the things that were 'bigger and stronger with sharp teeth' in *Deep Blue Sea* were sharks. Several of them. And not just any old sharks. Giant, bionic, evil scheming, twice as big as normal sharks. With a grudge.

Despite its action tag, *Deep Blue Sea* had its origin in science fact rather than science fiction, something which appealed to the oceanographer in its star. Its premise involved a group of scientists on a Caribbean research facility trying to cure Alzheimer's Disease by experimenting with sharks' brains – similar research has been undertaken for years in the real world. Despite all the known scary statistics about sharks – that they can smell blood a mile away, that their teeth grow back when they lose them in a fight with a particularly feisty seal, that they die if they stop swimming – it's less common knowledge that they have particularly speedy regenerative systems: they are just about the only form of life that doesn't succumb to some type of cancer. And they have teeny-weeny brains. By pumping the guinea-pig mako sharks with DNA goodies, scientists on the Aquatica base hope to test how the shark copes with the bad cells. What actually happens is the animals' brains grow to a hideous size. Not only are the humans sharing a small research facility in the middle of the ocean with some of the most efficient eating machines on the planet, but they've just made them a whole lot smarter. That's fine, unless, for some reason, an almighty storm brings a helicopter crashing down onto the computer system and suddenly the super fish are swimming through the humans' quarters looking for revenge . . .

Samuel Jackson plays billionaire philanthropist Russell Franklin whose dollars are funding the research. English rose Saffron Burrows is naughty geneticist Dr Susan McAlester, L.L. Cool J – yes, the rapper – is alcoholic chef Sherman Dudley, Stellan Skarsgård is Jim Whitlock and Thomas Jane is shark wrangler and resident hero, Carter Blake.

When he received the script, Jackson was not even sure if his character would make it through to the final reel or whether it would result in a bloodbath like that little dinosaur flick he had been a part of. 'Hollywood is calling it *Jurassic Shark*,' he laughed at the time. 'I don't know if my character gets "sharked" or not. I've never had a good limb-tearing death on screen before.'

What he did see of the script itself was scary enough. 'I read the script and it was like, "Oh yeah, I'd be scared." We've got bigger, smarter sharks and man, they are terrifying. Believe me, I worked with them, so I know.'

But are they real? 'Hell, no!' he says smiling, 'I have a career.'

The point of *Deep Blue Sea*, as Jackson appreciated, was to supply good, old-fashioned, seat-of-your-pants thrills. For all the DNA blurb, it wasn't rocket science. 'It's a popcorn movie, a monster movie, and there's nothing wrong with that,' he said at the time. 'I took the role because I never did a big monster movie and I always wanted to.' And what a monster movie, what with its genetically enhanced 25-ft villains. 'It's a shark movie for the millennium.'

Of course, with hardly any prompting, mention shark films and most people think of a certain movie put together by young director S. Spielberg back in 1975. It was called *Jaws* and it featured a big rubber fish with bendy teeth nicknamed Bruce by the shooting crew. Where *Jaws* succeeded – and even its three mostly dodgy sequels managed to keep this element – is that it chose as its villain something that really exists. Something that most people have seen footage or pictures of. Something that, if you live in Australia, you've probably seen for yourself anyway.

'With sharks you're dealing with creatures that are very real, since they're predators that share the environment openly with us,' says *Deep Blue Sea* director Renny Harlin. 'I felt that it was important to make the story and the characters very real, so the fact that the sharks are the threat is also real. In essence it's about you and me in that situation.'

Of more concern to Jackson than a few bloodthirsty killing machines was the fact that Harlin was helming the picture. Despite getting on fabulously during the filming of *The Long Kiss Goodnight*, Jackson had not forgotten the physical discomfort the Finn had put him through. One look at the script proved that this shoot would be no better, but the reality was even worse.

'I got a lot wetter than I figured that character was going to be,' he recalls. 'I was wet every day for two months.' Considering the movie was shot off the coast of Mexico at the height of summer, this doesn't sound like too much of a problem. 'I don't care that it was Mexico,' he moans, 'it was freezing cold ocean water. When you're wet all day long or all night long, it gets old after a while.'

So he didn't like it then? 'It's just the kind of thing Renny does to his actors, he always finds a way to make us uncomfortable.' Rumours that the recently separated Harlin was taking out his marital strife on his cast were unfounded.

Despite everything, Jackson had gone into the movie with his big expressive eyes wide open. *The Long Kiss Goodnight*, filmed in the zero-ish temperatures of Canada's winter, had been no picnic, after all. And, despite his name being slightly lower down the credits than some actors who had more screen time, he was being more than compensated dollar-wise to show his compadres how it should be done.

'The last time I worked with Renny, he tried to freeze me to death,' he recalls. 'I ended up being wet in that movie and being cold and wet in this one was part of the deal.' This time around, as what Jackson calls 'senior actor' and the highest-paid movie star on set, he felt a certain responsibility to lead from the front when spirits were starting to flag and another drenching was called for. 'Everyone else would see that was what we had to do – we have to suffer sometimes for the art.'

Even the Zen-like patience of Samuel Jackson was tested when one of the water stunts went wrong. Faced with the storm that was to wreck the computer systems and throw the actors into one-on-one combat with the brainiac sharks, nobody expected the wrong button to get pressed. With 'waves' meant to rush the actors off their feet during an outdoors scene, something went wrong and three tons of water, according to Jackson, were accidentally dropped instead, washing the cast towards the cargo bays. 'Everybody thought we were going into the drink,' he recalls. 'We didn't have safety harnesses on or anything. We managed to scramble up and keep acting, but everybody was pissed off.'

For all the experience and acting talent available to him, Harlin obviously decided you can't beat real emotion – especially fear. When Jackson saw the final edit of the movie, he discovered that the cheeky director had used the footage of the misfiring stunt. 'I thought it was pretty funny when I saw it,' he admits. 'I was like, "Oh they kept it? It looked that good?"'

For all his griping, Jackson admits that Harlin is his kind of film-maker. 'I enjoy Renny,' he says. 'You get to run and jump and dodge things. We're running from these giant sharks and we're out of our element and we have to use our wits to get away.'

Unlike Levinson's decision on *Sphere* to go only as close to water as he had to – the director called all the shots from above the tanks through earpieces linked inside each actor's helmet – Harlin felt that greater authenticity could be achieved through greater exposure. Of course, this was the man who had seen millions of dollars swallowed up by a live ocean shoot on *Cutthroat Island*; but even in artificial settings he felt you could achieve realism if you really wanted to. Thankfully, that master of realism, James Cameron, had already constructed the world's largest water tank to hold the 90 per cent scale model of *Titanic* for his little Atlantic adventure movie of the same name; rather than face the elements, Harlin opted to use the facilities down at Fox's Baja Studios just off the coast of Mexico.

'I've learned from past mistakes,' Harlin admits. 'I don't think anybody would want me to make another pirate movie.' Give him a few extra years, he said, and he could probably make another film using the ocean for real, but with the intricacies of the movie's sets and shark machines, this was not the time to experiment.

Unlike Spielberg's Bruce, the *Deep Blue* sharks were fully functioning, fully rounded, fully automatic beasts, controllable from above the tank. At least, that was the theory. Saffron Burrows, in her first action part, found the sheer relentlessness of the robot sharks scarier than the real thing. 'They were more of a nightmare,' she says. 'If you dropped into the pit where the mechanical ones were operating, you were mangled.' She points out that the actors' safety depended on the shark 'operator' not having an off day. 'He only has to blink or have a sip of tea and forget it's turned on . . .' Burrows, in actual fact, handled the dorsal dilemma better than some others. 'L.L. Cool J. got very scared because he got chased down corridors by it and had to wade through water very fast,' she laughs.

Big butch co-star Thomas Jane admits to his own wobbles when confronted by his automated screen-sharers. 'The first time I got into the water with a mechanical shark I stepped right out again,' he admits. 'Even though you know they're mechanical, they look very real.'

Strangely enough, Jane had fewer qualms filming with the real thing. Of all the cast, he was the only one required to go swimming among living, breathing – and, let's face it, killing – sharks. For some reason, those kind people in the production office scheduled his couple of days in the ocean for after he had completed all his other scenes. It was almost as though they were expecting him to be incapable of acting afterwards. Surely not . . .

'I signed my will and I jumped in the water with the sharks,' Jane says. 'I didn't have a cage; I didn't even have a wetsuit for some of the time. It was terrifying.' The nearby scuba divers with 'stun sticks' provided the scantest of comfort.

The resulting film is every inch the $80 million horror story Harlin was aiming for. The scenes where the sharks tear down flooded corridors are quite stomach-wrenching – although the death of L.L. Cool J.'s character can never be a bad thing. There's a breathless claustrophobia to the movie that is actually more reminiscent of *Alien* than *Jaws*, as the pathetic humans scramble their way through the holed sea station to safety and higher ground. In fact, there's more than a hint of *The Poseidon Adventure* or even parts of *Titanic* (not the steamy in-car sex scenes, obviously) to the cast's desperate race against nature. There are even a few deaths of major characters to jar audiences out of their action flick comfort zone.

'I worked hard to cast really good actors rather than big stars,' Harlin admits, 'because I don't want people to guess who's going to live.' Here's a clue. The delectable Dr McAlester ends up as shark food. Had you caught one of the test screenings, however, you might have seen a different ending, as Burrows admits. 'I originally survived in a lifeboat with L.L. and Thomas Jane,' she says. 'But at test screenings audiences were shouting, "Die bitch! Die!" at the screen so changes were made.'

Whether the hero of this book lives to swim another day I won't reveal. What can be said, however, was that he probably would not be rushing back to work with Harlin again, not unless he could be guaranteed some sunshine and solid ground.

For all the discomfort involved in making the picture, Jackson was actually proud of the result. As far as he was concerned, they set out to make a scary popcorn movie and they did. And as for that other little shark movie a quarter of a century earlier . . . 'I like to think of our movie as *Jaws Millennium*,' he boasts, 'because we've got bigger, badder sharks than Steven Spielberg ever dreamed of.' He's not wrong.

It was no surprise to Jackson when the box-office figures started rolling in for *Deep Blue Sea* the following year. Despite most of them having never been near the ocean, Americans liked the sharks-on-steroids romp. Like its star, it seemed the US public preferred its monster movies to have visible predators if the comparative takes were anything to go by: while *Sphere* enticed $37 million during its domestic release, *Deep Blue Sea* splashed in with exactly double that figure.

As with any action movie – think *Star Wars*, parts I, IV, V and VI to date – public support through the turnstiles was always going to be easier to attract than critical acclaim. *Sight and Sound* decided that, despite 'the cast diminishing in a quite unexpected order', 'what should have been gripping viewing often resembles an episode of the quiz show *Crystal Maze*'. Ouch. *Entertainment Weekly* got a little more into the spirit of the genre. 'As *Jaws* knockoffs go, *Deep Blue Sea* is certainly far superior to *Lake Placid*. That said, the sharks have far more personality than the people they are eating.' *Empire* noted Jackson's mocking allusion to Robert Shaw's *U.S.S. Indianapolis* speech from *Jaws*, and found the fin-ished fare satisfactory enough. 'It's unlikely to crash any parties come Oscar night, but *Deep Blue Sea* remains defiant. It's about giant sharks eating people. And that's exactly what you get.'

20. GO PLAY WAR

A man's fiftieth birthday is normally considered to be a time for reflection, for taking stock of one's past achievements and planning for the second phase of life. According to the textbooks, some men react to this milestone by embarking on a gradual winding down of their affairs, opting for a gentler way of living, with thoughts of early retirement and the holiday home on the coast. Others perhaps entertain their second crisis of identity (the first arriving on their fortieth) and go to egregious lengths to halt the flow of time's effects on their body: a change of hair colour, a change of style, maybe a change of partner. A third group weigh up the what-might-have-beens and condemn themselves as failures, doomed to burden the world further until they die. What practically none of them do, however, is embark on a two-week training programme at one of the United States' toughest boot camps.

Under the demanding tutelage of Captain Dale Dye, the military adviser who helped Oliver Stone recreate the Vietnam experience in *Platoon* and worked with Spielberg on *Saving Private Ryan*, Samuel L. Jackson spent the start of 1999 up to his elbows in mud; he spent it carrying heavy rucksacks over assault courses; he spent it any which way Captain Dye wanted him to.

There was a reason, of course, and as with all Jackson's reasons, it was a film. *Rules of Engagement* was the no-punches-pulled tale of the court martial of Marine Colonel Terry Childers, a decorated war hero with the blood of 73 'innocent' Yemenis on his hands following a botched embassy evacuation. On the face of it, the movie could be another *A Few Good Men*. But where that film dwelled largely on the courtroom action, relying on Tom Cruise and Demi Moore's enfeebled attempts at getting the better of Jack Nicholson for its drama, *Rules of Engagement* was going to be much more of a war film in the classic tradition; that is, with guns, with exploding heads, with panicked shouting into field telephones and with lots of running around.

As with the previous year's *Deep Blue Sea*, Jackson saw *Rules of Engagement* as yet another chance to live out his childhood dreams – a slightly more common trait for those recently chalking up their half century. 'As a kid, you always used to play war,' he says. 'That was the game. Go play war.' With Dye's help and the South Carolina boot camp, he – and co-star Tommy Lee Jones – could.

'Tommy Lee and I went into these units, walking the bush, laying an ambush, taking Capt. Dye's orders and making them happen. I ended up having a really great relationship with my company.' Jones reported the same response. 'We met a lot of marines and I really admire them and hope we serve them well with this movie,' he says.

As far as Dye was concerned, even actors of Jackson and Jones's calibre could not be expected to create characters with thirty years' service as active marines behind them. Up there on the big screen, any actor tricks would be exposed – they needed to know, from people who were there, just how horrific Vietnam was for the troops.

'They have to learn how to live in fear of constant attack, that sort of thing,' Dye explains. 'The hard part is working on their minds so that their eyes don't lie.'

'Dye dropped us in there like we were second lieutenants going to Vietnam,' Jackson says, 'and we had to earn the respect of those men and be leaders and survive.' They went on forced marches and, in age-old tradition, looked for 'Charlie' while Charlie looked for them. Staying alive was one thing, but there was also the matter of earning something like respect from the real soldiers they were training with. 'I think I did a pretty good job of that,' Jackson says. 'All my guys liked me. I don't know about T.L.' If he doesn't know about T.L., it's highly unlikely anyone else does. The possessor of 'practically no sense of humour' by his own admission, and the cause of more than one interviewer's Worst Day at the Office, it's fair to say that Tommy Lee Jones has something of a reputation for being irascible. And that's putting it politely.

Fortunately, like all good soldiers, Jackson was going into the situation fully briefed. He, after all, had a man – actually a woman – on the inside during filming of Lee's last movie. 'My wife had worked with Tommy Lee on US Marshals and said he was great to be around,' Jackson insists. 'I know others who've had a different experience, but that may be a personality thing.'

Whatever 'personality thing' drives Jones into his mien of seemingly permanent tetchiness is hard to fathom. He was a top grade student and roomed with Al Gore at Harvard; he played in one of the most famous and talked-about collegiate football games of all time; he won an Emmy for playing killer Gary Gilmore in The Executioner's Song; and, since The Fugitive in 1993, he has cornered the Hollywood market for grizzled old Texans who are employed to give the likes of Will Smith an edge. At two years Jackson's senior, he clearly cannot be another victim of the turning-fifty blues.

In truth, Jones has been in a bad mood since before he turned the big five-oh, and Jackson had got to hear about it, even the reputation for intimidating his co-stars. Nothing like that happened here, but then Jones and Jackson are probably better suited than Jones and the latest loudmouth comedian on the block. 'T.L. is a guy's guy,' Jackson says. 'He just does not tolerate bullshit of any sort. He doesn't like inane conversation. He doesn't like wasting your time.'

Like the finest words Robert Forster found for his gangsta-playing co-star, Jackson pays Jones the ultimate compliment by comparing him to . . . himself.

'Tommy comes to work as prepared as I usually am,' he gushes. 'He does his homework. He has lots of notes written all over his script just like me, saying these are things he wants to change.'

For all Jones's famed irascibility, Jackson won him over. 'He brings a lot of relaxation to the set,' Jones says. 'Everyone feels a lot of confidence knowing that Sam's there.'

The dynamic between the two men was so strong that director William Friedkin compared them to 'the modern equivalent of Spencer Tracy and Clark Gable, two tremendous actors and the most perfect cast I've ever had'.

If all was well professionally, there was one potential hiccough on the social side that could have wrecked the Jackson/Jones axis. Jones, he had to admit, just did not see the point of golf. 'I tried but I didn't have enough time to wait for the ball to stop rolling,' he admits. Polo, he reveals, is his rapid-action sport of choice.

Although he claimed his role was as a glorified casting director, Friedkin brought to *Rules of Engagement* a remarkable pedigree as a live action framer and an Oscar-winning director. Any man with *The French Connection* and *The Exorcist* on his CV is a force to be reckoned with, and any movie which required large scale recreations of Vietnam battles, major riots outside the American Embassy in Yemen and the marshalling of serving aircraft carriers and helicopters is in need of that force. Opting to stage the Yemeni mob scenes in Morocco because it was a safer option for the production, Friedkin was donated several helicopters from the Moroccan airforce – plus their pilots. Unfortunately, the pilots had minimal – i.e. no – experience of the kind of formation flying absolutely de rigueur in every major action film these days, requiring intensive training.

Marshalling the hundreds of extras, especially the crew of the carrier *USS Tarawa* who were employed as background actors for authenticity, was the sort of thing that only someone of Friedkin's experience could pull off. Of course, like all great talents who have prepped thoroughly before they even approach the set, he made it look easy. It was no surprise that his lead actors, equally fastidious in their preparation, found it suited them just fine.

'He's really willing and able to get the job done on the first take, or the second, sometimes the third, but very rarely the fourth,' Jones says. 'And I like that.'

'Working with Billy is kind of like a dream deal for me,' Jackson agrees, 'because I like to work efficiently and that's what he does. He sets up the shot and we shoot it.'

For all his behind-the-scenes industry, Friedkin was always open to new ideas. 'The idea is to come completely prepared,' he says, 'but to be flexible enough to allow your preparation to be altered by either good ideas, insights or flashes of genius which very often take place.'

Some of those insights could, in other circumstances, have caused ructions between the stars and their director. It is not, after all, everyone who welcomes occasionally wholesale changes once the script has been approved. Samuel L. Jackson, in fact, as was fast becoming his policy, only agreed to take part in *Rules of Engagement* once certain changes had been made to the screenplay he had originally been sent.

'I finally read a version of the script that made sense to me and made the character come to life in a much better way than I had read it before,' he says. Throw in William Friedkin and Tommy Lee Jones and 'it was win-win'.

Once Jackson had created his 'biography' for Childers, however, new problems arose. The new, improved script was out of sync with the way he saw his character's life. Now, you could take the view that 'it's only a movie and you're paid to do a job, Sam'. Or you could realise that this is one actor who is not going to budge until his character acts in a way consistent to his – in Jackson's mind – history.

One scene in particular bristled. The film starts in bloody technicolour with Jones's character, Hays Hodges, seriously wounded by snipers in Vietnam. Childers's quick – and brutal – thinking saves his life, but Hodges is forced to train as a military lawyer – a bad one – and take a desk job when they return if he is to play any further part in the marine way of life. As the film develops, and Childers becomes a political pawn for the US government, he enlists Hodges as his defence counsel in his forthcoming court martial. 'I'm a good enough lawyer to know you need a better lawyer,' Hodges says, but Childers will not take no for an answer. In any case, as he reminds him, Hodges owes him his life.

As the trial gets under way, the movie descends into slightly predictable territory by conspiring to have the old friends have a let's-settle-this-once-and-for-all punch-up. In the script, hopalong Hodges whips Childers's ass. In the original script, that is.

'Because his character is the star, he won the fight,' Jackson says with some disregard to the plot's subtle construction. 'But when we got ready to do it, logic told me Hodges was a desk jockey and my character was still out there in the field.' Jackson hadn't put in all that physical training to be beaten in a punch-up by a pensioned-off pen-pusher, and he let the rest of the team know. In the end, the fight was rewritten to resemble something closer to honours even. The actor remains unrepentant and plays down his part in it. 'Let's call my objection light controversy,' he says. 'But because Tommy Lee didn't want Hodges to lose either, we settled on a draw.'

Although both actors agreed to disagree on this one, there was obvious respect between them. If there weren't, Jackson reckons, and if Jones had lived up to even half his unpredictable billing, then this was the moment when things could have come to a head. 'If we didn't like each other, that scene would have been a perfect opportunity to take care of some business with each other,' he laughs.

While Jackson may have been happy to throw his above-the-title weight around regarding script, there were other areas where he was impressively just another one of the boys. Co-star Blair Underwood, who plays one of the marines under Jackson's command, was bowled over by the incredible stamina of this man who was allegedly fifty years old – fifteen years Underwood's senior.

'We were in Morocco filming in scorching heat running up and down stairs all day doing these battle scenes,' he recalls. 'Sam kept up with all of us and never complained once.'

As with his behaviour on the set of *Deep Blue Sea*, Jackson is not the kind of actor who takes liberties. In his logic, if he's being paid to front up the movie and be the star, then that's what he'll do. There's no skulking around hiding when the chips are down; to his way of thinking, he needs to show the rest of the cast and crew that, if he can do some extraordinarily taxing physical work, then so can everybody else. It's an unwritten part of the contract: he might get a little hissy over the script details, but when it comes to being a leader on set and making sure all the acting talent is pulling the same way, he's the man.

Of course, in the role of Colonel Childers, Jackson was acutely aware of the strictly professional and regimented behaviour required at all times of the real men being depicted up on screen. His own personal experience with the military had not, to date, been happy. Although draft age during the Vietnam War, he did not take part in combat. 'I just didn't want to go and fight,' he says. 'All my relatives had been in the military. My uncle was a marine, my cousin was a marine who was killed in Vietnam.' As he has said before, 'I wasn't anti-war, I just didn't want to die.'

If he was aware of it before he arrived, the shortest time in the company of real marines proved to Jackson that they really are a cut above the rest of us when it comes to dedication and selfless acts of courage. 'Once I actually started to spend time with these people, I started to get a different idea of what it must be like to be in the corps,' he told the *Evening Standard*. 'The marines are a special breed of young men and women and I'm proud to represent them in this film.'

Rules of Engagement was shot over two months from March 1999. It would be released the following year. As with *The Negotiator*, reviews were oddly mixed, ranging from the wildly ecstatic to the frankly bored. At a time when the public was so spoilt for choice with its war movies and courtroom dramas, there was a chance that *Rules of Engagement* struggled to find an audience interested in the subtleties of what it had to say. Box-office action was suitably robust, however, and the $80 million movie recouped its outgoings during the American run alone. Unusually for a Jackson picture, takings in Europe were less spectacular – as were the reviews.

'Largely crap,' was one *Empire* writer's succinct verdict. A colleague countered this with 'it has an acceptable solidness to it', but both were underwhelmed, both by the story and its execution. For once, even Jackson's mastery of his inherent acting gene hadn't been enough. American magazine *Entertainment Weekly* disagreed, at least on the subject of the top line talent. 'The commanding gravitas of Jackson, who always raises a movie's game, whether the project's worthy of him or not, is comfortably met by Jones's bulldog cussedness.'

USA Today wheeled out Larry King for his verdict: 'Wow! What a great film,' the great man raved. 'A forceful, powerful, thoroughly convincing film,' agreed *The Today Show*. There was less hyperbole from the *New York Times* and the *LA Times*. 'With actors like Mr Jones and Mr Jackson, *Rules of Engagement* doesn't need to stack the deck so heavily in its favour,' said the former of the too neat, too contrived ending. 'Let's start with the closing argument: *Rules of Engagement* is guilty of flagrantly formulaic behaviour,' said the latter. 'It is the verdict of this court that it be led to a stockade reserved exclusively for cheap, pandering movies and duly shot.'

As *Entertainment Weekly* had pointed out, there are a certain number of films in Samuel L. Jackson's back catalogue that are patently not worthy of his considerable talents. On *Rules of Engagement*, he flexed a little muscle and had changes made. But was the picture ever going to be as good as *Pulp Fiction, Die Hard: With a Vengeance* or *A Time to Kill*? Did Jackson believe it was something special or was he, as usual, solely interested in making his character work?

The consensus view on *Rules of Engagement*, especially in Europe where the ghost of Vietnam resonates considerably less than in America, was that here were two amazing actors outshining their movie. It was exactly the same view that greeted *The Negotiator*: two of the best performers on film, wasted in a below-par action flick. For the first time there was an argument building against Jackson's view that only the calibre of his own performance counted: that logic was fine if you were a bit part in somebody else's film. Then you would be credited with being the only bright light in the otherwise unimpressive work. But, as had recently been the case, when you were paid to be and promoted as the star of the show, and when the movie was sold on the strength of your name, it is possible that you will come out of it tarnished with the same critical brush as the whole picture. Good character actors will always find work; major stars are more likely to boom and bust as their pulling power rises then disappears. It happened to John Travolta (twice), it happened to Warren Beatty, it happened to Eddie Murphy, Kevin Costner, Steve Guttenberg – the list goes on.

To his credit, as he looked around for his next part in 1999, Jackson was aware of this. The last two years had seen a remarkable let-up in his phenomenal work-rate; he was doing far fewer pictures, but he was the star. Suddenly his profile was higher so he had to be seen to be more judicious in his role selection. Nobody recovers from too many flops as a leading man, however good they are, whoever they are. His next role, he realised, had to be in a film worthy of his talent. It had to be the one to make audiences sit up and take notice of Samuel L. Jackson, bona fide movie star and leading man.

21. I'D SHOOT INNOCENT BYSTANDERS IF THEY LET ME

It might be stating the obvious, but Arnold Schwarzenegger has never been nominated for an Oscar and yet has starred in several of the most successful – that is, profitable – movies of all time. Steven Spielberg, arguably the greatest film-maker alive, was serially blanked by the Academy for decades, despite churning out one record-breaking movie after another. And as for the *Star Wars* series . . .

There are two schools of film-making – the critical success and the commercial success – and Hollywood has great trouble combining them. Recently, only Peter Jackson's remarkable *Lord of the Rings* trilogy has come close to providing any crossover, although its lead actors still struggle for recognition in what's regarded as an 'effects' movie. Even *The Matrix*, for all the industry's technical worship, was only really appreciated after the first movie had been out for some time; and the later instalments never lived up to critical billing.

Of all the hard men of Hollywood – Arnie, Van Damme, Seagal etc. – only Sylvester Stallone has any legitimate Oscar experience. His self-scripted first *Rocky* film won the Best Picture Oscar in 1976. Interestingly, as soon as Hollywood realised it had a potential commercial superstar on its hands, he lost all critical credibility. The only awards Stallone picks up these days are the Razzies – the Raspberry Awards for worst acting/directing/writing etc.

In 1999, Samuel L. Jackson was beginning to feel a little of Stallone's dilemma. He had been in several big-budget, money-making pictures recently and, as a consequence, was aware that his chances on the awards circuit were close to nil. Of course, since the powers that be at the Academy had refused even to acknowledge his great work in movies like *Jackie Brown*, *A Time to Kill*, *187* and *Eve's Bayou* with even a nomination, there was a very strong argument for taking the 'fuck it' approach to his work.

Fortunately for Jackson, however, there will always be fans of action flicks. For all the movie's flaws as a piece, Jackson picked up a Best Actor nomination for his role as Danny Roman in *The Negotiator*. Admittedly it was only from the Blockbuster Entertainment Awards, but it was recognition of his commercial appeal. Of different significance to him, he also received the same nominations from the annual Black Film Awards and the Image Awards. While all three of those awards eventually went someone else's way, he was luckier elsewhere. The respected Hasty Pudding Theatricals company crowned Jackson their 'Man of the Year' for 1999, and the Acapulco Black Film Festival handed over a Career Achievement Award in recognition of his contribution to the advancement of black movie-making. They weren't the highest-profile trophies in the land, but they were all sincerely chosen, and equally sincerely received.

As far as the wider entertainment business went, however, Jackson was still left somewhat scratching his head, even after almost thirty years as a professional. 'I still don't know how the industry evaluates an actor's work,' he said at the time. 'I know it's all reflected in salaries, but I'm not sure that means they value or understand talent. I do know they don't know what to think about me. After all my years in Hollywood, I'm still considered a fringe player. I don't have studio deals. Everything is on a per-picture basis.'

In 1999, however, he was given the opportunity to address this slightly. Not only was he rumoured to be picking up almost $10 million for his next movie, but he was also being signed up for its two sequels. It wasn't quite a multi-picture deal of the type that George Clooney, for example, had with Warner's early in his career, but at least there was some sense of medium-term commitment. Of course, Jackson had had a similar three-picture deal to cover the *Patriot Games* series a decade earlier, and the producers had soon found a way to chop him out of that contract as soon as he stepped out of line. But this time it wouldn't be so easy; this time he was the star. The multiple deal was a good thing, the money was great – the only outstanding question was: would this be the movie, after all this time, that justified his talent?

While Sam Jackson was dividing his time at Morehouse College between terrorising the school governors and studying the craft that was to make his fortune, the Black Revolution was reaching out into all aspects of American society. As a student in the arts, he was able to spare the time and the brain power to immerse himself in the movement to a greater extent than those in full-time employment. Even so, apart from marches and demonstrations there was very little that the average guy could contribute to what was basically a political campaign.

That changed in 1971. In that year, Melvin Van Peebles and Gordon Parks almost single-handedly took the Black Revolution from a soapbox on the street corner to every inch of the country. Where politics had made noisy in-roads, they carved out vast motorways of new possibilities. Where politics had criticised and alienated its enemies, they ignored them. Where politics had struggled for a mass audience, they found it: in the movies.

Peebles' *Sweet Sweetback's Badasssss Song*, released in 1971, was the first major film to address black lives positively. If young black men like Jackson were impressed by the audacity of that film, however, nothing prepared them for what was to come with Parks's release later in the year. It was called *Shaft* and it marked the beginning of the Blaxploitation period of cinema. Between 1971 and 1975 a huge number of black exploitation movies were produced, some amazing, some called *Blacula* or *Boss Nigger*. In a way, however, the quality was almost secondary: through the power of movies, the Black Revolution had taken a detour from minority political nuisance to vast cultural powerhouse. In short, black people were trendy.

Sam Jackson was not on his own in being struck by the new dawn that *Shaft*, in particular, represented. 'I saw *Shaft* when I was in college,' he recalls. 'I remember that I was deeply affected by it.' For the first time he was watching an action movie hero who looked like him, sounded like him and even dressed and acted the way the young Sam always dreamed he would one day, money and chutzpah permitting. It was time to go shopping. 'It inspired me to get a leather jacket and a turtleneck, comb my afro out, and get a girl.'

The film didn't just improve Sam's chances with the ladies. It had wider social impact.

'*Shaft* was important for black actors,' he says. 'All of a sudden we had black characters doing things that white characters were doing in a world that we understood, and they were winning.' Suddenly, black actors were 'viable'. Suddenly there were career possibilities other than being John Wayne's lackey or another white actor's punch bag. From having only Poitier, Harry Belafonte and Bill Cosby in prominent screen roles, opportunities began to open up everywhere for black actors. And it was thanks to *Shaft*.

Jackson wasn't alone at being struck by the wealth of powerful opportunities shown in the film. John Shaft, played by Richard Roundtree, was a private eye who was not afraid to throw his weight around in the course of his work, or to take his chances with the ladies when they came along. You can look at Lawrence Reddick's nineteen roles for black movie stars, but anti-(white) establishment maverick detective with a libido as ferocious as his temper will not appear on it. This was something very new indeed.

As with anything new, there will always be imitators. As far as Roundtree is concerned, *Shaft* should actually be judged separately from the Blaxploitation movement it triggered. 'I'm vehemently opposed to any association of black exploitation with regard to *Shaft*,' he says. '[Director] Gordon Parks is such an incredibly class human being that to attach a negative label is really a slap in the face.'

Roundtree is being rather literal in his reading – Blaxploitation has come to define a genre that largely has little to do with its original definition of exploitation. Although at its worst, there were a large number of films made to cash in on the new funky vogue, there was still an undeniable majority that were made with the promulgation of the black community at heart. And that, surely, was no bad thing. Jackson certainly liked them. Tarantino was a fan. And Pam Grier starred in most of them.

Two follow-ups – *Shaft's Big Score* and *Shaft In Africa* – plus a 1973–74 TV series never managed to recreate the magic of the first movie once the original impact had been diluted by so many rip-offs. *Shaft* would always remain a classic, but obviously an unrepeatable one as its own spin-offs had proved. It was so clearly a one-off, that when *Boyz N the Hood* director John Singleton approached copyright holders Turner Classics for the rights to the movie in 1997, they sold them for an undisclosed but relatively minimal fee. In their minds, *Shaft*'s best days were behind it. It didn't take long before they realised their mistake, however, and soon after took the rest of the titles off the market. 'Turner realised too late the mistake they made,' Singleton says. He suspected the film still had a place in modern culture; and Turner had just realised it as well.

Singleton had plans for his new acquisition; big plans. No sooner had word got out that there was possibly a remake on the cards, he was bombarded by every black actor in America. Wesley Snipes appeared to become Singleton's stalker in his campaign for the part; other names like Ving Rhames, Delroy Lindo, John Leguizamo and Don Cheadle were all linked at one time or another with the role.

Singleton was in two minds about where to go with the look of the character. To date, he had cast unknowns in his work. 'But I needed to have a black man who could talk shit and still be likeable,' he explains. 'It came down to who really is the man, who has the style, the personality, the drive, who is the coolest?' There was only ever one answer.

'This whole film was all based on getting a guy that had the right attitude. If you look at all of Sam's work, the roles that stand out the most are the ones where he has this cool, bad-ass attitude.' For *Shaft*, Singleton knew Jackson would also find the right balance between jokey and serious, detached and accessible. And he was right.

Unlike Snipes and co., Jackson was not obsessed with getting the role. If he was honest, he wasn't sure the film should even be made. It was like trying to remake *Casablanca*.

'My first reaction was, "Why they gotta remake it? *Shaft* is *Shaft*," ' he admitted to the *Voice*. The only person he thought would stand a chance of pulling it off was Snipes. When a script found its way to him, he was interested to see which part Singleton had him down for.

Two guesses.

Jackson was eventually sold on the idea when he learned that the new *Shaft* was not going to be a remake, but rather an update. His John Shaft would be the nephew of the original Shaft. And, like the original, he would start out on the police force. Then, also like the original, he would go solo in order to pursue justice in his own inimitable fashion. Just in case anyone mistook the movie as a heretical piece of opportunism, it was important for Jackson to get Roundtree involved to prove that this film was not treading on anyone's toes.

'I didn't think we needed a remake of *Shaft*,' Jackson admits. 'No actor could possibly have accomplished what Richard Roundtree did in those original movies.' When Singleton assured Jackson it was not a remake, the actor reconsidered. Then it was just a case of convincing other people.

'The only way to clear that up was to find a way to put Richard Roundtree in this movie as John Shaft, so I could create something that was new and my own.'

Just to kill off any doubts about the two characters' relationship, new Shaft tells old Shaft, 'My mom really loved you, and she named me John Shaft. She was gonna name me Kunta Kinte, but . . .'

Like William Shatner or Leonard Nimoy – actors whose entire careers have been dominated by one particular character they played (Nimoy wrote a book called *I Am Not Spock*) – Roundtree has, over the years, become less fond of his 1971 creation than most of its audience would like. Ironically, he saw working on the new movie less as a regression than a step forward. 'I've been trying to distance myself from it for years,' he admits. 'But I like this new *Shaft*. It meant I was handing over the baton to someone else.'

Jackson and Singleton even found room for a cameo from Gordon Parks, who plays a Harlem bar customer.

Having found a role for Roundtree, the next thing Jackson did, of course, was arrange a few holes. 'It was kind of like, "Oh man, I'm playing golf with John Shaft!" So working with Richard was just like hanging out with a friend,' he says. Strangely enough, the subject of how each played Shaft never came up.

Lest anyone mistake Jackson for too much of a fan, it never occurred to him to let his idol win. 'Hell no,' he says. 'I beat Sidney Poitier the first time I played him. I can be all ga-ga goo-goo, but when I hit a golf shot, I'm hitting a good golf shot.'

With the words 'king of cool' often used in the same sentence as 'Samuel', 'L.' and 'Jackson', he also knew something of what Roundtree had been going through these last thirty years. 'He's still Shaft. He won't be able to get away from that but there was a lot of pressure on him for a long time to be this quintessentially cool character. Maybe that's over now.

'I get a lot of that "Oh you're so cool" stuff too. I guess there's a comfortable sort of arrogance in the way I am and what I do and I think I'm pretty good in what I do and I carry myself that way.'

Apart from his role in getting Roundtree involved, it was also Jackson who campaigned for the new Shaft not to be a member of the NYPD, what with the problems of police brutality raging at the time. The problem was, his Shaft was just as handy with his fists as the old one – and just as likely to use them. 'He's less than gentle with the scum he encounters,' Jackson explains. 'I told the studio it would be wrong for me to beat up people and still be a cop. It would send out the wrong message.'

Singleton, on the other hand, was less concerned about showing the city's guardians in a bad light. 'Yeah, I don't like cops,' he admits. 'I don't think any black person in America likes cops, but it was a matter of the story, of giving him somewhere to go.' While the original Shaft quit the force as a protest against its corruption, Singleton's hero becomes a private eye more with a view to giving any sequels 'somewhere to go'.

For all Jackson's good intentions, the movie starts with Shaft being less than restrained with a criminal – when he is still a cop. 'Yeah, he breaks his nose,' Jackson revels in the comic-book violence. 'He's been callous about this kid dying. It is one of those visceral reaction things.' Except he punches him twice. 'Well, the second time he does it for emphasis!'

As far as Jackson is concerned, the more violence the better. This is *Shaft*, after all. 'Come on. You've got to kill somebody,' he insists. 'I'm not politically correct in that way, you know. I'd shoot innocent bystanders if they let me.' Fortunately for the studio's peace of mind, they don't.

Clearly though, while Paramount seemed happy enough with the quite graphic violence on show in the movie, there were other issues on which the studio was just not going to budge. Not an inch. In the original *Shaft*, Roundtree spent every other scene negotiating safe passage from one naked lady to another. When Jackson read his script for the new version, he couldn't believe it: no sex scenes. Not even one. But wasn't this, according to Isaac Hayes's seminal theme song, 'the private dick who's a sex machine to all the chicks'?

There was talk about it not being the mature thing to do in the late 1990s – what with AIDS and other STDs running rampant through the first world – but realistically, there had to be another reason. For a society to be more comfortable with sickening unsolicited violence than a couple of adults rolling around in a bed, there had to be another agenda. John Singleton, ever the cynic, has a view.

'That was a big fight with the studio and we went down to the wire as to the sexual content,' Singleton says. 'Americans get away with more violence than sexual content now, especially with a black man. They're afraid of black sexuality.'

It was bad enough that Jackson's sex scenes were cut from *The Long Kiss Goodnight*, but to have them excised from this film was almost unfathomable. The official line, however, was that race was not an issue: if there were concerns at the studio it was with the idea of glorifying random sexual acts. 'Whenever Hollywood studios make a picture, they're really afraid to offend people, so they didn't want him, like, bedding three or four women,' Singleton says. 'They thought maybe some women would be offended.' The fact that *Shaft* cost $50 million might have made it a risk not worth taking, he said.

Even the legendary spy who shagged me had famously toned down his act, after all. In Timothy Dalton's *Living Daylights* he sleeps with only two women. The same in *Licence to Kill*. But times change and Pierce Brosnan's Bond has been rather more frisky.

'In the new millennium, it's politically incorrect to fall into bed with five different women in the same movie,' Jackson sighs, resigned to his Shaft's celibacy. 'Apart from James Bond. He has had that government injection. He can't catch anything.'

He's joking of course. When he first picked up the script he was horrified at its exclusion. 'I kept saying, "Where's the gratuitous sex scene?" I thought, "What part of the song do they not understand?" But hopefully, if this movie makes a lot of money, we'll do it again and get that part right next time.'

It is ironic that, given Shaft is Jackson's most overtly sexual character, he actually never gets to see the inside of anyone's bedroom. What's more ironic is that Mrs Jackson – Ms Richardson to you – should be as taken as anyone by his allure. 'It's his walk,' she says. 'Shaft is his sexiest role because I don't think there's anyone, any actor alive who can walk like Sam, because the brother can strut.'

If it worked on LaTanya, they must have been doing something right. Behind the cool dude swagger that Jackson brought to the role, no expense had been spared in crafting as close as possible a living, breathing, sex machine. It started with the hair – or lack of it. 'Sam Jackson is already the coolest actor on the planet,' Singleton says. 'My only suggestion to him was to have Shaft be bald. For African-Americans, the shaved head is currently the ultimate symbol of masculinity and Shaft is one sexy dude.' Fortunately, between the half-and-half disaster of *The Red Violin*'s geriatric styling and Ordell Robbie's rat-tail barnet in *Jackie Brown*, *Sphere* had shown the world just how striking a bald Samuel Jackson could look. He had grown his hair back for *Deep Blue Sea* and affected a ridiculous Grace Jones-style oblong cut for *Rules of Engagement*, but it was no hassle for him to whip it off again. But if it was cool you wanted, he saw no reason to stop there with the razor.

'It was my idea to add the sculpted beard,' he says of the severe triangular goatee grown for the part. 'I thought it was a great complement to the bald head.' Well, amusing facial hair had worked for Jules and Ordell, and to a lesser extent Franklin in *Deep Blue Sea* . . .

The next step for the new hero was his clothes. Roundtree had swung around in a cool but pretty much second-hand looking leather coat. Jackson's gear would be slightly less off the peg. Garbed in slick black, three-quarter-length leather jacket, high mock-neck, wool sweater, wool trousers and lace-front leather boots, Shaft 1999 dresses like no cop on the planet – no wonder he had to quit the force. But then, when did Giorgio Armani start designing police uniforms? 'I'll design the clothes. You'll create the attitude,' the Italian couturier told Jackson during a fitting. (The rest of the cast is dressed by Gucci, Kenzo, Dries Van Noten, Cerruti and Gianfranco Ferre – not exactly high street.)

Just as he found it easy to slip back into the character of Ordell as soon as he slipped into the wig and braid, Jackson was equally adroit at 'becoming' Shaft as soon as he stepped into his *Matrix*-style uniform. 'Once you have that look and you put on those designer clothes, it's easy to become Shaft,' he says. Easy and, it has to be said, surprisingly effective. Filming in New York, he recalls being complimented by women on a daily basis as he made the trip from his trailer to the various location shoots. 'Almost every day a woman would comment on how much better I looked in real life than I do in my movies,' he said. 'I never thought I looked like a troll, but this new look definitely works for the women.' Fortunately, LaTanya included.

Zoe, on the other hand, was as immune to the new look's charm as any daughter would be. 'It's not cool for her to think I'm cool,' he laughs. 'But she still thinks Richard is cool.' So much so, she has a poster of him on her wall – thirty years after his success. If Jackson's film has half the legs, he'll be grateful.

Apart from the obvious controversy about even trying to emulate Roundtree's version, Jackson soon became embroiled in another minor squabble. When he was a jobbing actor lower down the ladder, he often found himself presented with scripts that placed him further down the pecking order than the latest comedian, athlete or rapper chosen to front the film. It bugged him then and it bugs him now. Does he think he can play basketball or sing as well as Michael Jordan or Dr Dre? Maybe he could, but not just by turning up with no practice. But that's what so many wannabe actors do. Experience? Nah, everyone can act.

In 1999, Jackson was in a slightly conciliatory mood given his earlier outbursts on the subject over the years. While proud of the fact that the USA is the land of opportunity, a country where an actor can decide to run for president – and win – he doesn't believe that he should have to work with wannabe actors just to validate their careers. 'If somebody's building a film around some rapper and they want me to go with it, I have the right to say no,' he says.

As far as Jackson is concerned, rappers in particular come from a different culture to actors. There's a different work ethic for a start. 'It's a generalisation but the reality is, acting's a craft. It's a job. I love hip-hop. I love listening to it. But we work on a schedule and we are very disciplined people. It's a craft. It's not a whim.'

It was one particular incident a few years earlier that got him thinking. The rapper co-star in question just decided he was bored halfway through the movie shoot and didn't turn up for the second half. 'They had to hire a double and shoot him from the back because this dude just said, "I'm not coming back. I don't want to do that no more!" ' It's fun to surmise who he's talking about (although I think we all know it was Tupac).

Maybe part of Jackson's sudden change of heart towards the hip-hop brigade had something to do with his co-star on *Shaft*: none other than Busta Rhymes.

'I had no problem with him,' he insists. 'Busta came to the movie with a lot of humility. He would finish a scene and ask, "How was it?" He wouldn't just walk to his trailer and go, "Yeah, I knocked that out!"

'These rapper movies are crude business deals designed to target a music star's built-in, hip-hop audience,' Jackson said, years before the excellent *Eight Mile* disproved the theory. 'Even if the film is no good and people don't see it, they still get a great soundtrack out of it and they make money off the CD.'

While Busta Rhymes escaped the wrath of Shaft, others weren't so lucky. Surprisingly, given all the glowing compliments he is prepared to lob Jackson's way, it was John Singleton who copped a lot of the star's displeasure.

Christian Bale, who plays the bail-jumping, racist, white murderer Shaft is trying to bring to 'justice', spotted early on that things were not right between the two men.

'There was definitely tension,' says the *American Psycho* star. 'Some days considerably more than others. I had far less at stake than either Sam or John, so I'd just sit back and observe. It got rather entertaining at times.'

'John is like many young directors I've worked with recently,' Jackson explained. 'They've done five or eight films. I've made close to seventy. I know better than they do what works for Sam Jackson.' And when Sam Jackson knows what works for Sam Jackson, he refuses to do anything else. Fortunately for William Friedkin on the set of *Rules of Engagement*, on that occasion Jackson was prepared to compromise. But maybe he trusted the veteran director? Certainly he is wily and experienced enough to be wise to a lot of the tricks younger crews can use.

'They always try to con me by asking me to do a scene my way and then do another their way,' he explains. 'I refuse, because in the editing room they'll inevitably use their take.'

What about Jackson's fabled 'I'm the senior actor, I have to set an example' ethos? Well, that's still there – after a fashion. 'I try not to involve crew members and everyone else in a conflict,' he says. 'But I'm going to say what I want to say, and sometimes it's a compromise and sometimes it's an argument. And I win all of them.'

For the sake of on-set morale, if it does descend to argument Jackson tries not to be mistaken for a bully or prima donna. 'No, nobody says that about me,' he insists. 'I'm very diplomatic about it.' A lot of times, he says, it isn't actually the director who causes waves; it's the voice in his ear from the studio. When it comes to fighting his corner, though, Jackson has his own set of advisers. 'My agent, my manager, my lawyers – they love being the bad guy,' he says. 'They're all little women who love yelling at big men.'

Other sources had it that Jackson was less than impressed by his director's womanising during the three-month New York shoot. Jackson, of course, had given up such things in that city a decade earlier. Singleton is dismissive of the accusation. 'We have a scene in a club that demanded sexy extras and one day, we had one hundred of the hottest women in New York lined up outside my trailer so I could pick,' he says. What he describes as little more than shaking everyone's hands was spun into stories about serial womanising. On the other hand, he says, he is single: 'So it really wouldn't have been anyone's business if I had slept with all of them.'

To his eternal credit, Singleton is surprisingly defensive about accusations that the two did not hit it off. He could, after all, make serious mileage on the back of balloon-pricking Jackson's so-called 'cool' reputation. And it is not even as if he wants to present solidarity to protect his film – if there is a villain of the piece, he insists, it is someone else who worked on the picture.

'Sam is opinionated, but I respect that,' he told the *Calgary Sun*. It was actually producer Scott Rudin who the director claimed 'was the big problem'. When you have an independent film-maker and one of Hollywood's most powerful producers each used to getting their own way, there is bound to be trouble. And there was. 'That meant incredible growing pains for me,' Singleton says.

The single most explosive area of contention was dialogue. Rudin, in his wisdom, hired at great expense Richard Price to rework Singleton's original screenplay. As far as the director was concerned, Price may have written such dramas as *Clockers*, *Mad Dog and Glory*, *The Color of Money*, *Ransom* and *Sea of Love*, but at the end of the day he was white – and here he was writing the heavily jargonised dialogue for *Shaft*. 'I'm a kid from the ghetto,' Singleton says. 'I know how the African-American characters in *Shaft* should speak. I know much better than Richard what is hip, but he wouldn't listen to Sam or me.'

Jackson backs him up. 'Richard Price tried to put certain words in my mouth,' he says. 'I told John point-blank that I refused to say that white man's lines. I'd do it my way and poor John would have Scott Rudin breathing in his ear demanding that he make me say the lines they'd paid so much money for.

'If I think something is wrong ethnically and culturally, then I think you should listen to me because I've been in this skin a while,' he told *The Times*. 'And if that becomes an argument then I want it to be an argument that I win and not one that I lose.'

At the end of the day, Jackson says, it's his ass on the line. 'It comes down to a situation where, when the film is released, the result is on the screen and nobody is going to say, "Wow, Richard Price wrote that!" They're going to say, "What is Sam doing?" '

In the end, Jackson was coming up with his own words. He was most proud of a line his character says to his girlfriend: 'It's my duty to please the booty.' Maybe Tarantino has nothing to worry about yet . . .

The rapport between the film's actor and its director reached such a low that there were reports that Singleton shot the movie's opening sequence using a double for Jackson. Can communication have got that bad? Singleton admits to using the double. 'But it wasn't because Sam and I refused to be on the same set ever again as was reported,' he insists. 'Sam was in Toronto shooting a new movie. There was no easy way to get him off that set just to shoot a title sequence.' What a shame then, that the one scene Jackson doesn't appear in is the movie's only love sequence. What a coincidence. *Shaft* shot for three months in New York from September 1999, taking in such salubrious surroundings as Lenox Lounge, a classic Harlem hangout, and Brooklyn's Vinegar Hill, Red Hook, Bedford Stuyvesant and Crown Heights areas. Manhattan's Washington Heights doubled as the movie's Dominican drug lord's zone. For the crucial murder scene, seven blocks had to be closed while Singleton's crew moved slowly around. Oh to be a normal New Yorker trying to get anywhere at times like these.

Jackson, of course, used to be a normal New Yorker and so he enjoyed the trip to his adopted home town. It didn't hurt that he was shooting a movie he thoroughly got a kick out of. Like so many of his recent films, he relates this one to . . . you guessed it, running around as a boy. 'Shaft is the gun game I used to play as a kid,' he reminisces. It's also his second popcorn movie after *Deep Blue Sea*. 'It's not a cause movie. You don't have to sit there and try to figure, "Will this make society a better place?" '

After all the fun and games of actually getting the movie to happen, you would have bet money on Jackson never wanting to set foot in his Armani suit ever again. Not so. No sooner had episode one been completed than he was mulling over a possible sequel – he had signed a provisional contract for one, after all. 'What I'd like to see is for Richard [Roundtree] to have a much more proactive role in the next film,' he says. But more than that, there's something else that would tempt him back. 'I'd do *Shaft II* if they put a little sex in it.'

With or without sex, the first *Shaft* performed very healthily for a film targeted at 'black' audiences when it was first made thirty years earlier. In America alone it took $70 million, easily taking it $20 million into profit. Its crucial first weekend take of $21.1 million saw it sail past *Gone in 60 Seconds* and Martin Lawrence's *Big Momma's House* to claim the number one spot on its debut in June 2000.

Unfortunately, the movie's box-office success was marred by some audiences' objection to one of its characters' lines. Prior to the movie's grandstand shoot-out finale, Shaft yells, 'It's Giuliani time!' – a line originally attributed to one of the NYPD officers accused of torturing Haitian immigrant Abner Louima. The phrase was shrouded in controversy, however, since Louima himself denied that any officer ever spoke those words. What's more, Richard Price, screenwriter of *Shaft*, claimed that he'd never written them either. 'It surprised me,' he told the *New York Post*. 'That was adlibbed.'

Even more bad news was to come with the reviews for the movie. Yet again, the consensus seemed to be, here was a Samuel L. Jackson vehicle that just did not do the great actor justice. How many more times could this happen before his own contribution was questioned?

The *Washington Post* declared it 'a movie without spirit, stuck with a hero without heart and a villain without teeth'. Like most critics, the *New York Times*' Elvis Mitchell, himself black, said, 'Though an outrageous flirt, the nouveau Shaft has more affection for his wardrobe than anything else.'

'What happened to Shaft's prowess with the chicks?' asked the *Dallas Morning News*. 'Aside from the occasional flirtation, this is one neutered ladies' man. If Paramount or producer Scott Rudin were afraid to turn Mr Jackson into a sexual creature, then shame on them.'

In the opposing corner, both the *Chicago Sun-Times'* Roger Ebert and the *Boston Globe* praised the coming to terms with current mores. 'One thing modern about the movie is its low sexual quotient,' said the former. 'Blaxploitation came along at a time when American movies were sexy, with lots of nudity and bedroom time. Modern action pictures seem prudish by comparison.' The latter praised the film-makers for knowing 'when to low-key things'. The new *Shaft*, it said, 'has style, punch, and street cred. It's a hot cool update.'

When the movie opened in the UK a couple of months later, the reception was even more mixed. 'Bloody, gripping entertainment that refuses to let up,' said *Film Review*. Not so, said *Empire*. 'Jackson's great, but he's poorly served by an overstretched plot, lacklustre script and weary action scenes. Not good and not "bad", if you get the drift.'

If this, then, was the movie that was going to cement Jackson's name in the A-list firmament, it had probably failed. The question was: would he get another chance at heading up such a big budget extravaganza on his own? Not the next year he wouldn't. Nor the one after that . . .

22. I'M THINKING PURPLE

Nothing ever comes of striving for quantity over quality, isn't that what they say? Forget the length, feel the width, and all that? Samuel L. Jackson has always been a quantity sort of guy. It comes with his personality. As much sex, drugs and alcohol in the bad old days. As much golf, golf and golf today. And acting – 'I love my job so I'm happy to do it,' he says. 'When people call me a workaholic I have to smile.'

Regardless of what people call the hardest working non-workaholic in Hollywood, if there was any doubt that he was out there on his own in the movie-making stakes, it was certified by A.C. Neilson E.C.I., a company which provides continuous tracking of box-office receipts in eleven countries. In the 1990s, they concluded, Jackson appeared in more movies than any other actor. It was true: 36 in total, and this was in January 2000, so that didn't include *Shaft* and *Rules of Engagement* which had yet to be screened. Box office-wise, it accounted for $1.7 billion in America alone – and probably a few million dollars more for popcorn.

What did the man himself say? 'Thirty-six? I thought it was more than that.' And what did he do? He promptly announced a schedule of five new films for that year. When you're hot, you're hot. 'All it means is that I like to work and I do work,' he says. 'But with all those films, I still didn't make as much as they gave Jim Carrey to star in *The Cable Guy*. For me that puts it all in perspective.'

Without giving away too much, one of those films in his diary was rumoured to be a certain sci-fi flick being shot in Sydney. Jackson was non-committal although he did admit to speaking to a certain Mr Lucas. 'It wasn't a big conversation,' he said with a smile to one interviewer. 'I know when they're shooting. If I happen to be in Australia and stop by the set, George might find something for me to do. "Oh, George, I was in the neighbourhood – what's going on?" '

Given the fact that he only released one movie in 1999, the fin-tastic *Deep Blue Sea*, Jackson's awards season was shorter than usual. In fact, it didn't even start. But that isn't to say he wasn't honoured in other ways. January saw him invited to take a front row seat at the Armani fashion show in Milan. This was the fashion house that was dressing John Shaft, after all.

Film-work aside, there were other honours to be had, however. In February, LaTanya and Zoe joined their man at the Regent Beverly Wilshire Hotel in Beverly Hills where the whole family was recognised for its commitment in promoting social and economic justice in underserved communities through the West Angeles Community Development Corporation. The event was the 6th Annual Unity Awards Banquet, and for the Clan Jackson it was a Very Big Deal. As the acceptance speech goes, this award wasn't just for them, it was for all black people in the area.

The honours kept coming. In June, Jackson was accorded one of Hollywood's most famous and yet, most strangely abused, prizes: he got his own star on the LA Walk of Fame, at 7020 Hollywood Boulevard. If Zoe and LaTanya had any desire to see their man on his hands and knees, up to his wrists in cement, now was their opportunity.

The same month found Jackson slightly further from home, both geographically and logically. For some reason he appeared at the inaugural Laureus World Sports Awards in Monaco, along with other such sporting luminaries as Sylvester Stallone, Naomi Campbell and Jon Bon Jovi. At one point, it looked like some furious vengeance would be lain on a chap with a rich Afrikaans accent who had crept up behind Jackson, already a multiple target for celebrity hunters, and whipped his Kangol hat off him. As the room held its breath, Jackson managed to produce a smile and even let himself be hugged by the South African. It turned out to be Johann Rupert, the guy whose ideas and money were behind the awards. Not many people would have got away with it, televised show or not.

All became clear the next day when the celebrity circus reconvened on a cliff top overlooking Monaco. For Stallone, so notoriously scared of heights, to have ventured so high and for Jackson still to be in the company of the ursine Rupert, it could only mean one thing: golf. A phalanx of reporters and fans watched as the celebrity four of Stallone, Jackson, Sugar Ray Leonard and Rupert teed off. At the first tee there was something to see as Stallone pretended to spar with Leonard before remarking, 'Wait a minute, I just remembered. You're not an actor.' Leonard would say the same to him the next day . . . It was another seventeen holes before the next piece of entertainment for the non-golf crowd. With our man Jackson putting out on the last – if he can beat Poitier, he can beat this motley crew – he was transformed into a man proud to wave around three hundred-dollar bills signed by Leonard with such legends as 'Sam kicked my ass'. In classic sportsman style, Jackson was then able to take anyone who would listen through the entire story, with theatrical flourishes, of how he played every shot.

By the end of the year, Jackson would be involved in a movie where his character used golf clubs for a lot more than taking a couple of dollars from an old man. His first role of the five, however, would not have known what a golf club was if you told him.

When John Singleton said that Jackson was away shooting another movie in Toronto when they needed to shoot the opening credit sequence for

Shaft, it was for *The Caveman's Valentine*, a murder-mystery with a twist. The director of the film was Kasi Lemmons, and after the success of *Eve's Bayou*, it made perfect sense for her to enlist her old friend in the title role. As Romulus Ledbetter, Samuel Jackson lives in a cave in the heart of New York City. When a junkie hustler is found frozen (there's that Toronto winter again), hanging from a tree outside the cave, Romulus decides to solve the case. This is a bigger deal than you would think, considering Romulus had opted out of society once his paranoid schizophrenia had driven him to think a mysterious force was spying on him from the Chrysler building. The fact that his idea of language makes gobbledegook fathomable doesn't seem to hinder him either.

He also doesn't let a simple matter like the fact he looks like and acts like – and is – a smelly vagrant hold him from his purpose. For the part, Jackson wears a hat of greying dreadlocks that reach down to his waist, and the most unrealistic fuzzy beard since the stoning scene in *The Life of Brian*. Fortunately, once Romulus's case gathers pace and he manages to infiltrate the inner circles of his number-one suspect's social life, he is 'adopted' by a series of wealthy benefactors and given access to a razor. He also seems to find his way around a classical piano and said suspect's sister with slightly more knowledge than one would expect from your average down and out. The fact that the movie manages to sneak a little subject like miscegenation among its already complicated themes gives some idea of Lemmons's ambition.

But just when you think the movie is settling into a *Trading Places*-style transformation, Lemmons reminds her audience just who the protagonist is – and why he is living as a tramp in the first place. The movie flits from one take on reality to another – from the real world to the world that Romulus sees – complete with legions of moth seraphs serenading him. It was this aspect that drew Lemmons to want to work with George Dawes Green's 1994 Edgar Award-winning first novel. 'It touches on all my obsessions about what's real and what's not,' she says. 'I was fascinated by the concept of the character's insanity and his moments of genius and the interplay of the two.'

As soon as he read the novel, Jackson was equally taken – although he envisaged slightly different angels to his director. 'They should be women!' he laughs. But he eventually agreed that using male figures to portray his character's 'furies and his posse' would represent 'ancestors – the souls of black men who rise up and give courage'.

It took him less time to be persuaded that this was a novel that needed to be made into a movie. Its strong themes would make for compelling viewing, he felt. 'How intriguing to have someone that society has discarded because he's unstable and have him be the person who pieces together a murder mystery,' Jackson says.

Although set entirely in New York, the movie's tiny $13 million budget meant that the cheaper option of Toronto just could not be ignored for a lot of the shots. 'I wish America would work harder to get the film industry to stay here,' Lemmons says, 'but Toronto is so damn film-friendly, they make it so easy.' And when you have only 49 days to shoot 211 scenes on a (relative) shoestring, easy is important. Not everything went to plan, however. There was a blizzard while they were shooting in New York which, Lemmons says, 'looks pretty on the screen but was unpleasant to work in' – but when they needed snow in Canada it just didn't fall, so they had to manufacture it. In one nice irony, however, the film did start shooting on Valentine's Day. Aah.

After the terrific surprise that was *Eve's Bayou,* there were high hopes for *The Caveman's Valentine*, especially with Danny DeVito's Jersey Films behind this picture. Unfortunately those hopes were dashed when the first reviews appeared. The consensus was that Lemmons had bitten off a more impenetrable story than she could chew; and that another film was found not worthy of Jackson's participation.

'It's remarkable the way Jackson begins with the kind of character we'd avert our eyes from, and makes him fascinating and even likeable,' said the *Chicago Sun-Times*. 'An utterly fascinating film that would not work without Jackson,' agreed the *Hollywood Reporter*. 'Watching the film, it's easy to imagine how a novel might make the unlikely plot machinations less ludicrous,' crowed the *Houston Chronicle*, while the *Toronto Star*, eschewing any accusations of favouritism for those movies investing in the local economy, said, 'It is burdened by sloppy plot turns and unbelievable characters.' The public seemed to agree. *The Caveman's Valentine* earned less than a million dollars at the US box office on its initial release, the lowest for any Jackson film since 1996's *Hard Eight* and *Trees Lounge*.

If his next two projects couldn't do better, then the world was officially mad, he mused. Ever since *The Sixth Sense* had become the tenth-biggest grossing movie of all time, and in doing so rejuvenated Bruce Willis's career as a bona fide actor, Hollywood had been on tenterhooks awaiting the follow-up from its writer and director, the M Night Shyamalan. That was due to start shooting in Philadelphia on 25 April 2000. And Samuel Jackson was a major part of it.

Unbreakable would be many things, one of which was to serve as a Friends Reunited function for Willis. Having seen his acting choices step up a notch from cops and white vests to grey raincoats and psychologists in *The Sixth Sense*, he had more cause than most to want to hook back up with the director who had given him his biggest hit. *The Sixth Sense*, after all, had been nominated for five Oscars, two of them for Shyamalan, and had earned an amazing $600 million at the box office. That film's boy star, Haley Joel Osment, may have been famous for saying, 'I see dead people,' but as far as Hollywood was concerned, they saw big bucks.

As well as putting director and star together, it was also Willis's fourth outing alongside Jackson, after *Pulp Fiction*, *Die Hard* and *Loaded Weapon*.

One of the reason's for *The Sixth Sense*'s success was its interesting spin on supernatural themes; another was its unexpected plot twist at the end. (What else would you expect from the man who had scripted mouse movie *Stuart Little*?) *Unbreakable* follows a similar template in both respects. When unhappily married security guard David Dunn is involved in a train crash in his hometown of Philadephia, he doesn't expect his life to be so altered. In fact, given that every other passenger perishes, he doesn't even expect his life to continue. But somehow Dunn steps from the wreckage without a scratch on him – just as Willis has done so many times in other movies. Across the country, New York comic book art gallery owner Elijah Price is intrigued enough to make contact with Dunn. Price has a rare illness called osteogensis imperfecta, which renders his bones with the constitution of glass. He can't cross a room without damaging a joint. As soon as he hears of Dunn's exploits, he realises that if the world can produce someone as delicate and breakable as him, then it can also create his polar opposite: someone who is unbreakable.

With hindsight, casting for the picture seems perfect. Willis and Jackson have a tried and proven rapport when they share a screen, especially when their relationships swing from one character being in charge to another. Ironically, for all the talk of Shyamalan and Willis's relationship, it was actually Jackson who was the first name on the team sheet, according to the director.

'Everybody was unavailable, so I went with Bruce,' he smiles. Willis is unabashed. He signed up for *Unbreakable* even before the screenplay was finished. 'I couldn't wait to get started on this film,' he enthuses. 'I'd call Night saying, "When are we going to start shooting the movie?" ' Because of their friendship, Willis even felt comfortable enough with Shyamalan to let himself go a bit as an actor. 'Our relationship allowed me to really put a lot of my performance in Night's hands.'

Elijah Price's role had been written by Shyamalan with Jackson in mind. It's an inspired piece of casting. Not only could no one – but no one – carry off Price's dodgy Mr Whippy-meets-Douglas-Hurd hairstyle, but there were also so many similarities between the actor and his character that made it easier for Jackson to create his biography.

For a start, Jackson had spent ten-and-a-half weeks on crutches in New York City in the winter following knee surgery. 'So I kind of understand that dynamic of being bumped around and not having access to things,' he says. He also empathises with the feeling of ridicule experienced as a child. His character is called 'Mr Glass' by teen tormentors, but Jackson's pre-drama stutter attracted its own attention. 'Kids used to call me things like "Duh-dud" or "Ba-ba-ba", so I stayed in the house too, or I would go outside and beat people up.' Whatever route he took, the sense of isolation and being different was palpable, and something he knew he could draw on as Elijah. And, of course, there's the small matter that Jackson still reads and enjoys comic books. 'I relate to Elijah in a lot of ways that Night didn't know,' he reflected at the time. 'Karma-wise, maybe I was supposed to do this.'

There was also a certain empathy between director and actor. After the hard slog that was making *Shaft*, Jackson had enjoyed recharging his batteries with old friend Lemmons. Shyamalan was also up to scratch. Tarantino Jackson likes for his near-perfect scripts; William Friedkin he admires because he doesn't hang around on a shoot; M Night Shyamalan's claim to fame, however, is that he shoots his movies in chronological order so that everyone understands exactly what is going to be in the final version – it won't all be 'sorted out in the edit' like a lot of films.

'Night is one of the few people you can trust,' Jackson says, conjuring images of all those directors who haven't been so honest. '*Unbreakable* was shot in sequence, so when Night tells you what to do, you listen.' For once, just as Willis had put himself totally in Shyamalan's hands artistically, Jackson knew to pronounce every syllable as his director requested, no argument. 'If you put even the tiniest bit too much emphasis on a particular line, then you might give away the entire ending,' he explains. And Shyamalan, if his first film was anything to go by, is a director who likes to keep his endings pretty much under wraps.

Apart from its shared 'hidden' ending, *Unbreakable* is a lot darker than *The Sixth Sense*, which is odd considering it is a film about an invulnerable person where the earlier movie was about dying. Perhaps for that reason, but largely to do with ridiculously high expectations – think *Jackie Brown* following *Pulp Fiction*; think *The Phantom Menace* following the earlier trilogy – *Unbreakable*'s performance both critically and commercially paled in comparison. That is not to say it was a flop: when it opened over Thanksgiving weekend in the USA after an amazingly brief production period, it took an impressive $46 million. That soon more than doubled, and it was matched abroad. But another half-a-billion-dollar flick? Not this time.

In fact, the biggest criticism anyone could level at *Unbreakable* was that it wasn't *Sixth Sense Part II* – and imagine the heckles if it had have been. The *New York Times*, while not exactly satisfied by the end result, probably sums up the critics' mood: '*Unbreakable* is tidy and compact and seems to have been only grazed by plot. This is a superhero comic rendered as a haiku. It is Superman starring in *The Seventh Seal* with an inspired twist.'

If the expectation on Shyamalan was great, increase it tenfold and you might get to the weight of anticipation on George Lucas's shoulders as he ploughed through his second *Star Wars* trilogy. *The Phantom Menace* had earned half again what *The Sixth Sense* had brought in and the production line was showing no sign of letting up. Three years to the day that cameras had started rolling in Leavesden for *Episode I*, filming kicked off for the next instalment in Fox's studio in Sydney, Australia. The $115 million budget would see the action then transported over the next 61 days to Tunisia, Italy and Spain before winding up in good old Ealing for the final touches. (Coincidence II: the first day's footage on both films has been of English actor and Almeida head honcho Ian McDiarmid.)

While new Vader actor Hayden Christensen and Princess Leia's mum-to-be Natalie Portman swanned around the glorious countryside of various European and African countries, the film's star Ewan McGregor seemed forever stuck indoors. In the wet. 'They got to go to Italy and Tunisia,' he moans, 'while I got to be the only one in bluescreen and being poured on by rain most the time.' The rumour that this had something to do with his famously blurting out 'it's a terrible, terrible title' when first told by a journalist of *Attack of the Clones*' nomenclature is denied by LucasFilm.

Gripes aside, at least McGregor's boisterous Obi-Wan got to run around a lot and use his lightsaber, which is more than Jackson got to do in *The Phantom Menace*. But second time around, however, he was a very happy man. 'I'm totally stoked to pull that thing out and get it to come on,' he admits. Jackson being Jackson, however, and fresh from the design-conscious *Shaft* set, there was one little favour he wanted of Lucas. 'I'm trying to figure out what colour I want my light to be,' he had said earlier in the year. 'I'm thinking purple.' As all Jedi fans know, there isn't a weapon in the galaxy that is that colour. 'George was like, "Hmm, well there are only two colours. Bad guys have red and good guys have blue. Let me think about it."' Despite repeated pestering, Lucas would not be drawn on an answer. Then when the crew returned to London for a few touch-up shots, the director called Jackson over to a monitor. On it, Mace Windu was swinging a purple lightsaber around his head. 'I was like, "Is this just for this or is it going to be like that in the movie?" ' Jackson recalls. 'He goes, "No, you got it." '

Apart from his puckish desire to be different and the colour's regal overtones, there was another reason Jackson wanted purple. 'When I'm in the big battle scenes off in the distance, I can always say, "Look! There I am, over there." ' (Unfortunately, it looks like no one told the merchandise people: the action figure version of Mace Windu comes with a blue weapon.)

Jackson's contribution to his character's fight scenes didn't stop with the colour schemes. There was a very certain vibe he wanted to get across, based a lot on another of his hobbies – the martial arts flicks – and the type of guy he felt his character was. With stunt co-ordinator Nick Gillard he thrashed out a plan. Equal parts drawing on his fencing as a kid, kendo from his beloved samurai flicks and his admiration for the films of Errol Flynn, a style was born. 'My Hong Kong film collection came into play quite a bit – because we've pretty much all decided that Mace is the second baddest guy in the universe.' Number one, of course, is Yoda, Jackson says. 'Yoda is the man!'

As for the actual fight scenes, there was more than a hint of John Shaft in Windu's version of justice. 'Mace isn't necessarily one to do things the honourable way,' he reveals. 'He'd just as soon lightsaber you in the back.'

If you want proof of that, ask Jango Fett – Boba's dad – who goes one-on-one with the Jedi councillor. 'Facing off against Samuel L. Jackson?' says actor Temuera Morrison. 'Seriously, you try eyeballing that guy when all you can think about is *Pulp Fiction*. Don't even go there.'

Nick Gillard backs this up all the way. 'Mace is judge and jury,' he says. 'If you get near him, he'll kill you. He ain't gonna fuck about.'

It was Gillard's job to put the four main swordsmen through their paces ('Well, Yoda kind of knew what he was doing already'): Christensen, McGregor, *Lord of the Rings* villain Christopher Lee as Count Dokuu, and Jackson. Amusingly for Gillard, it was Jackson who showed the least aptitude at first. 'He talked the talk all right, but that was it,' he laughs. 'But I gave him one of the prop lightsabers to take home and the next day he was all over it.'

Jackson can put his overnight transformation down to, like most things, the sort of fun he used to have as a kid. 'Totally!' he says. 'I spent so much time in my room fighting off imaginary pirates and Basil Rathbone and all those guys. I had an active imagination.

'So, when George put me in that big empty room and said, "OK, lots of things are attacking you, fight 'em off!" I went straight to the place. It was great! I kind of turned my theme music on in my head and started looking around for them: OK, let's go!'

Never was his imagination so tested as when Mace lined up against the amazingly athletic fighting machine that was Yoda. 'It was just me in a room, but it's cool watching Yoda fighting in this movie, him being about one hundred years young and all.'

Despite starring in a film of the same name, it was the first time Jackson had worked in Sydney. Obviously it was a long way from home, but at least he could call on a few close friends for a spot of socialising. One of them, multiple Majors-winner Greg Norman, just happened to know a few local golf courses, which kept him busy. He still found time, occasionally, to lead the partying in town. 'We had our fun,' says Nick Gillard, 'not least the night me, Ewan, Sam Jackson, Jimmy Smits and a three-foot midget went out on the piss in Sydney. That got messy.' So messy, he didn't realise that Jackson wasn't touching a drop – imagine how he used to carry on when he was drinking. (Quite wisely, Hayden Christensen was often found partying with the more restrained Elijah Wood and his hobbit pals, seeking hedonistic refuge in the city during breaks in their New Zealand *Lord of the Rings* shoot.)

Star Wars: Episode II – Attack of the Clones would be released in 2002. Lucas wasn't holding his breath for the reviews. 'It's better than *The Phantom Menace*. But unless you're an absolute raving *Star Wars* junkie, it isn't much fun,' said the *South Florida Sun-Sentinel*. The *Kansas City Star* went further: 'An entertainment so in love with its over-inflated mythology that it no longer recognises the needs of moviegoers for real characters and compelling plots.'

With only $309 million taken at the US box office, the film was seen as less popular than its predecessor – but how many directors could be disappointed with a worldwide take of three quarters of a billion dollars? There was certainly no hint that Lucas would give up before he got round to making *Episode III*. Jackson, typically, was criticised in some quarters for giving the game away by saying that, not only would Mace Windu be back next time, but he would also meet his death. In his defence, since *A New Hope* starts with only two Jedi alive – Yoda and Obi-Wan who then train Luke – most people could work out that something happens to the rest of them in *Episode III*. 'All the other Jedi get wiped out in the Clone Wars,' Jackson explains. 'I told George I didn't mind dying, I just didn't want to go out like some punk.'

Jackson was called back for four re-shoots once the production wound up in London late in summer, although Lucas has another name for them. 'George refuses to call them re-shoots. He refers to them as ligaments,' Jackson says. 'For George, it's all about making things better.'

From a workaholic's point of view, the trip to England could not have been better because it gave Jackson the chance to do a lot of much-needed promotion with John Singleton in time for the opening of *Shaft* in Europe. It also gave both men the opportunity to check out the Notting Hill Carnival – although standing on the back of a float chucking out film freebies to a baying crowd may not be the ideal way to soak up the event's unique ambience. 'I've always got here a few days after carnival so I've always heard about it and seen pictures but it was good to finally see it,' Jackson says. 'They have something similar in Brooklyn – the West Indian Parade – but it's not as peaceful as yours.' Singleton's experience was tinged by an accident with his footwear. 'Those Trinis messed up my shoes,' he laughs. 'They got red paint everywhere, on my new Air Jordans.'

The London premiere went off without a hitch. The New York bash, on the other hand, could have turned nasty when *Shaft*'s star bumped into one of his leading rivals for the part. For a while during the 'audition' stage, Wesley Snipes had let it be known that he was the only man capable of stepping into Shaft's leather coat. 'There's no problem,' Jackson makes clear. 'I saw him at a premiere and said, "Wassup," and we talked about what we always do – we don't talk about work.' There's no competition between them, he insists, due to the amount of work around.

There may well be plenty of work, but perhaps not everyone is so keen as Jackson to take it. For his fourth movie of 2000 he would have to spend the winter in England's sunny Liverpool – wearing a kilt. Snipes was strangely silent when it came to casting this one. Can't imagine why.

23. A NIGGA IN A KILT

Kasi Lemmons had said it first – why can't other countries be as film-friendly as Canada? In October 2000, a movie shot in England was produced 'with the participation of the Canadian film and tax credit' in association with a pile of cash from the UK lottery. Why? Because they care about films and they are prepared to take risks on new and exciting ventures. It just so happens, so does Samuel L. Jackson.

'My wife always used to say, "Why are you taking that piddling-ass job?" ' he says. 'And I'm like, "Every piddling-ass job is a step to another place." ' Occasionally that place can be a creative cul-de-sac; but other times it leads to new and wondrous and, above all, better things. Jackson's career has been a series of, on the face of it, fairly random steps. But throughout every role he has strived to build a reputation as a versatile, talented and capable actor. And that has its own rewards.

One of the results of a good reputation is the opportunity to get involved with projects at a higher level. He had first acted as a producer for Kasi Lemmons's *Eve's Bayou*. Now he was putting on his Executive Producer Kangol for a new project that he was about to star in. Apart from all the added hassle, the joint role brought some perks. For a start, after all the friction he had experienced over the years with directors, he now had the chance to select someone to helm the new picture. Immediately he knew who he wanted.

'I love Hong Kong martial arts movies, so I wanted to get Ronny Yu who directed some of my favourite films,' he says. 'I love the way he directs action.' Yu was interested as soon as Jackson contacted him – especially with the star's logic. 'He said, "You've got to direct me – I'm going to be wearing a kilt." '

Released in the USA as *Formula 51* and in Europe as *The 51st State*, the movie that pitched one of Hollywood's coolest men as a gangster in a skirt was the usual tale of an LA drug dealer out to make a $20 million killing in the north-west of England who gets embroiled in the plans of a number of local villains, including those of Liverpool FC fan Felix DeSouza – he just wants a ticket to see his beloved team play Manchester United. For all of the plot's inventiveness, however, Jackson was more taken by his character's look.

'The first draft of the script I saw said my character, Elmo McElroy was this tall, bald black man in a kilt,' he recalls. 'The image just caught me and struck me as vivid.'

Much is made in the finished movie of the character's dress sense. As he lurches, under Yu's breathless direction, from one life-or-death scenario to another, Elmo at one point finds himself in a seduction situation gone wrong. 'Ain't that always the way,' he shrugs. 'Elevator music, a nigga in a kilt and a chick with a nickel-plated.' Every other major character in the movie refers to the 'skirt', and some of them live to laugh about it. An early scene on a heavily 'placed' Virgin Atlantic flight sees his would-be assassin trying to sneak a peak up his kilt while he sleeps, legs slightly akimbo.

Having worked with Obi-Wan actor McGregor, Jackson had experience of the fashion. 'I had seen Ewan at the *Star Wars* premiere wearing a kilt and, of course, I've seen Sean Connery,' he says. 'So I thought, "Yeah, I can pull it off." ' He was also helped by the fact that the costumiers for the picture were able to trace his heritage to provide a tartan from the 'clan' of his grandparents, the Montgomerys.

One of McGregor's fellow *Trainspotting* stars, Robert Carlyle, plays Elmo's Yank-loathing henchman. Like everyone else, he had been interested to see how the great Hollywood star would fare in the national costume of his and McGregor's homeland. 'I had seen some sketches of the costume design, but it didn't prepare me for seeing Sam dressed like it. He just looked so cool,' Carlyle admits. 'But then, he'd look cool in a bin bag.'

As Jackson has often said, being 'cool' to him is appearing comfortable in your own skin. Wearing a kilt in blustery Liverpool meant that there was a chance other people might have to get comfortable with his skin. As always, he had a plan, triggered by the costumier in Liverpool handing him a book on kilts. Page one, line one: 'Do not put on a kilt if you can't wear it with confidence.' Fortunately, confidence is something Jackson has never lacked. 'When I finally got the kilt and stood in front of the mirror looking at myself, it looked very cool,' he says. 'All of a sudden I had this whole sort of *Gladiator* thing going on.'

His director had other bravado-building suggestions.

'Yu told me to put on my lipstick, so every morning, before I put the kilt on, I'd do my lips, bend over and kiss myself – then put the kilt on.'

Elmo is obsessed with his Scottish ancestry, but Carlyle really is Scottish, hence a certain in-depth knowledge of his co-star's outfit. 'It's a casual style, it's not a dress kilt like the Alexander Brothers or Andy Stewart type of regalia,' he explains. 'It's a heavy blue woollen jersey and it's kind of looser, but he just looks brilliant.'

Even the local weather seemed to play to Jackson's advantage as far as embarrassing himself went. 'I know people don't wear anything under their kilts,' he told the *Independent*. 'It's pretty cold in Scotland, so I guess they don't have to worry about their dangly bits.' The same was probably true of Liverpool in October and November.

It was another bonus of being a producer that Jackson had a say in his co-stars. He was very happy that his first choice – Carlyle – came off. 'He is just so good, you know? He makes all this work,' Jackson says. 'We clicked the minute he walked into the room. I was like, "All riiight, this is going to be all right." '

The film also casts a whole array of actors known specifically for other parts. First there's Meat Loaf, the possessor of a fine voice and a finer pair of breasts in *Fight Club*, as psychotic villain of the piece, The Lizard. Then there's Rhys Ifans, wonderfully unhinged as Iki, and a thousand miles away from his dozy *Notting Hill* character. Sean Pertwee is a bent cop – 'an arsehole' according to the actor – and an array of *Full Monty* and *Brookside* faces add support, amomg them Ricky Tomlinson. *The Royle Family* star particularly made an impression on Jackson. 'I love his show,' he says. 'Try to get an American producer to wrap his mind around that. It's like, "Why would I watch that?" Because it's an interesting character study, stupid!' Almost overnight, Jackson had adopted the phrase 'my arse' into his speech.

It is a sign of Jackson's talent as an actor that even in this hotch-potch but thoroughly enjoyable romp, he never appears to be playing it by numbers as a lot of his contemporaries might. At no point do audiences sense that he is in it for the pay cheque; that he is the big American star come to shore up this humble little British picture. Apart from his opening scene as a 1971 hippie, everything else is played straight down the line. There's as much 'proper' acting from him here as there was in, say, *Pulp Fiction*. In fact, there's even the same facial hair as Jules, although this time his hair is stunningly corn-rowed with an end result to make even David Beckham jealous.

Apart from inserting his choice of director and lead actor, Jackson was able to wield influence in one other area. As if his character weren't different enough, he also wields a peculiar weapon of choice. Coming straight from the set of *Attack of the Clones*, it wasn't too much of a leap to adjust to, either. The first time audiences see Elmo, he is leaving his laboratory (having freed his test mice) carrying only his most precious possessions – a set of golf clubs. Various set pieces in the movie, in particular one where he and Carlyle are stuck on a ferry on the Mersey driving balls at a far-off buoy, utilise the character's golf obsession. But it is when Elmo starts flashing around his number three wood like it's a lightsaber that his character becomes really memorable, almost like a Bond villain. Of course, there was the odd mishap during filming and more than one extra needed treatment following a mistimed driving iron to the head (Ewan McGregor broke Nick Gillard's finger during *Star Wars*; and vice versa).

The 51st State attracted Jackson in other ways, other than golf. In particular he was taken by his chemist character's creation of a highly efficacious drug made only from legal substances. 'I liked the ambiguity of it: is it a drug, or isn't it?' he says. He remembers his own experiences of being so desperate for a hit that he'd accept anything from a dealer. 'You find the guy and before you even see him, you start getting high,' he says. 'He could give you some baking soda and you'd take it. All that's very true.'

Less attractive to the man from California was filming in Liverpool – at least at first. It may just have been named European City of Culture but it still has, let's face it, a certain reputation. 'It's not as depressing as people made it out to be,' he admits. 'By the time I got there my expectations were pretty low, but no one bothered me or anything like that – but it was always raining.'

Like a good tourist, he spent a lot of his time exploring the city. 'I was even driving,' he laughs. 'I finally figured out how to drive on the wrong side of the street! I went to bars, clubs, restaurants and the people were really cool, everybody was helpful.' As in Sydney, he even found himself taking in the local music scene. Not used to having anything more than a couple of teenage millionaire footballers in their midst, the local papers of course ran several stories about how Jackson was spotted off his tree here or there. He doesn't deny it – not all of it, anyway. 'I was in the clubs, dancing and hanging out, but I don't drink,' he says. 'There's good party life in Liverpool. The rave scene is incredible.'

Jackson even tried to take in the local culture: namely a trip to Anfield football stadium to watch the local team play a Champions League tie against Italy's mighty Roma. He wasn't impressed. Subtleties like the fact that the Reds only needed a draw (because of their 2–0 victory in the first leg) were lost on him. 'It was bad, man,' he says. 'I didn't know they didn't have to score. There is an inherent problem in any game where you don't have to score points.'

Jackson's lack of appreciation of the very subject that drives Carlyle's character should have been a clue. The fact that the movie ended up with different titles either side of the Atlantic was a bigger indicator of how difficult it would be to sell internationally. In the UK, it went on to become the ninth most successful film of 2001. In America, it was harder to shift, ostensibly because it was set in so alien a place, and $5.2 million represented the best it could do there. Jackson takes it in his stride. 'We weren't making *Gone with the Wind*,' he says. 'I learned when I was doing theatre that criticism is not general, it's very personal. Everybody's entitled to an opinion.'

His own opinion is that his favourite British gangster movies, *The Long Good Friday* and *The Krays*, needn't worry about their place in history since he was trying to do something different with the genre. 'I've always wanted to do one or be a part of one and this was kind of an opportunity to do one, but in a very different kind of way.' *Formula 51* was bought for American distribution by Sony. Having bought it, they sat on it for up to a year longer than was healthy for a movie shot in 2000. The reason: a bunch of strong British dialects and a major movie star in a frock. 'I don't know what they saw that they bought,' Jackson says sarcastically. ' "Well, we're not sure that an audience wants to see you in a kilt!" ' In their wisdom, a poll was paid for and, lo, Sony decided they didn't want to depict Jackson in his tartan on the poster. 'It was when they started talking about trying to digitally take the kilt out of the movie that I had to say, "Hold it!" '

Not that all critics are parochial, but just as the *New York Times* seems more favourable towards movies shot within its skyline, so this movie split reviewers on an international basis. English? You loved it. Yank? What a turkey.

'*Formula 51* is so trite that even Yu's high-energy action stylings can't break through the stupor,' said the *Miami Herald*. 'Just as the lousy Tarantino imitations have subsided, here comes the first lousy Guy Ritchie imitation,' sneered the *Illinois Northwest Herald*. The *Fort Worth Star-Telegram* was blunter: 'Excessive, profane, packed with cartoonish violence and comic-strip characters' – like that's a bad thing? *Fantastica Daily* were slightly more generous: '*Formula 51* is pretty much Quentin Tarantino meets Guy Ritchie, as directed by Ronny Yu. However, if you like that sort of thing, as I do, you just might have some fun with the chemical imbalance of *Formula 51*.'

Over to the Brits and *Total Film*'s emphatic defence: 'A British comedy thriller that says cobblers to reality but does it with so much wit, style and balls-out verve that you're far too busy enjoying yourself to care. See it.' *Empire* was equally effusive: 'The end result is full-on fun, a British movie with the guts to push beyond our humble industry's barriers.'

Hats off, then, to that British film made with Canadian money, directed by an Asian and starring and produced by an American. Rule Britannia.

Lest anyone think that the life of the internationally acclaimed movie star is hermetically divined years in advance, *Variety* reported an article on Samuel L. Jackson on the last day of August 2000. At the time, he was in Britain promoting *Shaft*; what he was doing though, the magazine said, was signing up for a new picture. Not something for next year, or the year after – but for this year; just a couple of months away.

Changing Lanes was a project that had been earmarked for new face on the block Ben Affleck for some time. While his *Good Will Hunting* co-writer and co-star Matt Damon had gone on to work with the likes of George Clooney and Brad Pitt on *Ocean's Eleven*, Affleck was winning more headlines for his will-they/won't-they dalliance with *Out of Sight* diva Jennifer Lopez. It didn't help that he was a far more wooden performer than Damon, albeit the more classically handsome of the pair. A lead turn in the Marvel Comics production of *DareDevil* gave him a shot at superhero glory, but he really needed a down-to-earth hit. And Paramount's *Changing Lanes* looked like supplying it.

There was a time that Jackson would have demurred on this project and let it go. What was his line about validating the careers of other lesser performers? But Affleck was a good egg as far as Jackson was concerned – more in the Busta Rhymes category than the Tupac mob. 'Ben's a cool guy and he comes really prepared to work which is far more important than an actor's cool quotient,' he says. And being prepared, as we know, is the highest compliment Jackson can give.

On the face of it, *Changing Lanes* is a nothing story: two strangers get involved in a fender bender. In the hands of *Notting Hill*'s Roger Michell, however, it soon spirals into a surprisingly plausible thriller. Even though Jackson's character, Doyle Gibson, was cast last, it is him audiences root for as the two leads conspire to destroy each other in New York. 'I'm the guy most people who come to the movie are going to relate to,' he says, assuming the majority of viewers aren't high-powered lawyers in Armani suits blessed with the kind of resources Affleck's character has. It's true. Although most audiences will not appreciate Doyle's position as a recovering alcoholic in quite the same technicolour as Jackson, they will no doubt empathise with his struggle as a father to try to win back custody of his kids by sorting his life out and securing a new family home. When Affleck's character interferes with this dream – first by crashing into his car and not giving him a lift home; then by getting mysterious 'fixers' to have Doyle declared bankrupt by all financiers – the sheer, almost tangible sense of Doyle's smallness in his struggle against 'the system' is engrossing.

'I understand how the bureaucracy of New York can drive someone crazy,' Jackson says. 'And I've worked on my share of movie sets where the bureaucracy nearly drove me crazy so it wasn't difficult getting into Doyle's mindset.'

Getting into character was a lot more tricky than with someone like Shaft or Elmo McElroy. Here was just an ordinary guy in ordinary clothes; no noticeable tics or quirks around which to hang a character. Some may have seen it as a problem, Jackson saw it as an opportunity to paint a character on a blank canvas. For him, finding the look of the character is the most important step, then building on that look to find the person within.

'I spent a lot of time talking with my stylist, make-up artists and costumier and only then did I try to tap into Doyle's frustration of not being able to access the resources he needs to solve his problems,' he says. A neat hairstyle that befits his character's position, plus a tamer moustache than Elmo sported completed the outfit of middle-class gent on his uppers.

'This guy was a good challenge for me as an actor, after having done all these other things for a while,' he says, 'so I kind of needed to just recharge my acting battery.'

Where others may have seen a dull, one-dimensional character – and that's Doyle, not Affleck – Jackson rose to the challenge of creating someone real, rounded and believable. 'I've never done a one-dimensional performance in my life, not that I know of,' he insists. Doyle has a lot going on, from trying to cling onto his family, his job and, at times, his sanity. It was all inner angst that Jackson needed to build on and somehow convey. Fortunately, Jackson felt he was up to it.

'I tend to think I have a facility for doing just about anything and I wanted to play a guy who was quietly raging in that way,' he says.

After the pushing-plausibility action sequences of *The 51st State*, the amazing internal anguish that Jackson manages to convey via Doyle is quite formidable. Unfortunately, yet again, his sum proved greater than the whole, a fact more noticeable than usual since he and his supposed leading man were barely on screen together. 'We were essentially making two different movies,' he reveals. 'We only interact three or four times in the film.'

Despite this sort of summing up from the *Los Angeles Daily News* – 'one of those movies where you walk out of the theatre not feeling cheated exactly, but feeling pandered to, which, in the end, might be all the more infuriating' – the star combination was enough to entice almost $70 million out of American cinema-goers, however. And that, for all its failings compared to the originality of *Formula 51*, is nothing to be sneezed at.

24. WE TOLD YOU SO

Every year, just prior to Oscar time, Graydon Carter's *Vanity Fair* publishes its 'Hollywood' issue. For one month only, the magazine becomes the movie bible as two hundred plus pages are devoted to interviews, photographs and articles featuring the world's leading stars. Like all publications, the cover is the most important selling tool and an actor's appearance on it can add another million dollars to his pay cheque. In April 2003, the magazine pulled off an amazing coup. The eleven most significant actors in town were brought together for a school photo-type shoot spread across a glossy, pull-out front cover. Tom Cruise, Tom Hanks, Brad Pitt, Jack Nicholson, Harrison Ford – it was a cover to make any PR firm cry. Oh, and Samuel L. Jackson.

There it was, in glorious poster-format technicolour: Samuel L. Jackson had made it. He was at the pinnacle of his career. Thirty years since leaving Morehouse College and aged 54, he was rightly and publicly hailed as one of the very best his industry had to offer.

For the shoot itself, Jackson turned up in a Day-Glo orange tracksuit topped off with fluorescent orange Kangol and shoes. Nice Mr *Vanity Fair* had laid on a room full of clothes from the world's leading designers, so by the time Jackson emerged from his dressing room, he was clad neck to foot in a suit from *Shaft* designer Armani. His hair for the occasion was shaped by Robert L. Stevenson, his *xXx* stylist, although hardly any was ultimately visible beneath another hat from his Kangol collection. Leaning against the back wall, effortlessly following snapper Annie Leibovitz's command to 'look good', he effuses style. At his feet, Hugh Grant sports odd coloured socks. To his right, Brad Pitt models the latest bum fashions from his private collection. Far left Tom Hanks sits politely in his tank top – clearly no one had told him it wasn't a real school picture.

Although it was a welcome public display of his standing in Hollywood, Jackson's appearance on the pull-out section the cover was not unexpected. The front five were the big ones, the nailed-on name-above-the-titles players who get multi-million-dollar movies greenlit just by agreeing to be in them. Jackson was paired with the likes of Ed Norton, Don Cheadle, Hugh Grant, Jude Law, Dennis Quaid and Harrison Ford's left arm; two Englishmen, two black guys, two 'interesting' character actors. All of them arguably better technically than some of the chaps round the flap, but commercially yet to come anywhere close.

While a minority fretted about what message *Vanity Fair* was sending out by relegating its two black cover stars to the second tier, most people, including Jackson, took his appearance as a compliment, as recognition of his place in the movie kingdom. But the minority was right to worry. Mainstream magazines are traditionally not inclined to use black stars as sales tools on their front covers. Black faces don't sell, goes the mantra. It is widely accepted that men are more likely to buy a magazine about movies. It is also widely accepted that those men prefer to buy magazines featuring scantily clad women on the covers. White women, at that. What the average male consumer does not want is a fully clothed, black, fifty-something male.

Samuel Jackson, however, appears to break that trend. According to its then editor Peter Howarth, an issue of the UK magazine *Esquire* featuring Jackson on its cover was the biggest selling issue of 2001. Appearing to plug *The 51st State*, Jackson's issue helped to sell more than 80,000 copies of the December issue, Howarth said, which was around 15,000 copy sales more than the second-best issue. 'To have a 52-year-old black man outselling the current crop of young, C-list blondes shows that readers aren't colour sensitive and gender sensitive,' he said at the time. Now, that is impressive.

Esquire would later go on to lose 13 per cent of its readership following its decision to use men as cover stars; Jackson, it seemed, was a one-off. Unfortunately, while it is a personal fillip for him, the fact remains that black faces in general are perceived not to be commercial winners, regardless of who they belong to. Black supermodel Naomi Campbell famously claimed she was dropped from the cover of American *Vogue* in 1996 because the American public was not ready for a black cover girl. 'This business is about selling,' she said, 'and blonde and blue-eyed girls are what sells.' Mrs David Bowie, Iman, went on to bring out a coffee table book in 2001 celebrating black models to emphasise the same lack of courage among publishers.

If *Vanity Fair* and his earlier statistics-defying *Esquire* appearance absolutely concretise Jackson's place in the Hollywood firmament, it has come as no surprise, either to him or to his audience. This, after all, was the hardest-working actor in the 1990s. This, after all, is the man seemingly hell-bent on maintaining that title at the end of the Noughties. Between his appearances in *Changing Lanes* and *Vanity Fair*, Jackson worked on another five movies.

In February 2003, however, he was in the news again for something entirely different, or at lease his name was. After a few years of sarcasm from the actor, Ice Cube (or was it Ice Pick or Ice Tray?) had decided to respond to Jackson's claims that rappers can't act. Of course, he did it in a song. In the track called 'Lights Out', he raps, 'You can tell Samuel L. I'm-a keep acting' over producer Damizza's popping funk track. Considering

Cube also compares himself to a young Osama, tells MCs to bow down to him as if he were Yoda and instructs the Reverend Jesse Jackson to 'put a rubber on' rather than sprinkle the planet with his illegitimate children, Jackson clearly came off lightly. As with most public spats, much was made of it, although no one seemed to recall the actor appearing in the video for Public Enemy's '911 is a Joke' – so much for him not supporting rap artists.

This time, Jackson (Samuel) refused to comment on the song, but he did speak out when similar comments were made about his co-star on new Bond film for the millennium, *xXx*. Vin Diesel, commentators felt, was not worthy of licking Jackson's boots, let alone having him play supporting cast in the ridiculously basso voice'd hunk's movie. Uh-ah, says Jackson. Diesel is the real deal. 'He's paid some dues,' he says, referring to the muscly one's background of New York theatre and several shorts which he wrote and directed. 'He has shown that there is a specific quality about him that is going to take him to the next place.'

In actual fact, clichéd though it seems, Diesel and Jackson had been looking for the right project to work on together, having become friends a few years earlier. They had met in London years before when Diesel was doing *Saving Private Ryan* and Jackson was working on *Star Wars: Episode I*. 'We accidentally ran into each other in a sushi bar and spent some time together,' the latter recalls. 'We've had some common experiences, and our relationship is such that we've wanted to work together for a while.'

As Augustus Gibbons, Jackson played a scar-faced straightman to Diesel's irrepressible extreme-ironing-type super spy – a disfigured M to his co-star's Bond, hence the 007-spoofing name of the film. Unfortunately, in the post-Austin Powers generation, there was also more than a hint of Michael York's Basil Exposition about him. *xXx*'s director, Rob Cohen, knew immediately that only one man could pull off the job of checking Diesel on screen – Jackson. 'He's the King of Cool,' Cohen says. 'He's self-confident, supremely talented, an ultimate gentleman. And he would be a trillionaire if he could just sell some of his charisma.'

Diesel agrees. 'He's always been one of my favourite actors,' he says. 'The idea of working with Sam was literally a dream come true.'

Of course, you hire the man, you get the package. Even for something as throwaway as this spaced-up spy romp, Jackson brought his full retinue of acting tricks, in particular a fully thought-out back story for his character. 'I wanted him to be badly scarred from some mission in the past,' he says, 'which Gibbons uses as a reminder of where he's been, who he is, what he sacrificed for his country and how proud he is of that.'

With the help of make-up artist, Allan Apone, and hair stylist Robert L. Stevenson, Gibbons's face gradually took shape. Four different facial looks were created and elements from each were chosen.

'Gibbons knows that you have to find someone who's on the same page as the bad guys. That's how he sees Xander – a renegade.'

Most reviewers picked up on the blatant attempt to build a Bond audience for a younger generation; for some this was a bad thing, others a boon. 'It's dumb fun slapped silly, a new franchise inspired by the Bond films that's not far from the porn its title promises; the film is a veritable orgy of outrageous stunts,' said the *Bangor Daily News*. 'For all its posturing, *xXx* essentially is a James Bond movie refitted for the Tony Hawk crowd,' reckoned the *Northwest Illinois Herald*. 'A mediocre exercise in target demographics, unaware that it's the butt of its own joke,' ranted the *Los Angeles Daily News*. The *Apollo Guide* was prescient in its verdict: 'Bond-inspired? Certainly. Likely to have decades of life as a classic movie franchise? Let's hope not.'

Others were more hopeful that there could be a lucrative serialisation, Jackson included. 'I haven't signed anything,' he says knowingly, 'but I did kind of make my character indispensable.' The only obstruction in the way of a lucrative long-running franchise (and the first attempt earned a not inconsiderable $142 million domestically) was the fact that the Bond film that came out shortly afterwards, *Die Another Day*, was the strongest for some time. 007 was still the one to beat.

One would think the same franchise plan would apply to *Shaft*. Despite doing better than most people budgeted for, and despite having all the major players signed to sequel options, there remains no whiff of an Episode II in the pipeline. 'I'd like to see me and Richard Roundtree team up to solve crimes – unfortunately, no one has even mentioned doing another picture,' Jackson says.

As reunion team-ups go, however, there has only ever been one partnership that movie audiences have really wanted to see recreated: Samuel L. Jackson and John Travolta – together again. In late 2001 it looked like it might happen when Jackson revealed in interviews that 'I've signed my contract but I don't know what John's plans are'. While he waited for the star of *Battlefield Earth* – arguably the worst film of all time – to make up his mind, Jackson was mollified by the news that he would be linking up with another old friend: *Die Hard: With a Vengeance* director John McTiernan.

The movie was *Basic*, less a whodunnit than a did-he-do-it? set within the sort of military environment that Jackson had explored with *Rules of Engagement* and Travolta had recently visited on *The General's Daughter*. Fitting it into his schedule for 2002 was tight for Jackson, but even though it meant one week he was in the Czech Republic working on *xXx* and the next he was suited and booted in Jacksonville for *Basic*, he wanted to do it. Eventually, so did Travolta too.

Unfortunately, it was a decision most audiences would regret on the actors' behalf. This was not how they wanted Jules and Vincent to reunite. There was only so far that a recently slimmed-down Travolta could carry the movie. Perhaps it was the 'follow that' syndrome that Jackson had experienced on *Star Wars* and *Unbreakable*, but *Basic* was pretty much hammered in all corners of the press. And rightly so. Between them, McTiernan and scripter James Vanderbilt attracted every negative phrase in the critics' phrasebook.

'McTiernan, still trying to wash the stink of *Rollerball* out of his clothes, tumbles further into the Abyss of Lost Film-makers,' said the *Dallas Observer*. 'Fumbling the set-up, the *Die Hard* helmer quickly loses his grip on the material, turning *Basic* into little more than a mechanical exercise in plotting,' scathed *BBCi*. 'Movie-goers aren't likely to be sold on the absurd plot twists doled out by screenwriter James Vanderbilt,' said *LA Weekly*. Last word to the *Philadelphia Daily News*: 'Conflicting point-of-view flashbacks defuse rather than raise tension, since any ultimate truth is going to be just another scenario.'

Several months after its national release in the US, *Basic* had earned just $26 million. To the average movie fan, this is a respectable enough figure. To the Hollywood glitterati, however, it really is a drop in the ocean, as Jackson revealed when he mocked Ordell Robbie's obsession with hoarding $1 million. As if to prove it, the *LA Times* revealed in June 2002 that he and LaTanya had just sold their Encino home for approximately $2 million. The interesting point of the story was the fact that the couple had already bought a replacement home two years earlier – and that had set them back a mighty $10 million. How many homeowners can afford to buy before they sell?

No prizes for guessing what caught Jackson's eye when he looked down the estate agent's spec for the property: two acres of land, nine bedrooms in 11,000 square feet, private pool, spa, tennis court and 2,300 square foot synthetic putting green. Clearly previous owner Roseanne Arnold had more taste than she ever let on in public.

With his own practice green, it is no wonder that Jackson has no qualms about turning out for various public golf tournaments. Along with the likes of Michael Douglas, he jetted into the UK in summer 2001 to take part in the Dunhill Links Pro-Am at St Andrews. August the same year found him lining up alongside the likes of *Formula 51* co-star Meat Loaf, Richard Roundtree and ex-husband of his new home's vendor, Tom Arnold to take part in the third annual NFL Celebrity Golf Shootout, in which stars paired up with various ball professionals. The pinnacle of Jackson's obsession came with the inaugural Samuel L. Jackson Celebrity Golf Classic, the profits from which all go to charity.

Away from the compliments earned from his sporting prowess, Jackson was also picking up a few plaudits in his day job. It may not have pleased everybody, but *Shaft* had a certain demographic appeal. The Blockbuster Entertainment Awards and the Image Awards both nominated him for Best Actor, but perhaps the MTV Movie Awards summed up the movie's success by nominating him as Best Dressed Movie Character for *Shaft*. It was a look that the *Matrix* boys would soon be copying. Blockbuster also nominated Jackson for Best Actor (Suspense) for *Unbreakable*.

Never one to shy away from work opportunities, Jackson had been quick to exploit the commercial possibilities for his *Shaft* look. When Reebok asked in 2000 if the character – rather than the actor –would appear in print adverts for their Classic trainers, he said yes. He has also lent his voice to pitches for KFC in the UK and Garden Burger in America. Considering that his first big success was for Krystal burgers more than thirty years earlier, it is interesting to see how fast food and him are automatically linked still, especially since Jules Winnfield's obsessive fascination with the various brands in *Pulp Fiction*.

Viewers of American television will vouch for the fact that Sarah, Duchess of York appears regularly on commercials for dietary products. Many major movie stars plug products in Japan. The basic rule of celebrity thumb appears to be: as long as you don't soil your credibility in your own backyard, be as shameless as you like. Having said that, the UK has been as good to Samuel L. Jackson as his home country; many of his films have been greater successes in Europe than in the US. For that reason, it is disappointing that arguably one of the greatest actors of his generation should have accepted the corporate dollar to advertise financial giant Barclays so brashly on British television. He may look cool walking up a long *O Brother, Where Art Thou*-type road with his tan Kangol and matching outfit, but he's talking about three little pigs for goodness' sake. Even though he doesn't actually mention Barclays – that's the voice-over man's job – it has Sell Out written all over it. There isn't a branch in the land that doesn't feature a giant poster of Jackson's smiling chops beneath a caption about smart investing. Congratulations to ad agency Bartle Bogle Hegarty for capturing him, but we would rather have had a sequel to *Amos and Andrew* than the never-ending Fluent in Finance campaign.

And yet . . . and yet, if anyone can pull off such a corporately clumsy stunt and still maintain his cred, it's Jackson. This is the man with some of the naffest hobbies around – golf, comic books, kung fu films – and yet in his hands, they all acquire unthinkable cachet. In 2002 it was time for his martial arts side to get a public airing as he hosted an HBO show called *The Art of Action*, 96 minutes of clips and interviews from one hundred of the best chocky sock flicks around – from *Crouching Tiger* to *Charlie's Angels*. On a more serious note, he also contributed, alongside Oprah Winfrey, Don Cheadle and many others, to a programme called *Unchained Memories: Readings from the Slave Narratives*, a collection of real-life stories told by the survivors of slavery and brought to life by actors. Rather than relying on voice-overs, each actor's face is in eerie close-up as they recount the first-person tales of terror and hardship.

In April, Jackson lent his name to another cause he believed in. The Screen Actors Guild had drawn up a contract clause that required member actors to be covered by the same working conditions overseas as they would enjoy in the US, aimed at curtailing studios' growing practice of using cheaper locations outside the US. Recent examples, according to SAG, included all three parts of *The Lord of the Rings*, shot in New Zealand. As Jackson and the likes of Sarah Michelle Gellar put their name to the campaign in full-page magazine adverts, it seemed that *The Caveman's Valentine* and other films which could never have been made at US prices had momentarily slipped his mind. Did anyone really think *The Lord of the Rings* would ever have been shot if Miramax had had to stump up Hollywood fees? Weinstein had wanted the trilogy condensed into one volume anyway.

Jackson is quite the evangelist when it comes to talking about his passions – and kung fu movies and anti-racism are certainly up there – but nothing drives him like his work. *xXx* and *Basic* were just two of the pictures put to bed in 2002; there were several others, plus promotional duties for a couple more. April 22 found him at the Paramount Theatre on the Paramount lot for the premiere of *Changing Lanes*. Along for the ride were LaTanya, Affleck and fellow co-stars Sydney Pollack and Amanda Peet. More pressing business, of course, was the worldwide round of premieres for *Attack of the Clones* shortly afterwards. Wowing heads of Londoners, Jackson turned up to the Leicester Square opening night with his date for the night, Halle Berry. The evening also marked Lucas's birthday, a fact recognised by 3,000 fans outside the cinema who burst into the time-honoured song. The Royal Philharmonic Orchestra was also on hand for the night to play endless versions of John Williams's theme music as the likes of Frank Skinner, Johnny Vegas, 'H' and Claire from Steps and Atomic Kitten drifted past to take their free celebrity seats.

Meanwhile, as Hayden Christensen told waiting journalists that he felt he had yet to master his Jedi weapon, Jackson was less reticent – after all, he had a pretty lady on his arm to impress. 'My lightsaber skills are impeccable,' he said. 'You want to take me on outside the theatre?'

Another project to test Jackson's schoolboy fighting fantasies was *S.W.A.T.*, a big screen adaptation of the 1970s TV series of the same name.

October 2002 found Jackson and co-stars Colin Farrell, Michelle Rodriguez, Olivier Martinez and old *Deep Blue Sea* pal, L.L. Cool J., raking through the streets of downtown LA in highly stylised car chases as principal photography began in earnest. The film follows Jackson's character, Hondo, as he is assigned to recruit and train five top-notch officers for a new Special Weapons and Tactics unit. Farrell stars as Jim Street, a Los Angeles Police Department officer whose recent demotion to a desk job leaves him desperate for a second chance to don the elite S.W.A.T. uniform.

After the lack of chemistry with Affleck, teaming up with current Britney-snogging bad boy Farrell gives Jackson a chance to give a spin to the Oscar-winning performance of Louis Gossett Jr in *An Officer and a Gentleman*, as he puts the surly Richard Gere-type through his arduous paces. We all know the relationship will end in much respect and mutual butt-saving, but it's how the movie takes us there that matters.

While *S.W.A.T.* has 'big box office' stamped all over it, it is commonly known that that has never been Jackson's main motivation for taking a job. No other leading actor so regularly mixes blockbuster-type cashability with such a range of diverse and interesting projects. Unfortunately, as he discovered with Sony's reaction to *Formula 51*, 'diverse and interesting' in Hollywood can be the kiss of death – it's film-parlance for 'impossible to sell'. Even so, the shoddy treatment to date of *The House on Turk Street* has defied expectations.

On the face of it, a crime thriller from *The Maltese Falcon* author Dashiell Hammett should be worthy of interest on its own. Throw in a cast which includes modern renaissance woman Milla Jovovich, another *Deep Blue Sea* alumnus Stellan Skarsgård, Britain's Joss Ackland and man of many hairpieces Samuel Jackson, a decently twisty plot involving a missing neighbour and a stumbled-upon bank heist – oh, and a cello – and there should be something for everyone.

Unfortunately, as in *Formula 51*, it appears there is too much for everyone. Where Sony couldn't handle Jackson in a kilt before, the hitch with this film appears to be his character's love of and dexterity on the cello. Despite all the other hooks in Bob Rafelson's flick, a large wooden instrument smacks of art house – and look what happened to *The Red Violin*. After what seemed like an age in the box marked 'finished movie', *Turk Street* had yet to see the light of day at the start of 2003. When it did emerge, it was with that same admission of mixed feelings that surrounded *Formula 51* – the double title. *No Good Deed* or *House on Turk Street* – take your pick, depending on where you see it. For its world premiere, *The House on Turk Street* led the pack at the 2003 Moscow International Film Festival – always the sign of quality distribution.

All of which is a shame. Hammett and Rafelson's pedigree – the latter directed the Nicholson classics *Five Easy Pieces* and *The Postman Always Rings Twice* – should have guaranteed greater respect. Even the plot stands up to scrutiny: Jackson is Jack Friar, a cello-playing San Francisco cop who is about to go on a long-awaited vacation when he is begged by a neighbour to go looking for her daughter, who has run off with her boyfriend. Armed only with a photograph (which he soon loses) and the address that gives the film its title (in some territories), Jack meets up with a charming elderly couple, the Quarres, played by Ackland and Rafelson regular Grace Zabriskie (the mad hitch-hiker in *Five Easy Pieces*). Realising he is a cop – and realising this might be bad for their general bank-robbing business – the Quarres and crooks Skarsgård and Jovovich go all out to manipulate Jack. In one of the movie's most crackling scenes, the scheming yet alluring Jovovich sits between Jackson and his cello as they embark on their own sweet music making. Unlike the interracial scenes in *The Caveman's Valentine*, any miscegenation is only hinted at here – but what hints. A candidate for the most erotic performance of Jackson's career, without a shadow of a doubt.

'My character Erin is definitely a product of her environment, which isn't a good one,' Jovovich says. 'For her, it's about lying, scheming and manipulating him for her benefit.' When she meets Jack, she realises there's another way and suddenly she can be herself. As she says, 'There's a lot of sexual tension in the air.'

Rafelson was delighted with the pair. 'Samuel Jackson brought a lot of dignity and a touch of vulnerability to his role,' he says, 'and Milla has great beauty and intelligence.'

Since robbery movie schemes never run to plan, Jackson is soon surrounded by the dead bodies of those trying to kill him – think Michael Palin's dog-assassin in *A Fish Called Wanda*. By the end of the movie, a heist has been foiled and he can walk into the distance with his cello, casting one last wistful glance back at the mischievous Jovovich.

For all the films Jackson does take on, it is amazing to think that some actually do escape his net. Trade bibles *Variety* and the *Hollywood Reporter* are forever linking actors to scripts; generally these happen. Every so often, one slips through. In November 2000, Jackson was linked to Peter Berg's *Truck 44*, in which a group of firefighters plan an elaborate heist in a New York high-rise, but end up setting off a fire with which they are forced to battle while trying to pull off their crime. By the end of 2003, not a word. Then there was *Training Day*. Jackson was the first name linked with this picture five years earlier; according to reports, he was reworking the script. The next time anyone heard of the film was when Denzel Washington stepped up to collect his Best Actor Oscar for the same part in 2002. Then there was a picture reuniting him with another actor from his past. In August 2001, Jackson was announced as starring opposite Ms Lopez in *Tick-Tock*, the everyday tale of an amnesiac who wakes up in the custody of the FBI and discovers that he is the prime suspect for a series of Los Angeles bombings. Think *Long Kiss Goodnight* in reverse. Late 2003, though, no sign of movement.

One movie that did follow up on its promise, however, was *Blackout*. Maybe it was in recognition of his age, but this was the second film in a few months to feature Jackson as a mentor to a younger star, and his fourth playing a man in uniform (his third copper). Shot in 2002, *Blackout* was the story of Ashley Judd's policewoman who becomes the target of a murder investigation when her former lovers start dropping dead around her. Think *The Negotiator* meets *The Dead Pool*. Lining up alongside Judd and Jackson is the underused Andy Garcia, under the direction of Philip Kaufman.

After the slapstick of filling his days with such easygoing blockbusters recently – including his work on *Episode III* of *Star Wars* during the summer and a small part in the second volume of Tarantino's long overdue *Kill Bill* – it was refreshing for Jackson to take a look at subjects closer to his heart late in 2003. On TV, he took part in *Fighting for Freedom: Revolution and Civil War*, contributing voice-overs to the tale of America's role as a beacon for immigrants, and her not always welcoming arms.

If the USA has had its race problems, then South Africa takes the biscuit. For his final role of 2003, Jackson announced that he would be travelling there to film *Country of my Skull*, a harrowing exposé of South Africa's Truth and Reconciliation Commission's investigation into human rights abuses during the years of apartheid. Joined by Juliette Binoche and director John Boorman, if the movie even half reflects the atrocities captured within Antjie Krog's book, *Country of my Skull: Guilt, Sorrow and the Limits of Forgiveness in the New South Africa*, then Jackson will have one of the most moving pictures of the decade on his hands. By comparison, the hardcore racism endemic in *A Time to Kill*'s Mississippi might look like schoolyard name-calling.

Three decades since Jackson had engaged in peaceful protest at Morehouse College on the subject of racism, and almost thirty years since he formed a 'hate whiteys' theatre group, *Country of my Skull* offered his first real chance to get a realistic eye-witness account of the horrors of segregation into the public domain. The only downside, as far as he was concerned, was that the movie dealt with the problems of another country, another continent. But evil is evil wherever it thrives. He may have become a household name the world over, he may have joined the middle-class golfing hierarchy, he may make a living from popcorn entertainment, but Samuel L. Jackson has never lost sight of his roots. He has never forgotten the very real danger of physical harm as a kid when he wolf-whistled the passing white girl. He has never got over the effrontery of so many white casting agents who refuse to pick him for a role because he is black. 'Sorry, Sam, we weren't going that way.' And to this day, he will not believe that the pathetic showing of black talent – himself very much included – at the Academy Awards over the last seventy years is not down to one reason only: bigotry.

Many people in public office or in positions of prominence have all sorts of views in private. What makes Samuel Jackson so admirable is his total disregard for the conventions of tradition when it comes to speaking his mind. Despite the multiple millions of dollars he has earned from an industry he seems to perceive as operating like a white man's cartel, it has never occurred to him to bite his tongue for fear of losing a job. (Being chucked off the *Patriot Games* series never did him any harm.) It doesn't matter who you are, he says, the truth is any man's right to speak. And he does speak. Jackson is out to be honest first, ingratiate himself later. One example: on the night of the opening ceremony of the 1996 Olympics, Jackson appeared on *The David Letterman Show* to promote *A Time to Kill*. This, according to tradition, is an occasion when Jackson would have been advised to be as personable and non-controversial as possible to win over audiences. Not Jackson. In due course Letterman asked if his guest had any interest in the games or even competing in them. The answer was barbed with years of anti-black sentiment. 'Yes, but if I was going to compete I would do one of those events like pole vault or swimming – one of those events you don't expect brothers to do,' he said to the dumbfounded host. Why? So black athletes could be the best at that event too. Cool.

Jackson is also honest about what he is trying to achieve through the Onyx Village – he wants black kids growing up black. It's not racism to his mind, it's being true to your culture and not kidding yourself that the world around you – the white world – has truly accepted you. It disturbs him that his daughter, Zoe, might be cocooned from a lot of the problems that affect other black kids in California just because she comes from a wealthy family. But he fears that her day of reckoning will come and he is not afraid to warn her about it in public, as he did in *Essence* magazine in 2002.

'Zoe is black and she hasn't had to be accountable for it yet, but she will,' he stated matter-of-factly. When she gets dragged from her car by the LAPD and treated like a second-class citizen, she might start to realise.

And his response if it happens?

'Say we told you so.'

Honest to the last.

BIBLIOGRAPHY AND PICTURE CREDITS

In the course of putting this biography together I have referred to many sources across several media to support my own research. Some texts or resources have been used for a general overview throughout, others have more specific reference to a particular chapter. The main sources are listed below.

BOOKS

Bogle, Donald, *Toms, Coons, Mulattoes, Mammies and Bucks: An Interpretive History of Blacks in American Films*, Penguin, 1973

Bourne, Stephen, *Black in the British Frame: Black People in British Film and Television 1896-1996*, Continuum International Publishing Group, 1998

James, Darius, *That's Blaxploitation: Roots of the Baadasssss 'tude*, St Martin's Press, 1995

Mapp, Edward, *Blacks in American Films Today and Yesterday*, Scarecrow Press, 1972

Noble, Peter, *The Negro in Films*, Arno P, 1976

Null, Gary, *Black Hollywood: Negro in Motion Pictures*, Citadel, 1975

Pines, Jim, *Blacks in Films*, Studio Vista, 1975

Rhines, Jesse Algernon, *Black Film/White Money*, Rutgers UP, 1996

Sampson, Henry T., *Blacks in Black and White: A Source Book on Black Films*, Scarecrow Press, 1993

Shepherd, Donald, *Jack Nicholson: An Unauthorised Biography*, Robson Books, 1991

WEBSITES

These include news sources and film-specific sites: BBC, CNN, IMDB.com, Warner Bros, Fox, Reuters, Amazon, E!Online, Hollywood.com, Virgin.com, Mr Showbiz.com, Jam!Movies.com, Ananova, eDrive, E-star and the various official sites for each Samuel L. Jackson movie.

TV/AUDIO

Interviews from the DVD editions of many Samuel L. Jackson movies, particularly *Pulp Fiction, Jackie Brown, The 51st State* and *Rules of Engagement*, are quoted.

NEWSPAPERS AND JOURNALS

Empire, Premiere, the *New York Times, Starburst, Variety*, the *Hollywood Reporter, Total Film, Sight and Sound, Entertainment Weekly, Toronto Sun* and

Calgary Sun and *Vanity Fair* were, along with the leading national and international daily newspapers, 'general' sources. However, the following publications/articles were of particular help:

Acting Workshop, 1999, Nasser Metcalfe; *American Cinematographer*, August 1996, Naomi Pfefferman; *American Film*, Jan/Feb 1988, Spike Lee; *Black Film Makers*, 18 December 2000, Pascoe Sawyer; *Calgary Sun*, 30 December 1997, Louis B. Hobson; *Calgary Sun*, 1 April 2000, Louis B. Hobson; *Creative Screenwriting*, Winter 1996, Erik Bauer; *Daily Variety*, 28 August 2000, David S. Cohen; *Edmonton Sun*, 11 June 2000, Steve Tilley; *Empire*, 1995, Mark Salisbury; *Empire*, 1995, Andrew Collins; *Empire*, 1998, Adam Smith; *Empire*, 1998, Andrew Collins; *Empire*, 1998, Jeff Dawson; *Empire*, 1999, Mark Dinning; *Empire*, August 1999, Adam Smith; *Empire*, January 2002, Mark Dinning; *Empire*, June 2002, Simon Braund; *Empire*, December 1997, Mark Dinning; *Empire*, June 2002, Mark Dinning; *Empire*, 1997, Mark Salisbury; *Empire*, 1995, Simon Braund; *Entertainment Weekly*, 14 April 2000, Lori T. Tharps; *Essence*, December 1999, Diane Weathers; *Evening Standard*, 13 February 1998; *Evening Standard*, 30 July 1998; *Evening Standard*, 4 December 2001, Jeff Dawson; *Evening Standard*, 6 September 2000, Andrew Billen; *Evening Standard*, 7 August 1998, Sarah Cassidy; *Evening Standard*, 'Hot Tickets', 3 August 2000, Lesley O'Toole; *Film Review Yearbook 2001*, Anwar Brett; *Film Review*, July 1999, Terry Richards; *Film Review*, November 1999, Ian Spelling and James Mottram; *Financial Times*, Weekend, 30 November 1996, Nigel Andrews; *Guardian Weekend*, 8 August 1998, Jim Shelley; *Guardian*, 17 August 1995, Sarah Gristwood; *Guardian*, 30 August 1997, Simon Hattenstone; *Guardian*, 27 June 2000, Andrew Anthony; *Guardian*, 14 December 2001, Jessica Hodgson; *Hollywood Reporter*, 3 August 1990, Christopher Vaughn; *Independent Review*, 10 August 1998, James Rampton; *Interview*, April 1992; *Movie Maker Magazine*, Lucky Star, Issue 21, Erich Leon Harris; *New York Post*, 2 October 1997; *New York Times*, 22 March 2002; *NME*, 20 September 1997, Gavin Martin; *Observer Review*, 8 March 1998, Andrew Anthony; *Observer*, 8 March 1998, Andrew Anthony; *Observer*, 20 August 2000, Trevor Phillips; *Positif*, 23 May 1994; *Premiere*, June 2002, Cheo Hodari Coker; *Premiere*, June 1995, Claudia Dreyfus; *Premiere*, September 1994, Malissa Thompson; *Premiere*, March 1996, Marc S. Malkin; *Premiere*, May 1992, Veronica Victoria Chambers; *Premiere*, April 1993, Michael Kaplan; *South China Morning Post*, 6 June 1998, David S. Cohen; *Starburst*, 1998, Lawrence French; *Starburst*, 1993, Edward Murphy and Alan Jones; *Starburst*, Special 40, Ian Spelling; *Sunday Herald*, September 2000, Robin Lynch; *Sunday Telegraph Review*, 22 February 1998, James Delingpole;

Sunday Times, 1 December 1996, Beverley D'Silva; *Time Out*, 11-18 September 1996, David Eimer; *The Times* magazine, 23 October 1999, Martyn Palmer; *The Times* Metro, 5 August 2000, Martyn Palmer; *The Times*, 12 March 1998, Carol Allen; *The Times*, 14 September 2000, Sean Macaulay; *Toronto Sun*, 26 July 1998, Natasha Stoynoff; *Toronto Sun*, 11 June 2000, Bob Thompson; *Toronto Sun*, 14 May 2002, Bruce Kirkland; *Toronto Sun*, 13 June 2000, Sylvi Capelaci; *Toronto Sun*, 17 November 1998, Wilder Penfield III; *Total Film*, 1998, Leesa Daniels; *Total Film*, September 2000, Charlie Tan; *Village Voice*, 2 July 2001; *Voice*, 10 September 1996, Allister Harry; *Voice*, 12 November 2001; *Voice*, 15 October 1994, Julia Toppin; *Voice*, 15 August 1995, Allister Harry; *Voice*, 17 August 1998, Lee Pinkerton; *Voice*, 23 February 1998, Dionne St Hill; *Voice*, 9 December 1996, Omega Douglas; *Winnipeg Sun*, 7 April 2000, Randall King

PICTURE CREDITS

The following pictures are from the Kobal collection:

Page 1 (bottom) Universal/The Kobal Collection/David Lee; Page 3 (top) Cinergi Pictures/The Kobal Collection/Barry Wetcher; (bottom) 20th Century Fox/The Kobal Collection; Page 4 (top) Warner Bros/The Kobal Collection/Christine Loss; (bottom) New Line/Ch4/Telefilm/The Kobal Collection/Bob Marshak; Page 5 (bottom) Paramount/The Kobal Collection/Sam Emerson; Page 6 (top) Paramount/The Kobal Collection/Eli Reed; Page 7 (top) LucasFilm/20th Century Fox/The Kobal Collection

The following pictures are from the Ronald Grant Archive:

Page 1 (top) courtesy 40 Acres and a Mule Filmworks; Page 2 (top) courtesy Jersey Films; (bottom) courtesy Miramax; Page 4 (middle) courtesy Addis Wechsler Pictures; Page 5 (top) courtesy Warner Bros; Page 6 (bottom) courtesy Alliance Atlantis Communications; Page 7 (bottom) courtesy Columbia TriStar

The following pictures are courtesy of Rex Features:

Page 8 (top and bottom)

INDEX